THE AMERICAN FAMILY

REFLECTING A CHANGING NATION

ISSN 1534-164X

THE AMERICAN FAMILY

REFLECTING A CHANGING NATION

Cynthia S. Becker

INFORMATION PLUS® REFERENCE SERIES
Formerly published by Information Plus, Wylie, Texas

THOMSON

GALE

Detroit • New York • San Francisco • San Diego • New Haven, Conn. • Waterville, Maine • London • Munich

THOMSON

GALE

™

The American Family: Reflecting a Changing Nation

Cynthia S. Becker

Paula Kepos, Series Editor

Project Editor
John McCoy

Permissions
Margaret Abendroth, Edna Hedblad, Emma Hull

Composition and Electronic Prepress
Evi Seoud

Manufacturing
Drew Kalasky

LIBRARY OF CONGRESS CATALOGING-IN-PUBLICATION DATA

ISBN 0-7876-5103-6 (set)
ISBN 0-7876-9066-X
ISSN 1534-164X

Printed in the United States of America
10 9 8 7 6 5 4 3 2 1

TABLE OF CONTENTS

PREFACE

The American Family: Reflecting a Changing Nation is part of the *Information Plus Reference Series*. The purpose of each volume of the series is to present the latest facts on a topic of pressing concern in modern American life. These topics include today's most controversial and most studied social issues: abortion, capital punishment, care for the elderly, crime, family issues, health care, the environment, immigration, minorities, social welfare, women, youth, and many more. Although written especially for the high school and undergraduate student, this series is an excellent resource for anyone in need of factual information on current affairs.

By presenting the facts, it is Thomson Gale's intention to provide its readers with everything they need to reach an informed opinion on current issues. To that end, there is a particular emphasis in this series on the presentation of scientific studies, surveys, and statistics. These data are generally presented in the form of tables, charts, and other graphics placed within the text of each book. Every graphic is directly referred to and carefully explained in the text. The source of each graphic is presented within the graphic itself. The data used in these graphics are drawn from the most reputable and reliable sources, in particular from the various branches of the U.S. government and from major independent polling organizations. Every effort was made to secure the most recent information available. The reader should bear in mind that many major studies take years to conduct, and that additional years often pass before the data from these studies are made available to the public. Therefore, in many cases the most recent information available in 2005 dated from 2002 or 2003. Older statistics are sometimes presented as well, if they are of particular interest and no more-recent information exists.

Although statistics are a major focus of the *Information Plus Reference Series* they are by no means its only content. Each book also presents the widely held positions and important ideas that shape how the book's subject is discussed in the United States. These positions are explained in detail and, where possible, in the words of those who support them. Some of the other material to be found in these books includes: historical background; descriptions of major events related to the subject; relevant laws and court cases; and examples of how these issues play out in American life. Some books also feature primary documents, or have pro and con debate sections giving the words and opinions of prominent Americans on both sides of a controversial topic. All material is presented in an even-handed and unbiased manner; the reader will never be encouraged to accept one view of an issue over another.

HOW TO USE THIS BOOK

Throughout history, the family has been seen as the basic social and economic unit of American life. Most people would agree that it continues to hold this status today. However, exactly what constitutes a family changed dramatically over the last half of the twentieth century. Some people believe that these changes have been for the worse, and conflict has arisen about different people's opinions concerning what makes a "good" family. This book presents the latest information available on America's families. Trends in American family size and structure are explored, and their effects examined. The significant racial and ethnic differences in family structure are also presented. Many theories explain these trends and differences; some of the most widely accepted are discussed. This includes coverage of such controversial topics as unwed mothers, same-sex couples, the roles of fathers and mothers in child care, and other issues.

The American Family: Reflecting a Changing Nation consists of seven chapters and three appendices. Each chapter covers a major issue related to families in the United States; for a summary of the information covered in each chapter, please see the synopses provided in the Table of Contents at the front of the book. Chapters generally begin with an overview of the basic facts and background information on the chapter's topic, then proceed to examine sub-topics of particular interest. For example, Chapter 3: The Children of America, begins by examining the declining proportion of the American population that is under age eighteen. It then moves on to describe the changing racial and ethnic distribution of America's children, followed by a similar examination of their living arrangements. The next section covers foster children and adopted children. Child care is covered extensively, especially the problems facing families where all of the caregivers work. The economic situation of children, children and school, and the cost of raising a child are also covered. Readers can find their way through a chapter by looking for the section and sub-section headings, which are clearly set off from the text. Or, they can refer to the book's extensive index, if they already know what they are looking for.

Statistical Information

The tables and figures featured throughout *The American Family: Reflecting a Changing Nation* will be of particular use to the reader in learning about this topic. These tables and figures represent an extensive collection of the most recent and valuable statistics on American families—for example the graphics in this book cover: the typical amount spent on raising a child for families of different income levels; public opinions regarding abortion; the fertility rate of American women, by age, race, and ethnicity; and housing costs for renters and homeowners, by state. Thomson Gale believes that making this information available to the reader is the most important way in which we fulfill the goal of this book: to help readers understand the topic of family life in America and reach their own conclusions about controversial issues related to it.

Each table or figure has a unique identifier appearing above it, for ease of identification and reference. Titles for the tables and figures explain their purpose. At the end of each table or figure, the original source of the data is provided.

In order to help readers understand these often complicated statistics, all tables and figures are explained in the text. References in the text direct the reader to the relevant statistics. Furthermore, the contents of all tables and figures are fully indexed. Please see the opening section of the index at the back of this volume for a description of how to find tables and figures within it.

Appendices

In addition to the main body text and images, *The American Family: Reflecting a Changing Nation* has three appendices. The first is the Important Names and Addresses directory. Here the reader will find contact information for a number of government and private organizations that can provide further information on aspects of families. The second appendix is the Resources section, which can also assist the reader in conducting his or her own research. In this section, the author and editors of *The American Family: Reflecting a Changing Nation* describe some of the sources that were most useful during the compilation of this book. The final appendix is the index.

ADVISORY BOARD CONTRIBUTIONS

The staff of Information Plus would like to extend their heartfelt appreciation to the Information Plus Advisory Board. This dedicated group of media professionals provides feedback on the series on an ongoing basis. Their comments allow the editorial staff who work on the project to make the series better and more user-friendly. Our top priorities are to produce the highest-quality and most useful books possible, and the Advisory Board's contributions to this process are invaluable.

The members of the Information Plus Advisory Board are:

- Kathleen R. Bonn, Librarian, Newbury Park High School, Newbury Park, California

- Madelyn Garner, Librarian, San Jacinto College—North Campus, Houston, Texas

- Anne Oxenrider, Media Specialist, Dundee High School, Dundee, Michigan

- Charles R. Rodgers, Director of Libraries, Pasco-Hernando Community College, Dade City, Florida

- James N. Zitzelsberger, Library Media Department Chairman, Oshkosh West High School, Oshkosh, Wisconsin

COMMENTS AND SUGGESTIONS

The editors of the *Information Plus Reference Series* welcome your feedback on *The American Family: Reflecting a Changing Nation*. Please direct all correspondence to:

Editors
Information Plus Reference Series
27500 Drake Rd.
Farmington Hills, MI, 48331-3535

CHAPTER 1
AMERICA'S FAMILIES

In virtually all cultures, the family is considered the basic societal unit. Because the U.S. Census Bureau provides the most comprehensive statistics available on families in America, this book uses its terms and definitions as they concern the American family. The Census Bureau conducts a nationwide population census every ten years. In addition, the Bureau gathers economic information and surveys state and local governments every five years. The Bureau completes more than a hundred annual surveys and publishes a wide variety of special reports each year.

The Census Bureau defines a family as two or more people related by blood, marriage, or adoption. To understand this definition of the family, one must first understand the terminology used by the Census Bureau to describe the wide variety of living arrangements in the United States. In gathering its statistics, the Census Bureau starts with the American "household"—a single housing unit occupied by a person or group of people. Group quarters, such as correctional institutions and nursing homes, are not counted as households.

The "householder" is the person in whose name the housing unit is owned, being purchased, or rented. A "family household" consists of a householder and one or more people who are related to the householder by blood, marriage, or adoption. A "nonfamily household" consists of a person living alone or living only with nonrelatives, such as boarders or roommates.

Family households are further divided into the traditional family maintained by a "married couple" and "other families" maintained by a male or female householder with no spouse present. These might include a single parent living with a child or children, siblings sharing a home, and any combination of relatives other than the householder's spouse.

HOUSEHOLDS

Historically, families have accounted for the majority of all households, but that picture changed significantly during the latter half of the twentieth century. According to the U.S. Census Bureau, by 2002 only 68% of households fit the bureau's definition of a family (with 52% constituting "family/married couples," 16% categorized as "other family," and 32% described as "nonfamily."

Americans began to live longer, marry later, or not marry at all, and had fewer children. Some married couples chose to remain childless. Since the 1960s an increasing number of couples chose to simply live together rather than formalize their union through marriage. Other individuals shared living space with roommates or boarders. More people who elected to remain single became parents through out-of-wedlock births, surrogate births, and adoption. Similarly, gay and lesbian couples established families. Divorce became more common and remarriage often created "yours-mine-and-ours" blended families. Adult offspring with personal or financial difficulties returned home to live with their parents. Grandparents looking forward to retirement sometimes found themselves raising grandchildren. Finally, increased longevity required some senior citizens to live with their children or other family members who could care for them. All of these factors contributed to the changing profile of the American family.

According to Census statistics, family households declined from 90% of all households in 1940 to 68% in 2002. There were 109.3 million households in the United States in 2002, about 74.3 million of which were family households. Of these, 56.7 million were designated "married couple" and 17.6 million were "other family" households in Census Bureau terminology. Another 34.9 million households fit the "nonfamily" category.

Household Size

Census data show a decrease in the number of people living together in households over the past century. In 1900 the average household included 4.6 people. Between 1960 and 2002 the total number of households more than

TABLE 1.1

Households by size, 1960–2002

(Numbers in thousands)

Year	All households	One person	Two persons	Three persons	Four persons	Five persons	Six persons	Seven or more persons	Persons per household
2002	109,297	28,775	36,240	17,742	15,794	6,948	2,438	1,360	2.58
2001ˢ	108,209	28,207	35,917	17,444	15,692	6,978	2,555	1,415	2.58
2000	104,705	26,724	34,666	17,172	15,309	6,981	2,445	1,428	2.62
1999	103,874	26,606	34,262	17,386	15,030	6,962	2,367	1,261	2.61
1998	102,528	26,327	32,965	17,331	15,358	7,048	2,232	1,267	2.62
1997	101,018	25,402	32,736	17,065	15,396	6,774	2,311	1,334	2.64
1996	99,627	24,900	32,526	16,724	15,118	6,631	2,357	1,372	2.65
1995	98,990	24,732	31,834	16,827	15,321	6,616	2,279	1,382	2.65
1994	97,107	23,611	31,211	16,898	15,073	6,749	2,186	1,379	2.67
1993ʳ	96,426	23,558	31,041	16,964	14,997	6,404	2,217	1,244	2.66
1993	96,391	23,642	31,175	16,895	14,926	6,357	2,180	1,215	2.63
1992	95,669	23,974	30,734	16,398	14,710	6,389	2,126	1,338	2.62
1991	94,312	23,590	30,181	16,082	14,556	6,206	2,237	1,459	2.63
1990	93,347	22,999	30,114	16,128	14,456	6,213	2,143	1,295	2.63
1989	92,830	22,708	29,976	16,276	14,550	6,232	2,003	1,084	2.62
1988	91,066	21,889	29,295	16,163	14,143	6,081	2,176	1,320	2.64
1987	89,479	21,128	28,602	16,159	13,984	6,162	2,176	1,268	2.66
1986	88,458	21,178	27,732	16,088	13,774	6,276	2,138	1,272	2.67
1985	86,789	20,602	27,389	15,465	13,631	6,108	2,299	1,296	2.69
1984	85,407	19,954	26,890	15,134	13,593	6,070	2,372	1,394	2.71
1983	83,918	19,250	26,439	14,793	13,303	6,105	2,460	1,568	2.73
1982	83,527	19,354	26,486	14,617	12,868	6,103	2,480	1,619	2.72
1981	82,368	18,936	25,787	14,569	12,768	6,117	2,549	1,643	2.73
1980	80,776	18,296	25,327	14,130	12,666	6,059	2,519	1,778	2.76
1979	77,330	17,201	23,928	13,392	12,274	6,187	2,573	1,774	2.78
1978	76,030	16,715	23,334	13,040	11,955	6,356	2,723	1,906	2.81
1977	74,142	15,532	22,775	12,794	11,630	6,285	2,864	2,263	2.86
1976	72,867	14,983	22,321	12,520	11,407	6,268	3,001	2,367	2.89
1975	71,120	13,939	21,753	12,384	11,103	6,399	3,059	2,484	2.94
1974	69,859	13,368	21,495	11,913	10,900	6,469	3,063	2,651	2.97
1973	68,251	12,635	20,632	11,804	10,739	6,426	3,245	2,769	3.01
1972	66,676	12,189	19,482	11,542	10,679	6,431	3,374	2,979	3.06
1971	64,778	11,446	18,892	11,071	10,059	6,640	3,435	3,234	3.11
1970	63,401	10,851	18,333	10,949	9,991	6,548	3,534	3,195	3.14
1969	62,214	10,401	18,034	10,769	9,778	6,387	3,557	3,288	3.21
1968	60,813	9,802	17,377	10,577	9,623	6,319	3,627	3,488	3.00
1967	59,236	9,200	16,770	10,403	9,559	6,276	3,491	3,550	3.30
1966	58,406	9,093	16,679	9,993	9,465	6,257	3,465	3,465	3.32
1965	57,436	8,631	16,119	10,263	9,269	6,313	3,327	3,514	3.32
1964	56,149	7,821	15,622	10,034	9,565	6,328	3,373	3,405	3.34
1963	55,270	7,501	15,279	9,989	9,445	6,240	3,473	3,342	3.33
1962	54,764	7,473	15,461	10,077	9,347	6,016	3,368	3,022	3.32
1961	53,557	7,112	15,185	9,780	9,390	6,052	3,085	2,953	3.38
1960	52,799	6,917	14,678	9,979	9,293	6,072	3,010	2,851	3.35

ʳRevised based on population from the decennial census for that year.
ˢData for March 2001 and later use population controls based on Census 2000 and an expanded sample of households designed to improve state estimates of children with health insurance.

SOURCE: "Households by Size, 1960–Present," in *Annual Social and Economic Supplement, 2003 Current Population Survey,* U.S. Census Bureau, 2003, http://www.census.gov/population/socdemo/hh-fam/tabHH-4.pdf (accessed July 16, 2004)

doubled from 52,799 to 109,297. During this same period, household size dropped 23%, from an average of 3.35 people per household in 1960 to 2.58 in 2002. The number of single-person households quadrupled. Three- and four-person families—couples with one or two children—remained relatively stable.

In 2002, Census data revealed that the percentage of six-person families was 19% lower than in 1960 and families with seven or more persons occurred 50% less frequently. (See Table 1.1.) Despite the smaller overall number of large families in 2000, the frequency of large families had begun to increase in 1989. Over the next twelve years, six-person families increased 20%, and families with seven or more persons increased more than 30%. (See Table 1.1.) This trend paralleled a growth in immigration during the same period.

IMMIGRATION AND LARGER HOUSEHOLD SIZE. According to the Census Bureau's report *The Foreign-Born Population in the United States: 2003,* 36.6% of the foreign-born population in the United States arrived in the decade 1990–99. Another 13.6% of the foreign-born population entered the United States after 1999. Of foreign-born households, 25% included five or more people compared to 12.5% of native households. (See Figure

TABLE 1.2

Family size in foreign-born households by geographic origin of householder, 2003 [1,2,3]

(Numbers in thousands)

| Household type and size | Foreign born | | World region of birth | | | | | | | |
| | | | Europe | | Asia | | Latin America | | Other areas | |
	Number	Percent	Number	Percent	Number	Percent	Number	Percent	Number	Percent
Total all households	**13,912**	**100.0**	**2,296**	**100.0**	**3,490**	**100.0**	**6,901**	**100.0**	**1,224**	**100.0**
One person	2,488	17.9	647	28.2	661	18.9	869	12.6	310	25.3
Two people	3,429	24.6	877	38.2	872	25.0	1,354	19.6	325	26.5
Three people	2,574	18.5	343	14.9	723	20.7	1,293	18.7	215	17.6
Four people	2,710	19.5	277	12.0	727	20.8	1,475	21.4	231	18.9
Five people	1,488	10.7	105	4.6	309	8.8	994	14.4	81	6.6
Six people	684	4.9	36	1.6	112	3.2	498	7.2	38	3.1
Seven or more people	540	3.9	11	0.5	87	2.5	419	6.1	24	1.9
Total family households [4]	**10,700**	**100.0**	**1,529**	**100.0**	**2,641**	**100.0**	**5,698**	**100.0**	**832**	**100.0**
Two people	2,952	27.6	783	51.2	725	27.4	1,182	20.7	262	31.5
Three people	2,434	22.7	326	21.4	693	26.2	1,211	21.3	203	24.4
Four people	2,642	24.7	269	17.6	717	27.1	1,430	25.1	227	27.3
Five people	1,468	13.7	103	6.7	307	11.6	980	17.2	77	9.3
Six people	667	6.2	36	2.4	112	4.2	481	8.4	38	4.6
Seven or more people	536	5.0	11	0.7	87	3.3	414	7.3	24	2.8
Total nonfamily households	**3,213**	**100.0**	**768**	**100.0**	**849**	**100.0**	**1,203**	**100.0**	**393**	**100.0**
One person	2,488	77.4	647	84.3	661	77.9	869	72.3	310	78.9
Two people	477	14.8	94	12.3	147	17.4	172	14.3	63	16.0
Three people	140	4.4	17	2.2	29	3.4	82	6.8	12	3.1
Four people	67	2.1	8	1.0	10	1.2	45	3.7	4	1.1
Five people	20	0.6	2	0.2	1	0.1	14	1.1	4	0.9
Six people	17	0.5	–	–	–	–	17	1.4	–	–
Seven or more people	4	0.1	–	–	–	–	4	0.4	–	–

–Represents or rounds to zero.

[1] Households with a foreign-born householder are defined as foreign-born households, regardless of the nativity of other household members.

[2] The majority of those born in 'Latin America' are from Mexico. Those born in 'Other Areas' are from Africa, Oceania, and Northern America.

[3] The data in this table do not include the population living in group quarters.

[4] Households in which at least one member is related to the person who owns or rents the house (householder).

SOURCE: "Table 3.4. Household Type among Foreign-Born Households by Size and by World Region of Birth of the Householder: 2003," in *Annual Social and Economic Supplement: 2003 Current Population Survey,* U.S. Census Bureau, 2003, http://www.census.gov/population/socdemo/foreign/ppl-174/tab03-04.pdf (accessed August 10. 2004)

1.1.) The largest number of foreign-born residents came from Latin American countries, and they had the largest families with five or more people in 32.9% of family households. They were also the only foreign-born group with more than five people reported in nonfamily households. (See Table 1.2.)

OTHER FACTORS INFLUENCED HOUSEHOLD SIZE. Changes in rates of fertility, marriage, divorce, and mortality all contributed to declines in the size of American households. Between 1950 and 2001 U.S. Census figures show the total death rate declined 11.5% and infant mortality rates plummeted 76.7%. Americans were healthier and lived longer. During this same period, however, the birth rate dropped 41.5%. The rate of marriage declined 24.3% while the divorce rate rose 53.8%. (See Table 1.3.)

In the twenty-first century, American life expectancy continued to increase. A baby boy born in 1900 could expect to live 46.3 years compared to 74.4 years for a boy born in 2001. (See Table 1.4.) In a February 2004 news release, the National Center for Health Statistics reported that life expectancy in the United States reached an all-time high in 2002, but the infant mortality rate increased for the

first time since 1958. The preliminary report noted increases in low birth-weight babies, preterm births, and multiple births as factors contributing to higher risk of infant death during the first twenty-eight days of life. Overall death rates continued to decline. The divorce rate fell, but so did the marriage rate. The live birth rate and fertility rate, however, both increased slightly. (See Table 1.5.)

CHANGING FAMILY STRUCTURE

The most noticeable long-term trend among American families has been the decline in the traditional family—a married couple with children. New terminology developed to describe the diverse types of families—single parent, stepparent, blended, unmarried partners, same-sex partners, and multigenerational.

The changes in the American family did not happen overnight but evolved after World War II. The uncertainty of the war drove many young couples to rush into marriage. At the war's end, returning soldiers married in record numbers and promptly began families. The "American Dream" became the security of a family in which the father's income provided for the household's needs, while

FIGURE 1.1

Family households with five or more people by nativity and by world region of birth, 2003

(In percent)*

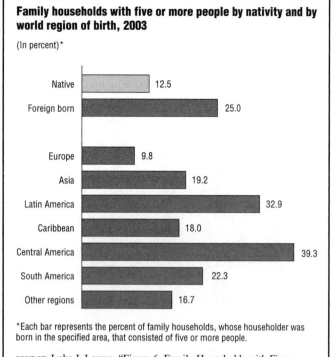

*Each bar represents the percent of family households, whose householder was born in the specified area, that consisted of five or more people.

SOURCE: Luke J. Larsen, "Figure 6. Family Households with Five or More People by Nativity and by World Region of Birth, 2003," in *The Foreign-Born Population in the United States: 2003,* Current Population Reports, P20-551, U.S. Department of Commerce, Economics and Statistics Administration, U.S. Census Bureau, August 2004, http://www.census.gov/prod/2004pubs/p20-551.pdf (accessed August 10, 2004)

TABLE 1.3

Rates of live births, deaths, marriages, and divorces, 1950–2001

[Prior to 1960, excludes Alaska and Hawaii. Beginning 1970, excludes births to and deaths of non-residents of the United States.]

Year	Births[1]	Deaths Total	Deaths Infant[2]	Marriages[3]	Divorces[4]
1950	24.1	9.6	29.2	11.1	2.6
1955	25.0	9.3	26.4	9.3	2.3
1957	25.3	9.6	26.3	8.9	2.2
1960	23.7	9.5	26.0	8.5	2.2
1965	19.4	9.4	24.7	9.3	2.5
1970	18.4	9.5	20.0	10.6	3.5
1971	17.2	9.3	19.1	10.6	3.7
1972	15.6	9.4	18.5	10.9	4.0
1973	14.8	9.3	17.7	10.8	4.3
1974	14.8	9.1	16.7	10.5	4.6
1975	14.6	8.8	16.1	10.0	4.8
1976	14.6	8.8	15.2	9.9	5.0
1977	15.1	8.6	14.1	9.9	5.0
1978	15.0	8.7	13.8	10.3	5.1
1979	15.6	8.5	13.1	10.4	5.3
1980	15.9	8.8	12.6	10.6	5.2
1981	15.8	8.6	11.9	10.6	5.3
1982	15.9	8.5	11.5	10.6	5.1
1983	15.6	8.6	11.2	10.5	5.0
1984	15.6	8.6	10.8	10.5	5.0
1985	15.8	8.8	10.6	10.1	5.0
1986	15.6	8.8	10.4	10.0	4.9
1987	15.7	8.8	10.1	9.9	4.8
1988	16.0	8.9	10.0	9.8	4.8
1989	16.4	8.7	9.8	9.7	4.7
1990	16.7	8.6	9.2	9.8	4.7
1991	16.3	8.6	8.9	9.4	4.7
1992	15.9	8.5	8.5	9.3	4.8
1993	15.5	8.8	8.4	9.0	4.6
1994	15.2	8.8	8.0	9.1	4.6
1995	14.8	8.8	7.6	8.9	4.4
1996	14.7	8.7	7.3	8.8	4.3
1997	14.5	8.6	7.2	8.9	4.3
1998[5]	14.6	8.6	7.2	8.3	4.2
1999[5]	14.5	8.8	7.1	8.6	4.1
2000[5]	14.4	8.7	6.9	8.5	4.2
2001[5]	14.1	8.5	6.8	8.4	4.0

Rate per 1,000 population

NA Not available.
[1]Prior to 1960, data adjusted for underregistration.
[2]Infants under 1 year excluding fetal deaths; rates per 1,000 registered live births.
[3]Includes estimates for some states through 1965 and also for 1976 and 1977 and marriage licenses for some states for all years except 1973 and 1975. Beginning 1978, includes nonlicensed marriages in California.
[4]Includes reported annulments and some estimated state figures for all years.
[5]Divorce rate excludes data for California, Colorado, Indiana, and Louisiana; population for this rate also excludes these states.

SOURCE: Adapted from "No. 83. Live Births, Deaths, Marriages, and Divorces, 1950–2001," in *Statistical Abstract of the United States, 2003,* U.S. Census Bureau, 2003, http://www.census.gov/prod/2004pubs/03statab/vitstat.pdf (accessed August 11, 2004)

---

the mother's workday was relegated to taking care of the children and house. Couples generally started families immediately, and women bore more children and in quicker succession than in previous generations. The seventy-seven million children born during the years 1946–64, the single largest generation in U.S. history, came to be known as the "baby boom generation."

Attitudes toward divorce began to relax as couples who rushed to marry during the war years went their separate ways. Divorces increased significantly in the 1950s and 1960s. The children of these divorced couples experienced new challenges brought on by the breakup of their families. They grew up questioning the value of marriage and launched a sexual revolution in which living together without being married became commonplace. The number of cohabiting couples continued to grow in the 1970s and 1980s, and young men and women further delayed marriage and having children. Women found careers and put off childbearing even into their forties. By the 1990s, the definition of "family" broadened to include married couples, cohabiting couples, same-sex couples, and single persons, any of whom might have children of their own, as well as stepchildren and adopted children. The ranks of those who chose to live alone—who were once considered odd or eccentric—swelled to record numbers.

Nonfamily Households

In 1950 only 10.6% of American households were nonfamily households. Census 2000 recorded 33.7 million nonfamilies—32% of all households. (See Table 1.6.) As traditional families declined, nonfamily households increased. The majority of this growth was due to more people living alone. In 1970 persons living alone represented 17.1% of all households. By 2000, single persons accounted for 25.5% of households. The Census Bureau reported that women represented 67% of one-person households in 1970

TABLE 1.4

Life expectancy, 1900–2001

[Data are based on death certificates]

Specified age and year	All races			White			Black or African American[1]		
	Both sexes	Male	Female	Both sexes	Male	Female	Both sexes	Male	Female
At birth				Remaining life expectancy in years					
1900[2,3]	47.3	46.3	48.3	47.6	46.6	48.7	33.0	32.5	33.5
1950[3]	68.2	65.6	71.1	69.1	66.5	72.2	60.8	59.1	62.9
1960[3]	69.7	66.6	73.1	70.6	67.4	74.1	63.6	61.1	66.3
1970	70.8	67.1	74.7	71.7	68.0	75.6	64.1	60.0	68.3
1980	73.7	70.0	77.4	74.4	70.7	78.1	68.1	63.8	72.5
1985	74.7	71.1	78.2	75.3	71.8	78.7	69.3	65.0	73.4
1990	75.4	71.8	78.8	76.1	72.7	79.4	69.1	64.5	73.6
1991	75.5	72.0	78.9	76.3	72.9	79.6	69.3	64.6	73.8
1992	75.8	72.3	79.1	76.5	73.2	79.8	69.6	65.0	73.9
1993	75.5	72.2	78.8	76.3	73.1	79.5	69.2	64.6	73.7
1994	75.7	72.4	79.0	76.5	73.3	79.6	69.5	64.9	73.9
1995	75.8	72.5	78.9	76.5	73.4	79.6	69.6	65.2	73.9
1996	76.1	73.1	79.1	76.8	73.9	79.7	70.2	66.1	74.2
1997	76.5	73.6	79.4	77.1	74.3	79.9	71.1	67.2	74.7
1998	76.7	73.8	79.5	77.3	74.5	80.0	71.3	67.6	74.8
1999	76.7	73.9	79.4	77.3	74.6	79.9	71.4	67.8	74.7
2000[4]	77.0	74.3	79.7	77.6	74.9	80.1	71.9	68.3	75.2
2001[5]	77.2	74.4	79.8	77.7	75.0	80.2	72.2	68.6	75.5

[1]Data shown for 1900–60 are for the nonwhite population.
[2]Death registration area only. The death registration area increased from 10 States and the District of Columbia in 1900 to the coterminous United States in 1933.
[3]Includes deaths of persons who were not residents of the 50 States and the District of Columbia.
[4]Life expectancies (LEs) for 2000 were revised and may differ from those shown previously. LEs for 2000 were computed using population counts from Census 2000 and replace LEs for 2000 using 1990-based postcensal estimates.
[5]Life expectancies for 2001 were computed using 2000-based postcensal estimates.

SOURCE: Adapted from "Life Expectancy at Birth and at 65 Years of Age and at 75 Years of Age, According to Race and Sex, United States, Selected Years 1900–2001," in *Health, United States, 2003,* U.S. Department of Health and Human Services, Centers for Disease Control and Prevention, National Center for Health Statistics, 2003, http://www.cdc.gov/nchs/data/hus/tables/2003/03hus027.pdf (accessed August 11, 2004)

TABLE 1.5

Births, marriages, divorces, and deaths, 2003

(Rates for infant deaths are deaths under 1 year per 1,000 live births; fertility rates are live births per 1,000 women aged 15–44 years; all other rates are per 1,000 total population. National data are bases on events occurring in the United States, regardless of place of residence.)

Item	December				12 months ending with December				
	Number		Rate		Number		Rate		
	2003	2002	2003	2002	2003	2002	2003	2002	2001
Live births	342,000	330,000	13.8	13.4	4,093,000	4,022,000	14.0	13.9	14.1
Fertility rate	. . .	. . .	64.7	62.5	. . .	. . .	65.8	64.8	65.1
Deaths	230,000	215,000	9.3	8.7	2,423,000	2,438,000	8.3	8.5	8.5
Infant deaths	2,300	2,300	6.6	6.9	27,500	27,600	6.7	6.9	6.9
Natural increase	112,000	115,000	4.5	4.7	1,670,000	1,584,000	5.7	5.4	5.6
Marriages[1]	158,000	165,000	6.3	6.7	2,187,000	2,254,000	7.5	7.8	8.2
Divorces[2]	—	—	—	—	—	—	3.8	4.0	4.0
Population base (in millions)	. . .	. . .	292.7	289.7	. . .	. . .	291.4	288.4	285.3

. . . Category not applicable.
— Data not available.
[1]Marriage rates may be underestimated due to incomplete reporting in Oklahoma.
[2]Divorce rates exclude data for California, Hawaii, Indiana, Louisiana, and Oklahoma. Populations for these rates also exclude these states.
Note: Figures include all revisions received from the states and, therefore, may differ from those previously published. National data are based on events occurring in the United States, regardless of place of residence.

SOURCE: M.L. Munson and P.D. Sutton, "Births, Marriages, Divorces, and Deaths: Provisional Data for 2003," in *National Vital Statistics Report,* vol. 52, no. 22, National Center for Health Statistics, 2004, http://www.cdc.gov/nchs/data/nvsr/nvsr52/nvsr52_22.pdf (accessed July 16, 2004)

but only 58% of one-person households by 2000. Householders who lived with nonrelatives made up the other growing nonfamily household type. In 1970 householders with roommates or boarders accounted for 1.7% of all households, but by 2000 they represented 5.7%.

Women Had Fewer Children

The number of women of childbearing age increased substantially from the mid-1960s until the early 1980s as the baby boom generation matured. The decline in large families during this period was evident in the decreasing percent-

TABLE 1.6

Households by type and size, 1900–2000

		Family households				Nonfamily households			Average size household
					Other family				
					Male householder*	Female householder*		Male householder	Female householder	
Year	Total households	Total	Married couples	Male householder*	Female householder*	Total	Male householder	Female householder	Average size household
Number (1,000)									
Census									
1900	15,964	(NA)	(NA)	(NA)	(NA)	(NA)	(NA)	(NA)	4.60
1910	20,256	(NA)	16,250	(NA)	(NA)	(NA)	(NA)	(NA)	4.54
1920	24,352	(NA)	(NA)	(NA)	(NA)	(NA)	(NA)	(NA)	4.34
1930	29,905	(NA)	23,649	(NA)	(NA)	(NA)	(NA)	(NA)	4.01
1940	34,949	31,491	26,571	1,510	3,410	3,458	1,599	1,859	3.68
1950	42,251	37,775	33,019	1,331	3,425	4,476	(NA)	(NA)	3.38
1960	53,024	45,027	39,657	1,295	4,196	7,997	(NA)	(NA)	3.29
1970	63,450	50,969	44,062	1,402	5,504	12,481	(NA)	(NA)	3.11
1980	80,390	58,882	48,371	2,102	8,409	21,508	9,187	12,320	2.75
1990	91,947	64,518	50,708	3,144	10,666	27,429	12,142	15,288	2.63
2000	105,480	71,787	54,493	4,394	12,900	33,693	15,556	18,137	2.59
Highest value	105,480	71,787	54,493	4,394	12,900	33,693	15,556	18,137	4.60
Lowest value	15,964	31,491	26,571	1,510	3,410	3,458	1,599	1,859	2.59

*No spouse present

NA Not available. X Not applicable. No spouse present. Revised using population controls based on the 1980 census. Revised using population controls based on the 1990 census. Covers all years from 1947 to present.

SOURCE: Adapted from "HS-12. Households by Type and Size, 1900–2002," in *Statistical Abstract of the United States: 2003,* U.S. Census Bureau, 2003, http://www.census.gov/statab/hist/HS-12.pdf (accessed August 11, 2004)

TABLE 1.7

Children ever born per 1,000 women 40–44 years old, selected years, 1976–2002

(Numbers in thousands)

			Percent distribution of women by number of children ever born						
Year	Number of women	Children ever born per 1,000 women	Total	None	1 child	2 children	3 children	4 children	5 or more children
1976	5,684	3,091	100.0	10.2	9.6	21.7	22.7	15.8	20.1
1980	5,983	2,988	100.0	10.1	9.6	24.6	22.6	15.5	17.6
1985	7,226	2,447	100.0	11.4	12.6	32.9	23.1	10.9	9.1
1990	8,905	2,045	100.0	16.0	16.9	35.0	19.4	8.0	4.8
1995	10,244	1,961	100.0	17.5	17.6	35.2	18.5	7.4	3.9
1998	11,113	1,877	100.0	19.0	17.3	35.8	18.2	6.1	3.5
2000	11,447	1,913	100.0	19.0	16.4	35.0	19.1	7.2	3.3
2002	11,561	1,930	100.0	17.9	17.4	35.4	18.9	6.8	3.6

SOURCE: Barbara Downs, "Table 2. Children Ever Born per 1,000 Women 40–44 Years Old, Selected Years, 1976–2002," in *Fertility of American Women, June 2002,* Current Population Reports, P20-548, U.S. Department of Commerce, Economics and Statistics Administration, U.S. Census Bureau, October 2003, http://www.census.gov/prod/2003pubs/p20-548.pdf (accessed July 19, 2004)

age of women having three or more children. The percent of women who had given birth to five or more children dropped from 20.1% in 1976 to 3.6% in 2002. (See Table 1.7.) Between 1976 and 2002 the percentage of women who had one child nearly doubled, and the percentage of women with two children increased from 21.7% to 35.4%.

In *Fertility of American Women* the Census Bureau estimated that women in the forty to forty-four age range in 2002 would end their childbearing years with an average of 1.9 children. As recently as 1976 the average was 3.1 children per woman. In the span of less than two generations the size of the average family dropped by one full child.

With greater acceptance of women remaining single and pursuing careers, more women chose to remain childless. In 1976 only 10.2% of women age forty to forty-four were childless compared to 17.9% in 2002. (See Table 1.7.) Of the 61.4 million women in the fifteen to forty-four age range in June 2002, 3.8 million gave birth in the preceding twelve months. The birth rate for first-born children was highest among women in the twenty to twenty-four age range with 45.3 births per one thousand women. African-American women in this age range had a birth rate of 61.2 and Hispanic women had a rate of 70.8. Among Asian women, the highest birth rate (45.2) came in the twenty-five to twenty-nine age range. (See Table 1.8.)

TABLE 1.8

Fertility indicators for women 15–44 years old by age, race, and Hispanic origin, June 2002

(Numbers in thousands)

Characteristic	Number of women	Percent childless	Women who had a child in the last year			First births per 1,000 women	Children ever born per 1,000 women
			Number with a birth	Births per 1,000 women			
				Rate	90-percent confidence interval		
Age							
Total	**61,361**	**43.5**	**3,766**	**61.4**	**59.4–63.4**	**23.1**	**1,211**
15 to 19 years	9,809	91.2	549	55.9	50.9–60.9	27.7	140
20 to 24 years	9,683	67.0	872	90.0	83.0–97.0	45.3	525
25 to 29 years	9,221	45.2	897	97.2	90.2–104.2	33.2	1,050
30 to 34 years	10,284	27.6	859	83.6	77.6–89.6	26.4	1,543
35 to 39 years	10,803	20.2	452	41.9	36.9–46.9	7.9	1,849
40 to 44 years	1,561	17.9	137	11.9	9.9–13.9	3.6	1,930
Race and ethnicity							
White							
Total	**48,481**	**43.9**	**2,958**	**61.0**	**58.0–64.0**	**22.9**	**1,196**
15 to 19 years	7,699	91.9	394	51.1	45.1–57.1	24.7	129
20 to 24 years	7,604	69.5	631	83.0	76.0–90.0	42.8	473
25 to 29 years	7,151	46.6	723	101.1	93.1–109.1	34.7	1,018
30 to 34 years	8,057	27.2	717	88.9	81.7–95.1	29.5	1,530
35 to 39 years	8,658	20.2	374	43.2	38.2–48.2	7.9	1,842
40 to 44 years	9,313	17.9	120	12.8	9.8–15.8	4.2	1,917
White, non-Hispanic							
Total	**40,017**	**45.6**	**2,262**	**56.5**	**53.5–59.5**	**21.3**	**1,130**
15 to 19 years	6,296	93.0	289	45.8	39.8–51.8	21.7	116
20 to 24 years	6,138	73.2	437	71.1	63.1–79.1	37.4	406
25 to 29 years	5,599	51.1	555	99.2	90.2–108.2	37.4	881
30 to 34 years	6,544	29.9	576	88.0	80.0–96.0	28.7	1,413
35 to 39 years	7,281	21.5	300	41.2	36.2–46.2	7.7	1,755
40 to 44 years	8,160	18.5	106	13.0	10.0–16.0	4.2	1,842
Black							
Total	**8,846**	**39.0**	**571**	**64.6**	**58.6–70.6**	**22.3**	**1,354**
15 to 19 years	1,535	86.7	125	81.4	65.4–97.4	38.0	214
20 to 24 years	1,497	51.1	193	128.9	108.9–148.9	61.2	828
25 to 29 years	1,351	31.6	98	72.7	56.7–88.7	18.6	1,392
30 to 34 years	1,440	23.9	95	66.1	51.1–81.1	10.1	1,790
35 to 39 years	1,506	19.7	52	34.2	23.2–45.2	5.0	1,942
40 to 44 years	1,518	19.2	8	5.6	1.6–9.6	—	1,991
Asian and Pacific islander							
Total	**3,267**	**50.8**	**181**	**55.4**	**46.4–64.4**	**27.3**	**994**
15 to 19 years	447	94.2	23	51.1	27.1–75.1	34.9	86
20 to 24 years	481	81.0	22	45.1	23.1–67.1	29.5	297
25 to 29 years	608	60.7	66	109.1	79.1–139.1	45.2	631
30 to 34 years	632	41.2	40	62.5	40.5–84.5	31.3	1,124
35 to 39 years	530	23.3	21	40.6	20.6–60.6	17.7	1,605
40 to 44 years	568	16.8	9	15.7	3.7–27.7	4.8	1,974
Hispanic (of any race)							
Total	**9,141**	**35.8**	**750**	**82.0**	**73.0–91.0**	**30.4**	**1,511**
15 to 19 years	1,517	87.8	105	69.3	48.3–90.3	35.4	172
20 to 24 years	1,574	52.9	226	143.7	115.7–171.7	70.8	768
25 to 29 years	1,682	29.5	176	104.6	80.6–128.6	25.8	1,522
30 to 34 years	1,620	15.6	152	93.7	70.7–116.7	32.6	2,043
35 to 39 years	1,481	13.4	77	52.1	34.1–70.1	8.1	2,287
40 to 44 years	1,266	13.1	14	10.9	1.9–19.9	3.8	2,437

— Represents zero or rounds to zero.

SOURCE: Barbara Downs, "Table 1. Fertility Indicators for Women 15–44 Years Old by Age, Race, and Hispanic Origin, June 2002," in *Fertility of American Women, June 2002,* Current Population Reports, P20-548, U.S. Department of Commerce, Economics and Statistics Administration, U.S. Census Bureau, October 2003, http://www.census.gov/prod/2003pubs/p20-548.pdf (accessed July 19, 2004)

Births to Teenagers and Unmarried Women

In 1940 the birth rate per one thousand women age fifteen to nineteen was 54.1. In the post–World War II years the rate for this age group jumped from 59.3 in 1946 to 79.3 in 1947 and continued to rise to a high of 96.3 in 1957. From that peak, births to teenage mothers began a gradual decline to a record low of 42.9 per one thousand births in 2002. While teen births declined significantly, the number of unmarried teens giving birth increased. In 1940 only 13.6% of women age fifteen to

TABLE 1.9

Births to teenagers and to unmarried women, 1940–2002

[Represents registered births. Excludes births to nonresidents of the United States. Beginning 1980, data for states in which marital status was not reported, are inferred from other items on the birth certificate. Prior to 1980, births to unmarried women are estimated based on data for registration areas.]

Year	Teen childbearing			Nonmarital childbearing		
	Total number of births to women 15–19 years	Birth rate per 1,000 women 15–19 years	Percent of teen births to unmarried women	Total number of births to unmarried women	Birth rate per 1,000 unmarried women 15–44 years	Percent of all births to unmarried
1940	300,747	54.1	13.6	89,500	7.1	3.8
1941	316,685	56.9	13.7	95,700	7.8	3.8
1942	341,315	61.1	13.0	95,500	8.0	3.4
1943	343,550	61.7	13.5	98,100	8.3	3.3
1944	301,130	54.3	16.6	105,200	9.0	3.8
1945	280,997	51.1	17.5	117,400	10.1	4.3
1946	322,381	59.3	18.4	125,200	10.9	3.8
1947	425,845	79.3	12.4	131,900	12.1	3.6
1948	431,933	81.8	15.3	129,700	12.5	3.7
1949	433,028	83.4	15.9	133,200	13.3	3.7
1950	419,535	81.6	13.4	141,600	14.1	4.0
1951	443,872	87.6	12.9	146,500	15.1	3.9
1952	438,046	86.1	13.4	150,300	15.8	3.9
1953	455,878	88.2	13.5	160,800	16.9	4.1
1954	477,880	90.6	14.1	176,600	18.7	4.4
1955	484,097	90.3	14.2	183,300	19.3	4.5
1956	520,422	94.6	14.0	193,500	20.4	4.7
1957	550,212	96.3	13.9	201,700	21.0	4.7
1958	554,184	91.4	14.3	208,700	21.2	5.0
1959	571,048	90.4	14.8	220,600	21.9	5.2
1960	586,966	89.1	14.8	224,300	21.6	5.3
1961	601,720	88.6	15.5	240,200	22.7	5.6
1962	600,298	81.4	15.7	245,100	21.9	5.9
1963	586,454	76.7	17.4	259,400	22.5	6.3
1964	585,710	73.1	19.0	275,700	23.0	6.9
1965	590,894	70.5	20.8	291,200	23.4	7.7
1966	621,426	70.3	21.9	302,400	23.3	8.4
1967	596,445	67.5	24.2	318,100	23.7	9.0
1968	591,312	65.6	26.7	339,200	24.3	9.7
1969	604,654	65.5	27.8	360,800	24.8	10.0
1970	644,708	68.3	29.5	398,700	26.4	10.7
1971	627,942	64.5	30.9	401,400	25.5	11.3
1972	616,280	61.7	32.8	403,200	24.8	12.4
1973	604,096	59.3	33.9	407,300	24.3	13.0
1974	595,449	57.5	35.4	418,100	23.9	13.2
1975	582,238	55.6	38.2	447,900	24.5	14.3
1976	558,744	52.8	40.3	468,100	24.3	14.8
1977	559,154	52.8	42.9	515,700	25.6	15.5
1978	543,407	51.5	44.1	543,900	25.7	16.3
1979	549,472	52.3	46.1	597,800	27.2	17.1
1980	552,161	53.0	47.6	665,747	29.4	18.4
1981	527,392	52.2	49.2	686,605	29.5	18.9
1982	513,758	52.4	50.7	715,227	30.0	19.4
1983	489,286	51.4	53.4	737,893	30.3	20.3
1984	469,582	50.6	55.6	770,355	31.0	21.0
1985	467,485	51.0	58.0	828,174	32.8	22.0
1986	461,905	50.2	60.8	878,477	34.2	23.4
1987	462,312	50.6	63.4	933,013	36.0	24.5
1988	478,353	53.0	65.3	1,005,299	38.5	25.7
1989	506,503	57.3	66.6	1,094,169	41.6	27.1
1990	521,826	59.9	67.1	1,165,384	43.8	28.0
1991	519,577	62.1	68.8	1,213,769	45.2	29.5
1992	505,415	60.7	70.0	1,224,876	45.2	30.1
1993	501,093	59.6	71.3	1,240,172	45.3	31.0
1994	505,488	58.9	75.5	1,289,592	46.9	32.6
1995	499,873	56.8	75.2	1,253,976	45.1	32.2

nineteen were unmarried when they gave birth. When the teen birth rate peaked in 1957, only 13.9% of births were to unmarried teens. By 2001, however, unmarried mothers accounted for 78.9% of all births to teens. (See Table 1.9.)

As attitudes toward marriage changed and more couples began to cohabit, attitudes toward births to unmarried women relaxed. In 1940 the birth rate for all unmarried women age fifteen to forty-four was 7.1 per one thousand. Contrary to the peak and decline pattern of births to teenagers, births to unmarried adult women continued a steady increase to forty-five births per one thousand in 2001. By 2002 one-third of all births were to unmarried women. (See Table 1.9.)

The American Family: Reflecting a Changing Nation

TABLE 1.9

Births to teenagers and to unmarried women, 1940–2002 [CONTINUED]

[Represents registered births. Excludes births to nonresidents of the United States. Beginning 1980, data for states in which marital status was not reported, are inferred from other items on the birth certificate. Prior to 1980, births to unmarried women are estimated based on data for registration areas.]

Year	Teen childbearing			Nonmarital childbearing		
	Total number of births to women 15–19 years	Birth rate per 1,000 women 15–19 years	Percent of teen births to unmarried women	Total number of births to unmarried women	Birth rate per 1,000 unmarried women 15–44 years	Percent of all births to unmarried
1996	491,577	54.4	75.9	1,260,306	44.8	32.4
1997	483,220	52.3	77.8	1,257,444	44.0	32.4
1998	484,895	51.1	78.5	1,293,567	44.3	32.8
1999	476,050	49.6	78.7	1,308,560	43.9	33.0
2000	468,990	48.5	78.8	1,347,043	45.2	33.2
2001	445,944	42.9	78.9	(NA)	45.0	33.5
2002*	424,670	45.3	(NA)	1,349,249	(NA)	33.8
Highest value	644,708	96.3	78.9	1,349,249	46.9	33.8
Lowest value	280,997	42.9	12.4	89,500	7.1	3.3

NA Not available.
*Preliminary data.

SOURCE: "HS-14. Births to Teenagers and to Unmarried Women, 1940–2002," in *Statistical Abstract of the United States: 2003,* U.S. Census Bureau, 2003, http://www.census.gov/statab/hist/HS-14.pdf (accessed August 11, 2004)

Abortions Declined

The Centers for Disease Control and Prevention (CDC) reported that 853,485 legal induced abortions were performed in the United States in 2001 compared to 857,475 in 2000. The 2001 abortion ratio (the number of legal induced abortions per one thousand live births) was 246. This was a slight increase from 245 in 2000 but a decrease from 256 in 1999. The CDC noted that the national abortion ratio increased from 196 per one thousand live births in 1973 to a peak of 364 per one thousand in 1984 and since then has steadily declined. Most abortions in 2001 were obtained by white, unmarried women less than twenty-five years of age. As in previous years, about one-fifth of women who had abortions were nineteen years old or younger. Of the women who had abortions, 45% were known to have had no previous live births.

The CDC noted a number of factors that may have contributed to the overall decline in the abortion ratio. These factors included a decrease in the number of unintended pregnancies; a shift in the age distribution of women (women are living longer and women past childbearing years make up a greater percentage of the female population); limited access to abortion services, including the passage of abortion laws that affect adolescents (parental consent or notification laws and mandatory waiting periods); and increased use of contraceptives (condoms and long-acting hormonal contraceptive methods for women that were introduced in the early 1990s).

Young Adults Delayed Marriage

Beginning in the mid-1960s, an increasing proportion of women and men postponed marriage. Many women began to focus attention on building careers. In 1950 14.4 million men (26.4%) and 11.4 million women (20%) had never been married. By 2002, 32% of men and 25.2% of women had never married. (See Table 1.10.)

The median age at first marriage in 1970 was 23.2 years old for men and 20.8 for women. As women found increasing opportunity in the workplace, they delayed marriage almost as long as men. By 2000 the median age at first marriage rose to 26.8 years old for men and 25.1 for women. (See Figure 1.2.)

Adult Children Living with Parents

Delays in marriage increased the number of one-person households or prompted adult children to continue living with their parents. Census 2000 reported 56% of men and 43% of women age eighteen to twenty-four lived at home with one or both parents. Both men and women in this age group were more likely to cohabit, live with roommates, or live with people other than spouses rather than live alone. Thirty percent of men and 35% of women in this age group lived with others who were neither spouses nor parents.

Single-Parent Households Increased

According to the Census Bureau's report *America's Families and Living Arrangements 2000,* single-mother households increased from 12% of family households in 1970 to 26% in 2000. In the same period single-father households grew from 1% to 5% of all family households. The sharp rise in birth rates among unmarried women between the mid-1970s and mid-1990s raised the proportion of children living with a single parent.

Divorces Continued

Before World War II divorces were difficult to obtain, and a divorce in a family was considered a scandalous

TABLE 1.10

Marital status of population 15 years old and over, by sex, 1950–2002

(Numbers in thousands)

			Males			
				Unmarried		
Year	Total	Married	Total unmarried	Never married	Widowed	Divorced
All races						
2002	106,819	61,268	45,551	34,229	2,636	8,686
2001*	105,584	61,209	44,375	33,077	2,540	8,758
2000	103,114	59,684	43,429	32,253	2,604	8,572
1999	102,048	59,039	43,010	31,912	2,542	8,556
1998	101,123	58,633	42,491	31,591	2,569	8,331
1997	100,159	57,923	42,236	31,315	2,690	8,231
1996	98,593	57,656	40,937	30,691	2,478	7,768
1995	97,704	57,570	39,953	30,286	2,284	7,383
1994	96,768	57,068	39,700	30,228	2,222	7,250
1993	94,854	56,833	38,021	28,775	2,468	6,778
1990	91,955	55,833	36,121	27,505	2,333	6,283
1980	81,947	51,813	30,134	24,227	1,977	3,930
1970	70,559	47,109	23,450	19,832	2,051	1,567
1960	60,273	41,781	18,492	15,274	2,112	1,106
1950	54,601	36,866	17,735	14,400	2,264	1,071

			Females			
				Unmarried		
Year	Total	Married	Total unmarried	Never married	Widowed	Divorced
All races						
2002	114,639	62,102	52,537	28,861	11,408	12,268
2001*	113,451	61,889	51,562	28,056	11,526	11,980
2000	110,660	60,527	50,133	27,763	11,061	11,309
1999	109,628	60,001	49,626	27,520	10,944	11,162
1998	108,168	59,333	48,835	26,713	11,029	11,093
1997	107,076	58,829	48,247	26,073	11,058	11,116
1996	106,031	58,905	47,127	25,528	11,078	10,521
1995	105,028	58,984	46,045	24,693	11,082	10,270
1994	104,032	58,185	45,847	24,645	11,073	10,129
1993	102,400	57,768	44,631	23,534	11,214	9,883
1990	99,838	56,797	43,040	22,718	11,477	8,845
1980	89,914	52,965	36,950	20,226	10,758	5,966
1970	77,766	48,148	29,618	17,167	9,734	2,717
1960	64,607	42,583	22,024	12,252	8,064	1,708
1950	57,102	37,577	19,525	11,418	6,734	1,373

*Data for March 2001 and later use population controls based on Census 2000 and an expanded sample of households designed to improve state estimates of children with health insurance.

SOURCE: Adapted from "Table MS-1. Marital Status of the Population 15 Years Old and Over, by Sex and Race, 1950–Present," in *Annual Social and Economic Supplement: 2003 Current Population Survey,* Series P20-553, U.S. Census Bureau, 2003, http://www.census.gov/population/socdemo/hh-fam/tabMS-1.pdf (accessed August 10, 2004)

event. The Census Bureau reported that in 1950 only 2% of men and 2.4% of women were divorced. No-fault divorce laws introduced in most states in the mid-1970s made divorces easier to obtain. Divorce rates soared in the 1970s, reaching a peak of 5.3 divorces per one thousand population in about 1979. *The Statistical Abstract of the United States 2003* reported a declining divorce rate as the nation entered the twenty-first century. There were 4.7 divorces per one thousand population in 1990; 4.5 in 1995; and 4.0 in 2001. By 2002, 8.1% of men and 10.7% of women identified their current status as divorced. (See Table 1.10.) (These figures did not account for people who had been divorced but were subsequently remarried.)

Divorce reduced the size of households when one household separated into two smaller ones. Remarriage by divorced persons, however, often brought stepchildren into the new household, sometimes creating larger families. It should be noted that stepchildren were counted as "own children" by the Census Bureau.

SAME-SEX PARTNERS AND FAMILIES

In Census 2000, 5.2 million households were classified as unmarried-partner households, representing 4.7% of all households in the United States. According to the Census Bureau, these figures may have underrepresented

FIGURE 1.2

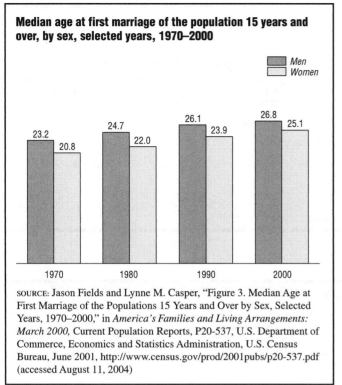

Median age at first marriage of the population 15 years and over, by sex, selected years, 1970–2000

Men
Women

	1970	1980	1990	2000
Men	23.2	24.7	26.1	26.8
Women	20.8	22.0	23.9	25.1

SOURCE: Jason Fields and Lynne M. Casper, "Figure 3. Median Age at First Marriage of the Populations 15 Years and Over by Sex, Selected Years, 1970–2000," in *America's Families and Living Arrangements: March 2000,* Current Population Reports, P20-537, U.S. Department of Commerce, Economics and Statistics Administration, U.S. Census Bureau, June 2001, http://www.census.gov/prod/2001pubs/p20-537.pdf (accessed August 11, 2004)

TABLE 1.11

Unmarried partner households, by sex of partners, 2000

Total	5,230,703	100
Male and female	4,571,992	87.4
Both male	332,645	6.4
Both female	326,066	6.2

SOURCE: Adapted from "QT-P18. Marital Status by Sex, Unmarried-Partner Households, and Grandparents as Caregivers, 2000," in *American Fact Finder,* U.S. Census Bureau, http://factfinder.census.gov/servlet/QTTable?_bm=y&-geo_id=01000US&-qr_name=DEC_2000_SF3_U_QTP18&-ds_name=DEC_2000_SF3_U&-_lang=en&-_sse=on (accessed August 5, 2004)

the true number of cohabiting couples. Same-sex partners in particular may have been reluctant to identify themselves as such and thus described themselves as roommates or friends. Census 2000 counted a little more than 650,000 households, or 12.6% of unmarried partner households, as same-sex partners. (See Table 1.11.)

The sexual revolution of the 1960s ushered in an era of more liberal societal attitudes about male and female relationships, and it also brought a new tolerance toward the gay community. The Lambda Legal Defense and Education Fund, an advocacy organization supporting the civil rights of gay men and women, sought to have same-sex couples included in the popular definition of family. It claimed there were between six and ten million same-sex parents in the United States who were the mothers and fathers of an estimated six to fourteen million children.

MULTIGENERATIONAL FAMILIES

Census 2000 recorded 3.9 million American households, or 4% of all households, that were composed of three or more generations living together. In 2000 there were 2.6 million multigenerational families that included children and grandchildren living with the householder. Nearly 1.3 million multigenerational families included the householder, his or her children, and his or her parents. Another seventy-eight thousand households, about 2% of all multigenerational family households, consisted of four generations. (See Table 1.12.)

The Census Bureau reported that multigenerational families were most common in areas where recent immi-

grants lived with relatives, housing shortages or high costs forced families to share living space, and teenage birth rates were high. As older adults lived longer, the need for family caregiving also created multigenerational households.

In 2000 children under age eighteen represented 26.3% of the population. They lived in diverse households. While 90% lived with at least one parent, 6.1% resided with a grandparent, 2% lived with other relatives, 0.4% lived with a foster family, and 1.4% lived with other nonrelatives. The South had the highest percentage of children living with grandparents (7.3%), while more children in the West (2.8%) lived with other relatives. (See Table 1.13.)

MILITARY FAMILIES IN WARTIME

In September 2003 America's active-duty military personnel had slightly more than two million dependents. While 749,000 dependents were spouses, 1.2 million (62%) were children. Another 11,600 military dependents were parents of active-duty personnel. Nine percent of military dependents lived in foreign countries and U.S. territories overseas. Typically, military families lived on or near military bases. Most knew the challenges of frequent relocations and the extended absences of husbands or wives, mothers or fathers.

Following the terrorist attacks of September 11, 2001, American military intervention in Afghanistan and Iraq required expanded troop strength. On March 12, 2003, the Pentagon reported 188,592 Reserve and National Guard members on active duty. By May 2003 that number had increased to 220,000. More than half of these men and women had never before been called to active duty. Others had been activated only for short-duration assignments. More than a year later, Reserve and National Guard members remained a vital part of U.S. troop strength in Afghanistan and Iraq and in support roles in other countries.

In June 2003 the Department of Defense released a survey of spouses of activated National Guard and Reserve members. Three-fourths of the activated National Guard and Reserve members had held full-time jobs. Of

TABLE 1.12

Multigenerational households, 2000

	All households	Total[2]	Multigenerational households by type[1]		
			Householder with child and grandchild	Householder with parent and child	Householder with parent, child, and grandchild
United States	105,480,101	3,929,122	2,561,637	1,289,159	78,326

Note: Parent may be either parent or parent-in-law of the householder. Child may be the natural born, adopted, or stepchild of the householder. Relationship refers to how each person is related to the householder.
[1]Individual types may include a small number of households with members from additional generations, for example, grandparents or great-grandparents of the householders for which tabulated data are not available.
[2]Total represents only those three types of households specified in the table.

SOURCE: Adapted from "PHC-T-17. Multigenerational Households for the United States, States, and for Puerto Rico, 2000," in *U.S. Census 2000*, U.S. Census Bureau, September 2001, http://www.census.gov/population/cen2000/phc-t17.pdf (accessed August 11, 2004)

TABLE 1.13

Relationship to householder for children under 18 years, by region, 2000

	Population under 18 years		Percent of population under 18 years						
Area	Number	Percent of total population	Total	Son or daughter	Grandchild	Householder/ spouse	Other relatives[1]	Foster child	Other nonrelatives[2]
United States	71,843,425	26.3	100.0	90.0	6.1	0.1	2.0	0.4	1.4
Region									
Northeast	12,950,914	24.9	100.0	91.1	5.5	0.1	1.7	0.5	1.2
Midwest	16,564,597	26.5	100.0	92.0	4.8	0.1	1.4	0.4	1.4
South	25,420,728	26.1	100.0	88.8	7.3	0.1	2.1	0.3	1.3
West	16,907,186	27.4	100.0	89.0	6.0	0.1	2.8	0.4	1.6

— Represents or rounds to zero.
[1]Other relatives include brother/sister, nephew/niece, cousin, brother/sister-in-law, son/daughter-in-law, and the category "other relative." An example of a relationship in the latter category would be great-grandchild.
[2]Other nonrelatives include roomer/boarder, housemate/roommate, unmarried partners, and the category "other nonrelative." An example of the latter category would be a child of an unmarried partner or roommate but not a related child of the householder.

SOURCE: Adapted from Terry Lugaila and Julia Overturf, "Table 2. Relationship to Householder for Children under 18 Years for the United States, Regions, States, and for Puerto Rico, 2000," in *Children and the Households They Live In, 2000*, Current Population Reports, CENSR-14, U.S. Department of Commerce, Economics and Statistics Administration, U.S. Census Bureau, February 2004, http://www.census.gov/prod/2004pubs/censr-14.pdf (accessed July 19, 2004)

the spouses unexpectedly left in charge of the family and all family affairs, less than half were employed. (See Figure 1.3.) Fifteen percent of reservists were activated with twenty-four hours or less notice. Health insurance, finances, dependent care, and legal matters were identified as the primary types of arrangement the family needed to make prior to deployment. Dependent care was the most frequently cited concern, reported by 74.6% of respondents. (See Figure 1.4.) According to the survey, thirty percent of spouses reported family income had decreased, while 58% reported an increase in family income while the reservist was on active duty. Despite the challenges of family disruption and concerns for the safety of the active-duty family member, 61% of spouses said they were coping "very well" or "well"; 15% said they were coping "poorly" or "very poorly."

FIGURE 1.3

Civilian employment of National Guard member's spouse, 2002*

(respondent n=3,777)

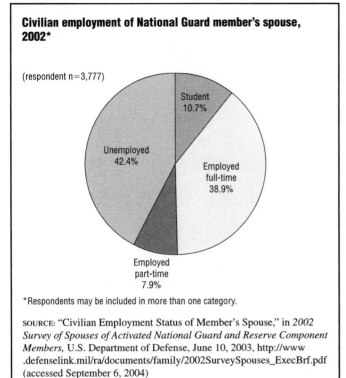

*Respondents may be included in more than one category.

SOURCE: "Civilian Employment Status of Member's Spouse," in *2002 Survey of Spouses of Activated National Guard and Reserve Component Members,* U.S. Department of Defense, June 10, 2003, http://www .defenselink.mil/ra/documents/family/2002SurveySpouses_ExecBrf.pdf (accessed September 6, 2004)

FIGURE 1.4

Tasks to be completed before activation in the National Guard, 2002*

(respondent n=3,811)

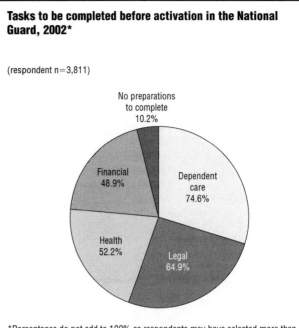

*Percentages do not add to 100% as respondents may have selected more than one preparation to complete.

SOURCE: "Types of Preparation Tasks to Be Completed before Activation," in *2002 Survey of Spouses of Activated National Guard and Reserve Component Members,* U.S. Department of Defense, June 10, 2003, http://www.defenselink.mil/ra/documents/family/ 2002SurveySpouses_ExecBrf.pdf (accessed September 6, 2004)

CHAPTER 2

WOMEN, MEN, AND THE FAMILY

Three trends greatly changed the composition of the American family beginning in the early 1960s: a lower fertility rate; an increase in the number of births among young unmarried women; and women—especially working women—delaying childbearing.

According to data from the National Center for Health Statistics (NCHS), in 2002 there were 4,021,726 live births in the United States, 136,485 fewer than 1990. Between 1990 and 2002 the crude birth rate fell 17%, from 16.7 to 13.9 births per one thousand population. The fertility rate declined 9%, from 70.9 to 64.8 live births per one thousand women aged fifteen to forty-four. The most dramatic decline in fertility rate was the 24% drop among African-American women. (See Figure 2.1.)

DECLINING BIRTH RATES

The National Vital Statistics Reports, published by the NCHS, showed that birth rates shifted significantly by age groups between 1990 and 2002. Teenage birth rates dropped continuously in the twelve-year period. For the fifteen to nineteen age group, the rate of first births reached a record low of thirty-four per one thousand births in 2002. The decline in first births applied to teenagers of all races and to those of Hispanic origin. The most dramatic change was the drop of 31.1 points for African-American teens age fifteen to seventeen.

An important trend in addition to the decline in teen birth rates was the decline in second births to teenagers. At its peak in the early 1990s, for every one thousand women age fifteen to nineteen who had given birth to a child, 220 gave birth to a second child while still a teenager. This trend dropped dramatically to about 173 second births per one thousand by 2000.

Between 1990 and 2002 the rate of first births increased for all women over age thirty. The increase was most dramatic in the thirty to thirty-four age group, which rose from a rate of 21.2 per one thousand births in 1990 to 26.6 per one thousand births by 2002. Asian-American women had the most stable first birth rate during the period, with an overall decline of just three-tenths of a point between 1990 and 2002.

Extending the Childbearing Years

Before the 1960s, when larger families were more common, it was not unusual for a woman to continue having babies well into her thirties or even her forties. However, as family size decreased, it became more common to have the typical two or three children during the first years of marriage when the woman was generally in her twenties. While most women still gave birth while in their twenties, a significant proportion began to wait until their thirties to have their first child. In the 1950s, women bearing children in their thirties were generally having their third or fourth child. Half a century later, many women who gave birth in their thirties were typically having their first or second child.

Historically, ages fifteen to forty-four were considered the childbearing years for record-keeping purposes. But women in the 1990s began to push that age forward, often with the help of new technological advances in reproductive medicine. The Bureau of Vital Statistics reported that between 1990 and 2002 the birth rate for women age forty to forty-four increased 51%, from 5.5 to 8.3 births per one thousand women. For women in the forty-five to forty-nine age group, the rate more than doubled from 0.2 to 0.5. Data for women past the age of fifty has been limited, but births have extended into that age group.

Nonmarital Childbearing

Prior to the 1970s the typical pregnant, unmarried woman either got married or gave the child up for adoption. Some women had abortions. However it was handled, the pregnancy was often cloaked in secrecy. An

FIGURE 2.1

Fertility rate by race, 1990 and 2002

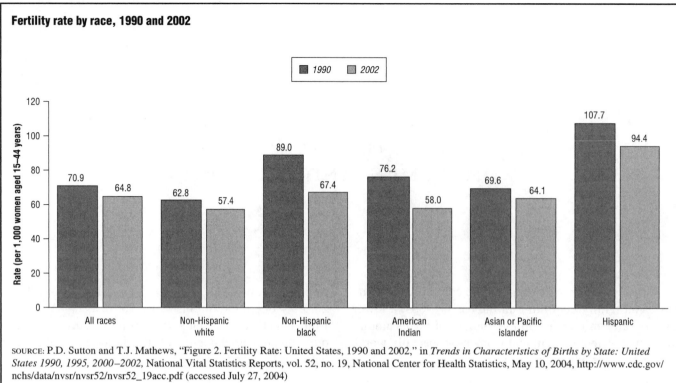

SOURCE: P.D. Sutton and T.J. Mathews, "Figure 2. Fertility Rate: United States, 1990 and 2002," in *Trends in Characteristics of Births by State: United States 1990, 1995, 2000–2002,* National Vital Statistics Reports, vol. 52, no. 19, National Center for Health Statistics, May 10, 2004, http://www.cdc.gov/nchs/data/nvsr/nvsr52/nvsr52_19acc.pdf (accessed July 27, 2004)

unmarried pregnant woman often left her family's home and community during the pregnancy to stay with a relative or entered a home for unwed mothers; in each case, her family made some excuse for her absence. The infant was given up for adoption and never openly discussed. Few women risked the social stigma of raising a child alone, at least without concocting a story of a husband who abandoned the woman or met an untimely death.

REUNITING ADOPTEES WITH THEIR PARENTS. Although young unmarried women who gave up their babies for adoption often suffered great guilt and wondered about the quality of the child's life, they never expected to meet that child in the future. Adoption records were sealed and the mothers expected to remain forever anonymous. In an unexpected twist, as these adopted children married and began their own families, many wanted to know their personal heritage. In some cases they wanted to know family medical history, including genetic conditions that might affect the adopted person's health or that of his or her own biological children. Other adoptees wanted to understand the circumstances that resulted in their adoption or to know general family information and family traits.

In January 2004 the American Adoption Information Clearinghouse reported that the percentage of adults searching for their birth parents continued to increase. The organization estimated that half of all adopted persons searched for their birth parents at some time in their lives. In addition, a growing number of birth parents searched

for their adult children who were placed for adoption many years earlier. New legislation in some states allowed greater access to adoption information, and computer and Internet technology expanded and speeded the search options. A variety of organizations emerged to assist with searches and serve as go-betweens in making contact. While many birth parents and natural children were pleased to be reunited, the new relationships added one more complexity to the profile of the American family.

TO MARRY OR NOT TO MARRY. According to the Federal Interagency Forum on Child and Family Statistics, the period 1960–64 was the peak for pregnant women choosing marriage. During that time, 60% of women who were unmarried at the time of conception married before the births of their babies. Immediately prior to and immediately following those years, about 54% of pregnant women wed before giving birth. That rate had dropped significantly by the late 1970s. Between 1975 and 1979, just 32% of unmarried, pregnant women chose marriage. Societal and family pressures on unexpectedly expectant couples to marry quickly had diminished, and other factors may have played a role in the drop as well—including women's increased earning power and the number of couples who chose to cohabit rather than marry.

A report from the Federal Interagency Forum on Child and Family Statistics tracked birthrates for children born to unmarried American women since 1980. Between that year and 2002 the percentage of births to unmarried mothers nearly doubled, from 18.4% to 34%. Births to unmarried women in their twenties generally increased at a steady rate during this period. The greatest rise in non-marital births was a thirty-five percentage point increase in the eighteen to nineteen age group. The year 1994 marked the high point for births to unmarried women age thirty and over. After decreasing by 1–1.5 percentage points by 1999 and 2000, the birth rate for the over-thirty group rose slightly in 2001 and 2002.

According to data published by the U.S. Census Bureau, between June 2001 and June 2002 1.3 million unmarried women gave birth. They represented 33% of all births during that twelve-month period. The highest proportions of out-of-wedlock births were to young women age fifteen to nineteen (89%), African-American women (65%), and women who had not graduated from high school (63%). (See Figure 2.2.)

The birth rate among women living with an unmarried partner (eighty-seven per one thousand women) was almost the same as for women living with a husband (eighty-six per one thousand). The birth rate for unmarried women not living with a partner (thirty-six per one thousand) was less than half of that for cohabiting women. (See Table 2.1.)

ARTIFICIAL REPRODUCTION

In the late 1980s and early 1990s, when an estimated four thousand women became surrogate mothers by being artificially inseminated with sperm from men whose wives were infertile, many people were concerned that surrogate motherhood might threaten family stability. Who would be considered the child's mother? Also, some surrogate mothers refused to relinquish the child after delivery, resulting in long, bitter fights for custody of the child.

Rapid advances in fertility technology made such family matters even more complicated. The use of donor sperm and/or eggs could mean a child might have three or four parents—the donor or donors, the mother who carried the transplanted embryo in her uterus, and her spouse. While federal funding for human embryo research was banned during the administration of President Ronald Reagan, private fertility enterprises continued to be unregulated, and each fertility clinic operated under its own guidelines. Critics feared that fertility patients as well as donors might fall victim to unscrupulous clinics and doctors who did not have to answer to scientific and ethical review boards. To further complicate the issues, initial successes with cloning of sheep led to rumors about the cloning of humans.

Monitoring Fertility Technology

Because of the expense of in vitro fertility treatments (about $8,000 for each attempt), couples wanted to ensure a successful pregnancy. In most cases the procedure had

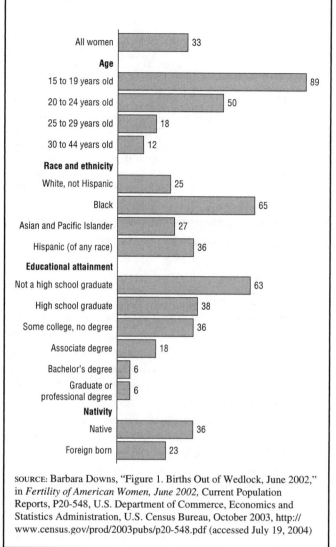

FIGURE 2.2

Births out of wedlock, June 2002

(Percent of births born out of wedlock in the preceding 12 months to women in specified categories)

Category	Percent
All women	33
Age	
15 to 19 years old	89
20 to 24 years old	50
25 to 29 years old	18
30 to 44 years old	12
Race and ethnicity	
White, not Hispanic	25
Black	65
Asian and Pacific Islander	27
Hispanic (of any race)	36
Educational attainment	
Not a high school graduate	63
High school graduate	38
Some college, no degree	36
Associate degree	18
Bachelor's degree	6
Graduate or professional degree	6
Nativity	
Native	36
Foreign born	23

SOURCE: Barbara Downs, "Figure 1. Births Out of Wedlock, June 2002," in *Fertility of American Women, June 2002,* Current Population Reports, P20-548, U.S. Department of Commerce, Economics and Statistics Administration, U.S. Census Bureau, October 2003, http://www.census.gov/prod/2003pubs/p20-548.pdf (accessed July 19, 2004)

to be repeated several times. Through ultrasound imaging, doctors could keep track of the number of maturing eggs. If too many eggs had matured, the doctor typically advised against continuing the treatment. Once sperm had been introduced, in cases in which it could be determined that a higher-order multiple birth was likely to occur, many doctors considered destroying some of the embryos in order to improve viability of the remaining embryos. Generally, this was not done without the permission of the parents. Some parents considered this act an abortion and refused to permit it, a stance that often led to a much higher level of multiple births. In the National Vital Statistics Report dated February 12, 2002, the Centers for Disease Control and Prevention (CDC) reported that from 1980 to 2000 the rate of twin births rose 55% from a rate of 18.9 per 1,000 total births to 29.3. From 1980 to 1998 the rate of higher order births (triplets or greater) surged from

TABLE 2.1

Fertility indicators for women 15–44 years old by cohabitation status, June 2002

(Numbers in thousands)

| Cohabitation status | Number of women | Mean age in years | Percent childless | Women who had a child in the last year | | | Children ever born per 1,000 women |
				Number with a birth	Births per 1,000 women	First births per 1,000 women	
Total	61,361	30.0	43.5	3,766	61.4	23.1	1,211
Married, spouse in household	27,828	34.5	18.5	2,382	85.6	29.6	1,784
Unmarried partner in household[1]	3,531	29.2	45.0	307	87.0	42.8	1,124
No partner in household[2]	30,001	26.0	66.5	1,077	35.9	14.6	689

[1]Includes women of any marital status who were living with an opposite sex unmarried partner at the time of the survey.
[2]Includes women of any marital status who were not living with an opposite sex partner at the time of the survey.

SOURCE: Barbara Downs, "Table 4. Fertility Indicators for Women 15–44 Years Old by Cohabitation Status, June 2002," in *Fertility of American Women, June 2002*, Current Population Reports, P20-548, U.S. Department of Commerce, Economics and Statistics Administration, U.S. Census Bureau, October 2003, http://www.census.gov/prod/2003pubs/p20-548.pdf (accessed July 19, 2004)

37.0 per 1,000 total births to 193.5. In 1999 and 2000 the rate of higher order births dropped to 180.5.

WOMEN REDEFINE THEIR ROLE

While the husband's main role had traditionally been that of breadwinner, by the 1960s many women were redefining their own roles as homemakers. Women who had experienced the economic independence of a paying job during World War II, and who had attained personal satisfaction from working, reentered the labor force. The availability of contraceptives enabled many young married women to postpone childbearing. The mothers of baby boomers, most of whom had given birth at a young age, saw the last of their children leave the nest. These mothers were ready to start a new chapter in life, which for many meant finding a career.

More Education

Most working women prior to the 1960s held secretarial and sales clerk positions, while nursing and teaching were the two primary career options for those wishing to pursue a professional degree. But their daughters aspired to different careers. Realizing that higher education meant better wages, these young women pursued postsecondary education. In 1960 women earned about one-third of all bachelor's (35.3%) and master's degrees (31.6%). By 1985, women earned fully half of these degrees. The increase in women earning degrees in medicine and law was even more dramatic, doubling from 12.4% in 1975 to 32.8% by 1985. According to the August 2004 *Chronicle of Higher Education,* in the 2001–02 academic year women earned 57% of bachelor's degrees, 59% of master's degrees, and 46% of doctoral degrees. Forty-four percent of medical degrees and 48% of law degrees were conferred on women.

Into the Labor Force

In 1950 about one in three women participated in the labor force—or, in other words, worked outside the home,

according to the Bureau of Labor Statistics. By 2002, three of every five women of working age were in the workforce, an increase from a 33.9% participation rate in 1950 to 59.8% in 1998. The most significant increase was among those women in the twenty-five to thirty-four age range, who more than doubled their participation in the workforce after 1950.

In 2002 women represented 47% of employed persons. The increase in women serving in managerial and professional positions, while partly the result of increased education, was boosted significantly by the Civil Rights Act of 1964, which forced businesses to recruit and promote qualified women and minorities. In 1983 women accounted for 45.8% of people employed in technical, sales, and administrative support positions and 21.9% of managerial and professional positions. By 2002, 33.7% of managers and professionals were women, while their representation in traditional women's roles as support staff had declined to 38.8%.

While women increased their education and moved into higher-paying careers, their earnings continued to trail those of their male counterparts. In a 2004 report the Bureau of Labor Statistics revealed that the median weekly wage of women working full-time in 2002 was 77.9% of the median weekly earnings of men working full-time. This represented an improvement from 1980, when women earned 64.2% of men's median pay.

The Bureau of Labor Statistics reported that between 1975 and 2002 the labor force participation of women with children under age eighteen grew from 47% to 72%. The most significant increase was among women with very young children. In 1976 just 31% of women with children under the age of one were part of the workforce. By 2002 54.6% of working mothers with infants were in the workforce. (See Figure 2.3.) In 2002 34% of women with infants were employed full-time compared to 51% of women without infants. Sixteen percent of both groups

FIGURE 2.3

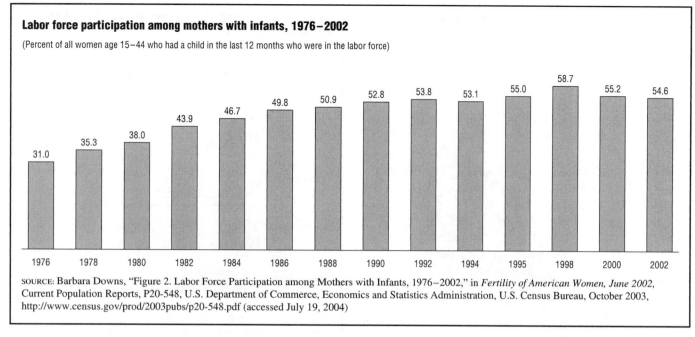

Labor force participation among mothers with infants, 1976–2002

(Percent of all women age 15–44 who had a child in the last 12 months who were in the labor force)

SOURCE: Barbara Downs, "Figure 2. Labor Force Participation among Mothers with Infants, 1976–2002," in *Fertility of American Women, June 2002,* Current Population Reports, P20-548, U.S. Department of Commerce, Economics and Statistics Administration, U.S. Census Bureau, October 2003, http://www.census.gov/prod/2003pubs/p20-548.pdf (accessed July 19, 2004)

were employed part-time, while mothers with infants had a 5% unemployment rate compared to 4% for women without infants. (See Figure 2.4.)

WORKING FAMILIES

According to the Bureau of Labor Statistics (BLS) report "Employment Characteristics of Families," in 2003, 82% of families had at least one employed member. Asian families were most likely to have someone in the family working (89.1%), followed by Hispanic families (86.1%) and white families (82.3%). African-American families were the least likely to contain an employed member (77.9%).

Among married-couple families, 83.3% had an employed member in 2003, down by 0.2% from 2002. This proportion had declined each year since 1999. Both the husband and wife worked in 50.9% of married-couple families in 2003. This proportion had declined since 1997, when it was 53.4%. The proportion of married-couple families in which only the wife worked rose for the third straight year, to 6.8% in 2003. The proportion of families in which only the husband worked was relatively unchanged at 20%; however, this statistic had risen by 0.8% since 2000.

The BLS reported 35.4 million families with children under age eighteen in 2003. Of these, 90.3% had at least one parent employed, down from 90.7% percent in 2002. All of the decline was among single-parent families.

Employer Assistance for Working Parents

Parents, and particularly working mothers, look to employers to offer family-friendly benefits such as flexible work schedules and time off for certain family needs. In order to attract new employees and retain existing ones, many employers have implemented creative options to assist working parents. Consolidated annual leave plans no longer categorized available paid leave time into vacation, personal, and sick time. This gave employees discretion about how best to use paid leave time to meet their individual circumstances. Some companies offer on-site day-care centers for children of employees. Part-time work, job sharing, and flexible work schedules help parents accommodate the needs of the job and the family. Telecommuting options allow parents to perform part or all of their work from home. Employer-sponsored flexible spending accounts allow working parents to set aside part of their pretax earnings (money not subject to income taxes) to pay for specified medical and dependent-care expenses.

Economic and Financial Pressures

Changes in the cost of goods and services can quickly upset tight family budgets. Rising energy costs topped a list of national concerns in a 2001 survey by the Pew Research Center. About half of Americans listed the rising cost of gasoline as serious, and four in ten were concerned about the cost of electricity and other home utilities. Almost 40% of parents in the survey reported they had changed summer vacation plans and cut back on long-distance driving because of the increased cost of gasoline, compared to 26% of nonparents. Hardest hit were low-income families; 52% of families with incomes below $20,000 rated increased utility costs as a serious problem. Many families, especially those with children, struggled to meet basic expenses of living and worried about their financial safety.

Financial concerns drive many difficult family decisions. For 27% of those surveyed in 2001, money was

FIGURE 2.4

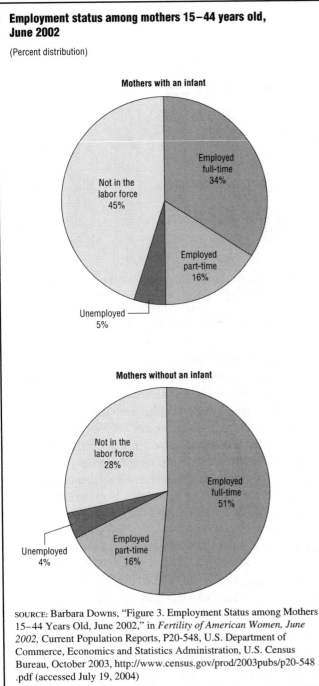

Employment status among mothers 15–44 years old, June 2002

(Percent distribution)

Mothers with an infant

Employed full-time 34%

Employed part-time 16%

Unemployed 5%

Not in the labor force 45%

Mothers without an infant

Employed full-time 51%

Employed part-time 16%

Unemployed 4%

Not in the labor force 28%

SOURCE: Barbara Downs, "Figure 3. Employment Status among Mothers 15–44 Years Old, June 2002," in *Fertility of American Women, June 2002,* Current Population Reports, P20-548, U.S. Department of Commerce, Economics and Statistics Administration, U.S. Census Bureau, October 2003, http://www.census.gov/prod/2003pubs/p20-548 .pdf (accessed July 19, 2004).

FIGURE 2.5

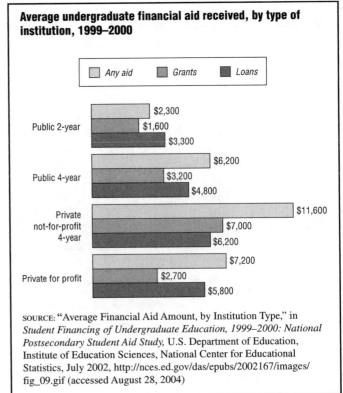

Average undergraduate financial aid received, by type of institution, 1999–2000

Legend: Any aid, Grants, Loans

Public 2-year: $2,300 / $1,600 / $3,300

Public 4-year: $6,200 / $3,200 / $4,800

Private not-for-profit 4-year: $11,600 / $7,000 / $6,200

Private for profit: $7,200 / $2,700 / $5,800

SOURCE: "Average Financial Aid Amount, by Institution Type," in *Student Financing of Undergraduate Education, 1999–2000: National Postsecondary Student Aid Study,* U.S. Department of Education, Institute of Education Sciences, National Center for Educational Statistics, July 2002, http://nces.ed.gov/das/epubs/2002167/images/ fig_09.gif (accessed August 28, 2004)

$11,600 in total aid, compared to $6,200 for public four-year institutions. (See Figure 2.5.) The differences in tuition for these two types of institutions, however, were similar. According to the August 2004 issue of the *Chronicle of Higher Education,* the average cost for tuition plus room and board at a private college in 2002 was $29,541, compared to $13,833 at a public institution. The percentage of students who received aid was less disparate than the amount of aid. In the private, not-for-profit colleges and universities, 76% of students received financial aid compared to 62% in public institutions. (See Figure 2.6.)

CUSTODIAL PARENTS

Custodial parent is the term used by the government to describe a single parent who has been awarded legal custody of one or more of his or her children, usually as part of a divorce. The Census Bureau reported that in the spring of 2002 an estimated 13.4 million parents had custody of 21.5 million children under the age twenty-one. About 84% of custodial parents were mothers and 15% were fathers, a proportion that had not changed since 1994. Between 1993 and 2001 the percentage of custodial parents employed in full-time, year-round jobs rose from 45.6% to 55.3%. Throughout that same time period, as employment of custodial mothers increased, the employment of custodial fathers remained relatively stable. (See Figure 2.7.)

With increased employment, the proportion of custodial parents living below the poverty level dropped from

cited in their decision whether or not to have, or to postpone having, a baby. The most frequent financial decision for 34% of parents was whether to work or stay at home with children. Finances played a large role in decisions about attending college for 24% of families ("Decisions Because of Lack of Money," *Money and the American Family,* Modern Maturity Magazine, AARP, May 2000).

The high cost of a college education presented challenges for parents who wanted to attend or complete college themselves or provide for their children's college education. Private, not-for-profit four-year colleges and universities offered the greatest amount of financial aid, an average of

FIGURE 2.6

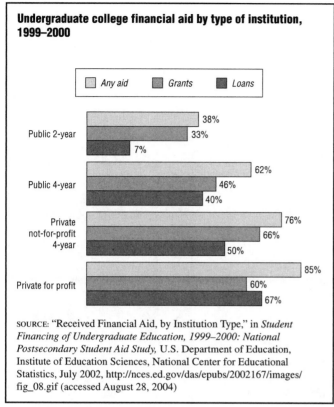

Undergraduate college financial aid by type of institution, 1999–2000

Legend: Any aid · Grants · Loans

Public 2-year
- Any aid: 38%
- Grants: 33%
- Loans: 7%

Public 4-year
- Any aid: 62%
- Grants: 46%
- Loans: 40%

Private not-for-profit 4-year
- Any aid: 76%
- Grants: 66%
- Loans: 50%

Private for profit
- Any aid: 85%
- Grants: 60%
- Loans: 67%

SOURCE: "Received Financial Aid, by Institution Type," in *Student Financing of Undergraduate Education, 1999–2000: National Postsecondary Student Aid Study,* U.S. Department of Education, Institute of Education Sciences, National Center for Educational Statistics, July 2002, http://nces.ed.gov/das/epubs/2002167/images/fig_08.gif (accessed August 28, 2004)

33.3% in 1993 to 23.4% by 2001, according to U.S. Census data. (See Figure 2.8.) Despite the steady decline in poverty for custodial parent families, their poverty rate was still four times that of married-couple families. Increased unemployment since 2001 may have changed the number of custodial parents living below the poverty level. The BLS reported that the jobless rate rose from 4.7% in 2001 to a peak of 6.5% in mid-2003. By November 2004 the jobless rate hovered near 5.5%.

The Census Bureau reported that about 63% of custodial mothers and 38.6% of custodial fathers had agreements or awards for child support payments from the other parent. The majority of them were waiting for past-due payments in 2001. The average annual amount of partial payments received was $4,300 and did not differ between mothers and fathers. The proportion of custodial parents receiving every payment they were due increased from 36.9% in 1993 to 46.2% in 1997 then slipped to 44.8% by 2001. (See Figure 2.9.) When there were no delinquent payments, custodial parents received an average of $5,800 per year.

CAREGIVERS

A somewhat unexpected result of better medical care and increased longevity is the phenomenon of the "sandwich generation"—adults who still have children living at home but who are also attending to the needs of their aging parents. While an increasing number of men

had primary parental responsibility, women remained the traditional caregivers, according to a survey published in April 2004 by the National Alliance for Caregiving and the American Association of Retired Persons. In most cases these women were also employed outside the home and had to meet the challenge of both family and work obligations.

The demands of caregiving usually required some adjustments at work. Nearly two-thirds (64.1%) of caregivers surveyed in the aforementioned study were employed, most (51.8%) full-time. More than one-half (54.2%) reported having to make some type of adjustments at work as a result of caregiving responsibilities. Overall, nearly half (49.4%) of caregivers had to make changes to their daily work schedule, such as coming in later, leaving earlier, or taking time off during the day. Some caregivers reported giving up their job either temporarily or permanently—10.9% took a leave of absence, 3.6% took early retirement, and 6.4% gave up their jobs altogether. About 7% worked fewer hours or took a less demanding job. A smaller percentage reported having lost some job benefits (4.2%) or having turned down a promotion (3.1%) because of caregiving.

MEN'S CHANGING ROLE

In a "Facts for Features" press release for Father's Day 2004, the U.S. Census Bureau provided a profile of contemporary fathers. Of the 25.8 million fathers who were part of a married-couple family with its own children under age eighteen:

- 12% were under age thirty; 4% were over age fifty-five.
- 22% were raising three or more children under age eighteen.
- 9% were raising infants under age one.
- 61% had an annual family income of $50,000 or more.

Of the two million single fathers with their own children under age eighteen:

- 22% were under age thirty; 5% were over age fifty-five.
- 10% were raising three of more children under age eighteen.
- 1% were raising infants under age one.
- 24% had an annual family income of $50,000 or more.
- 45% were divorced; 34% had never been married; 17% were married but the spouse was absent; 4% were widowed.

The Future of Fatherhood

Researchers believe that more changes would occur in the roles of men and women in the twenty-first century. If mothers of young children continue to join the labor

FIGURE 2.7

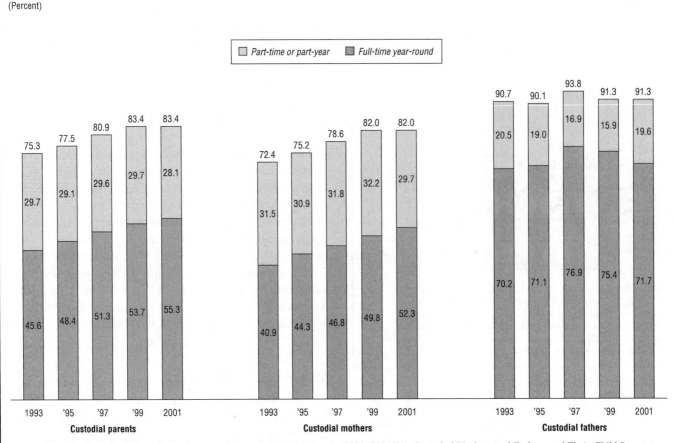

Employment status of custodial parents, 1993–2001

(Percent)

Legend: ☐ Part-time or part-year   ■ Full-time year-round

SOURCE: Timothy S. Grall, "Figure 1. Employment Status of Custodial Parents, 1993–2001," in *Custodial Mothers and Fathers and Their Child Support, 2001,* Current Populations Reports, P60-225, U.S. Department of Commerce, Economics and Statistics Administration, U.S. Census Bureau, October 2003, http://www.census.gov/prod/2003pubs/p60-225.pdf (accessed July 19, 2004)

FIGURE 2.8

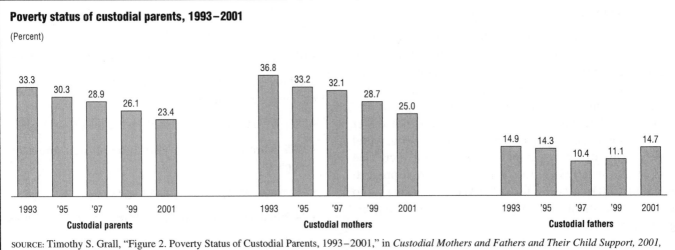

Poverty status of custodial parents, 1993–2001

(Percent)

SOURCE: Timothy S. Grall, "Figure 2. Poverty Status of Custodial Parents, 1993–2001," in *Custodial Mothers and Fathers and Their Child Support, 2001,* Current Populations Reports, P60-225, U.S. Department of Commerce, Economics and Statistics Administration, U.S. Census Bureau, October 2003, http://www.census.gov/prod/2003pubs/p60-225.pdf (accessed July 19, 2004)

force, fathers might have to assume more child-care tasks. Researchers asked whether modern fathers would accept an increasing share of child-rearing responsibili- ties or flee from them. One indicator of fathers' interest in their child-rearing role was the increase in single fathers raising their own children. According to Census

FIGURE 2.9

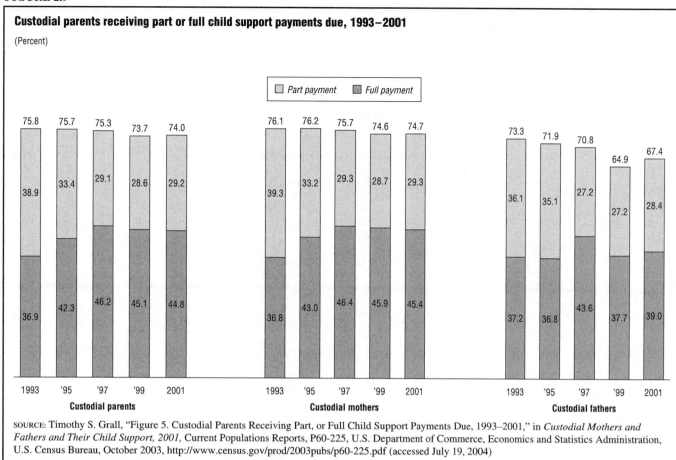

Custodial parents receiving part or full child support payments due, 1993–2001

(Percent)

SOURCE: Timothy S. Grall, "Figure 5. Custodial Parents Receiving Part, or Full Child Support Payments Due, 1993–2001," in *Custodial Mothers and Fathers and Their Child Support, 2001,* Current Populations Reports, P60-225, U.S. Department of Commerce, Economics and Statistics Administration, U.S. Census Bureau, October 2003, http://www.census.gov/prod/2003pubs/p60-225.pdf (accessed July 19, 2004)

Bureau data, in 1970 only one in ten single parents was a father; by 2004 the share of single fathers had increased to one in six.

A bigger issue concerned the role and/or the commitment of noncustodial fathers in divorced families and fathers of children born out-of-wedlock. According to the U.S. Department of Health and Human Services (HHS), the number of children growing up in homes without fathers increased dramatically from 1960. By 2000 nearly twenty-five million children did not live with their fathers, compared to fewer than ten million in 1960. More than one-third of these children did not see their fathers at all during the course of a year.

On the National Fatherhood Initiative (NFI) Web site, Roland Warren, NFI's president, stated that violent criminals are overwhelmingly males who grew up without fathers (72% of adolescent murderers and 70% of long-term prison inmates). Warren also noted that children living in homes without a father are "more likely to experience poverty; be suspended from school, or to drop out; be treated for an emotional or behavioral problem; commit suicide as adolescents; and be victims of child abuse or neglect." The Fatherhood Initiative sought to increase public awareness of the importance of fathers in children's lives, promote a national public agenda of policies supportive of

families and fathers, and provide resources to help men be better fathers.

HOW MEN AND WOMEN SPENT THEIR TIME

In September 2004 the Bureau of Labor Statistics released the first of a series of new studies tracking trends in how Americans spent their time. For the *American Time Use Survey,* twenty-one thousand participants kept a record of how they spent every hour in a single twenty-four-hour period. The survey confirmed that many traditional divisions of labor between men and women had not changed very much over the past few generations. While 78% of women and 85% of men were part of the workforce, two-thirds of women said they prepared meals and did housework on an average day compared to 34% of men who said they helped with meals or cleanup and 19% of men who said they did housework.

Table 2.2 provides a picture of the activities of the average American during a typical twenty-four-hour period, with separate columns showing how men and women used their time differently. For most people, sleep consumed more than one-third of the time. The adult respondents averaged about five hours of leisure time per day, with more than half of it spent watching television. Women spent an average of 138 minutes per day on

TABLE 2.2

Average hours per day spent in primary activities for the total population and by sex, 2003[1]

Activities	Hours per day, total population		
	Total	Men	Women
Total, all activities[2]	24.00	24.00	24.00
Personal care activities	9.34	9.13	9.54
Sleeping	8.57	8.48	8.65
Eating and drinking	1.21	1.24	1.18
Household activities	1.83	1.33	2.30
Housework	0.62	0.23	0.98
Food preparation and cleanup	0.53	0.25	0.79
Lawn and garden care	0.20	0.26	0.14
Household management	0.13	0.11	0.15
Purchasing goods and services	0.81	0.68	0.94
Consumer goods purchases	0.40	0.32	0.48
Professional and personal care services	0.09	0.07	0.11
Caring for and helping household members	0.55	0.34	0.75
Caring for and helping household children	0.42	0.24	0.58
Caring for and helping non-household members	0.29	0.26	0.31
Caring for and helping non-household adults	0.11	0.11	0.10
Working and work-related activities	3.69	4.57	2.87
Working	3.32	4.09	2.60
Education activities	0.47	0.45	0.50
Attending class	0.29	0.28	0.29
Homework and research	0.14	0.12	0.15
Organizational, civic, and religious activities	0.32	0.29	0.35
Religious and spiritual activities	0.14	0.12	0.16
Volunteering (organizational and civic activities)	0.14	0.13	0.14
Leisure and sports	5.11	5.41	4.83
Socializing and communicating	0.78	0.72	0.83
Watching television	2.57	2.75	2.41
Participating in sports, excercise, and recreation	0.30	0.39	0.21
Telephone calls, mail, and e-mail	0.19	0.13	0.24
Other activities, not elsewhere classified	0.19	0.18	0.20

[1]Primary activities are those respondents identify as their main activity. Other activities done simultaneously are not included.
[2]All major activity categories include related travel time.
Note: Data refer to respondents 15 years and over.

SOURCE: Adapted from "Table 1. Average Hours per Day Spent in Primary Activities for the Total Population and for Persons Reporting the Activity on the Diary Day by Activity Category and Sex, 2003 Annual Averages," in *American Time-Use Survey*, U.S. Department of Labor, Bureau of Labor Statistics, 2004, http://www.bls.gov/news.release/pdf/atus.pdf (accessed September 16, 2004)

TABLE 2.3

Average hours spent in primary activities on weekdays and weekends, 2003[1]

Activity	Hours per day, total population	
	Weekdays	Weekends and holidays[2]
Total, all activities[3]	24.00	24.00
Personal care activities	9.04	10.04
Sleeping	8.26	9.30
Eating and drinking	1.16	1.32
Household activities	1.69	2.18
Housework	0.57	0.73
Food preparation and cleanup	0.51	0.57
Lawn and garden care	0.16	0.28
Household management	0.13	0.13
Purchasing goods and services	0.76	0.95
Consumer goods purchases	0.34	0.57
Professional and personal care services	0.11	0.05
Caring for and helping household members	0.59	0.46
Caring for and helping household children	0.43	0.38
Caring for and helping non-household members	0.28	0.30
Caring for and helping non-household adults	0.10	0.13
Working and work-related activities	4.68	1.33
Working	4.22	1.19
Educational activities	0.61	0.14
Attending class	0.40	[4]
Homework and research	0.14	0.12
Organizational, civic, and religious activities	0.22	0.55
Religious and spiritual activities	0.06	0.34
Volunteering (organizational and civic activities)	0.14	0.14
Leisure and sports	4.59	6.35
Socializing and communicating	0.61	1.18
Watching television	2.39	3.01
Participating in sports, exercise, and recreation	0.26	0.37
Telephone calls, mail, and e-mail	0.20	0.16
Other activities, not elsewhere classified	0.18	0.20

[1]Primary activities are those respondents identify as their main activity. Other activities done simultaneously are not included.
[2]Holidays are New Year's Day, Easter, Memorial Day, the Fourth of July, Labor Day, Thanksgiving Day, and Christmas Day. In 2003, data were not collected about Thanksgiving Day or Christmas Day.
[3]All major activity categories include related travel time.
[4]Data not shown where base is less than 800,000.
Note: Data refer to respondents 15 years and over.

SOURCE: Adapted from "Table 2. Average Hours per Day Spent in Primary Activities for the Total Population and for Persons Reporting the Activity on the Diary Day by Activity Category and Weekdays and Weekends, 2003 Annual Averages," in *American Time-Use Survey*, U.S. Department of Labor, Bureau of Labor Statistics, 2004, http://www.bls.gov/news.release/pdf/atus .pdf (accessed September 16, 2004)

household activities, while for the men this figure was just 80 minutes. Men tended to spend an extra half an hour per day on leisure activities, while women spent that half hour caring for family members and communicating by telephone, mail, and e-mail.

Activities varied for the average adult on weekdays compared to weekends and holidays. On weekend days and holidays people reported getting over an hour more of additional sleep. They also spent one and three-quarters hours more time in leisure activities. The average adult watched thirty minutes more television on weekends and holidays and enjoyed an extra thirty minutes of social time. (See Table 2.3.)

Factors such as age, race, presence of children, and educational level determined how people spent their leisure time. For example, adults in the typical child-raising years of twenty-five to forty-four spent less than four and one-half hours in leisure activities, while people under age twenty-four and over age fifty-five found five and one-half hours for sports and leisure. People over age sixty-five enjoyed more than seven hours of daily leisure activity. Both men and women with less than a high school education were more likely to spend leisure time socializing and watching television. Of people who participated in sports or enjoyed reading, men and women with a bachelor's degree or higher spent the most time in those activities. Of people who enjoyed playing games or using the computer for fun, men and women with high school diplomas but less than a college degree most frequently chose those activities. (See Table 2.4.)

Not surprisingly, as people aged they spent less time working and more time eating and drinking (1.52 hours per day at age sixty-five and over compared to .96 hours per day at age fifteen to twenty-four), taking care of household activities (2.55 at age sixty-five and over compared to .82 hours at age fifteen to twenty-four), and enjoying leisure activities (7.16 hours at age sixty-five and over compared to 4.20 at age thirty-five to forty-four). (See Table 2.5.)

TABLE 2.4

Average hours per day spent in leisure and sports activities, 2003

Characteristic	Total, all leisure and sports activities			Participating in sports, exercise, and recreation		Socializing and communicating		Watching TV		Reading		Relaxing/thinking		Playing games and computer use for leisure		Other leisure and sports activities, including travel[1]	
	Total, both sexes	Men	Women	Men	Women	Men	Women	Men	Women	Men	Women	Men	Women	Men	Women	Men	Women
Age																	
Total, 15 years and over	5.11	5.41	4.83	0.39	0.21	0.72	0.83	2.75	2.41	0.33	0.40	0.34	0.32	0.36	0.23	0.52	0.43
15 to 24 years	5.46	5.92	4.99	0.67	0.36	1.00	1.02	2.29	2.17	0.14	0.14	0.22	0.22	0.80	0.43	0.79	0.65
25 to 34 years	4.30	4.58	4.03	0.37	0.22	0.72	0.83	2.33	2.01	0.14	0.18	0.24	0.24	0.36	0.19	0.42	0.37
35 to 44 years	4.20	4.60	3.81	0.32	0.19	0.63	0.72	2.54	1.87	0.20	0.26	0.26	0.22	0.21	0.16	0.45	0.38
45 to 54 years	4.67	4.89	4.46	0.27	0.18	0.60	0.83	2.65	2.26	0.30	0.34	0.38	0.30	0.24	0.18	0.45	0.37
55 to 64 years	5.27	5.55	5.02	0.34	0.18	0.63	0.78	3.06	2.53	0.43	0.55	0.39	0.34	0.25	0.21	0.45	0.42
65 years and over	7.16	7.52	6.88	0.33	0.13	0.73	0.81	4.05	3.70	0.94	1.01	0.66	0.63	0.26	0.24	0.54	0.37
Race and Hispanic or Latino ethnicity																	
White	5.07	5.32	4.83	0.39	0.23	0.71	0.83	2.69	2.39	0.35	0.44	0.31	0.29	0.34	0.23	0.53	0.43
Black or African American	5.55	6.13	5.09	0.32	0.12	0.77	0.84	3.35	2.72	0.19	0.18	0.58	0.56	0.45	0.28	0.47	0.38
Hispanic or Latino ethnicity	4.85	5.28	4.41	0.46	0.19	0.76	0.79	2.78	2.53	0.15	0.13	0.33	0.24	0.27	0.12	0.53	0.41
Employment status																	
Employed	4.23	4.53	3.89	0.35	0.21	0.65	0.74	2.26	1.83	0.23	0.28	0.28	0.23	0.30	0.19	0.45	0.41
Employed full-time	4.06	4.33	3.66	0.32	0.19	0.64	0.67	2.21	1.76	0.21	0.26	0.28	0.23	0.26	0.16	0.42	0.39
Employed part-time	4.83	5.60	4.40	0.52	0.24	0.75	0.91	2.55	2.00	0.34	0.32	0.31	0.23	0.50	0.24	0.64	0.46
Not employed	6.71	7.66	6.12	0.48	0.21	0.90	0.95	3.98	3.19	0.57	0.57	0.50	0.44	0.52	0.30	0.70	0.45
Presence of children																	
No household children under 18	5.62	5.87	5.36	0.39	0.21	0.71	0.84	3.07	2.69	0.40	0.54	0.38	0.38	0.37	0.25	0.55	0.44
Household children under 18	4.35	4.64	4.10	0.39	0.20	0.74	0.82	2.21	2.02	0.20	0.21	0.28	0.23	0.35	0.21	0.47	0.41
Children 13 to 17 years, none younger	4.77	5.14	4.45	0.47	0.22	0.78	0.84	2.26	2.18	0.28	0.29	0.30	0.26	0.55	0.22	0.49	0.44
Children 6 to 12 years, none younger	4.44	4.76	4.18	0.43	0.25	0.76	0.80	2.27	2.01	0.19	0.23	0.27	0.22	0.33	0.21	0.51	0.46
Youngest child under 6 years	4.02	4.23	3.84	0.30	0.16	0.70	0.83	2.14	1.93	0.15	0.14	0.27	0.23	0.25	0.20	0.43	0.35
Educational attainment, 25 years and over																	
Less than high school	6.29	6.75	5.87	0.32	0.11	0.76	0.85	3.94	3.47	0.29	0.35	0.79	0.65	0.19	0.12	0.44	0.31
High school diploma[2]	5.36	5.52	5.21	0.32	0.13	0.68	0.84	3.19	2.81	0.25	0.45	0.41	0.41	0.23	0.21	0.44	0.37
Less than a bachelor's degree	4.78	5.08	4.53	0.26	0.17	0.63	0.76	2.70	2.28	0.37	0.44	0.31	0.27	0.33	0.23	0.47	0.38
Bachelor's degree or higher[3]	4.29	4.56	4.01	0.38	0.28	0.62	0.74	2.11	1.66	0.52	0.54	0.18	0.17	0.27	0.17	0.48	0.44

Hours per day spent in leisure and sports activities

[1]Includes other leisure and sports activities, not elsewhere classified, and travel related to leisure and sports activities.
[2]Includes persons with a high school diploma or equivalent.
[3]Includes persons with bachelor's, master's, professional, and doctoral degrees.
Note: Unless otherwise specified, data refer to respondents 15 years and over. Persons whose ethnicity is identified as Hispanic or Latino may be of any race and, therefore, are classified by ethnicity as well as by race.

SOURCE: "Table 9. Average Hours Per Day Spent in Leisure and Sports Activities for the Total Population by Selected Characteristics, 2003 Annual Averages," in *American Time-Use Survey*, U.S. Department of Labor, Bureau of Labor Statistics, 2004, http://www.bls.gov/news.release/pdf/atus.pdf (accessed September 16, 2004)

TABLE 2.5

Average hours spent in primary activities by age and sex, 2003

Characteristic	Hours per day spent in primary activities											
	Personal care activities	Eating and drinking	Household activities	Purchasing goods and services	Caring for and helping household members	Caring for and helping non household members	Working and work-related activities	Educational activities	Organizational, civic, and religious activities	Leisure and sports	Telephone calls, mail, and e-mail	Other activities not elsewhere classified
Total, 15 years and over	9.34	1.21	1.83	0.81	0.55	0.29	3.69	0.47	0.32	5.11	0.19	0.19
15 to 24 years	9.95	0.96	0.82	0.69	0.27	0.32	2.65	2.20	0.26	5.46	0.24	0.18
25 to 34 years	9.25	1.17	1.59	0.78	1.11	0.23	4.78	0.29	0.21	4.30	0.13	0.16
35 to 44 years	9.07	1.16	1.99	0.82	1.05	0.19	4.81	0.10	0.34	4.20	0.13	0.16
45 to 54 years	9.00	1.19	1.97	0.84	0.38	0.31	4.91	0.06	0.34	4.67	0.17	0.17
55 to 64 years	9.13	1.35	2.28	0.90	0.15	0.40	3.70	*	0.37	5.27	0.21	0.20
65 years and over	9.65	1.52	2.55	0.89	0.13	0.31	0.77	*	0.44	7.16	0.27	0.28
Men, 15 years and over	9.13	1.24	1.33	0.68	0.34	0.26	4.57	0.45	0.29	5.41	0.13	0.18
15 to 24 years	9.85	0.94	0.65	0.54	0.10	0.37	2.95	2.06	0.26	5.92	0.19	0.16
25 to 34 years	8.93	1.21	1.10	0.70	0.58	0.24	5.95	*	0.21	4.58	0.10	0.14
35 to 44 years	8.82	1.19	1.40	0.67	0.68	0.17	5.84	*	0.31	4.60	0.10	0.16
45 to 54 years	8.76	1.22	1.45	0.66	0.27	0.23	5.93	*	0.27	4.89	0.12	0.14
55 to 64 years	8.93	1.40	1.79	0.68	0.09	0.27	4.64	*	0.32	5.55	0.13	0.20
65 years and over	9.51	1.65	1.89	0.90	0.15	0.31	1.20	*	0.41	7.52	0.16	0.29
Women, 15 years and over	9.54	1.18	2.30	0.94	0.75	0.31	2.87	0.50	0.35	4.83	0.24	0.20
15 to 24 years	10.06	0.97	1.00	0.83	0.45	0.27	2.35	2.33	0.25	4.99	0.30	0.21
25 to 34 years	9.55	1.12	2.08	0.86	1.64	0.22	3.62	0.31	0.22	4.03	0.16	0.17
35 to 44 years	9.31	1.13	2.56	0.96	1.40	0.20	3.81	0.14	0.36	3.81	0.16	0.16
45 to 54 years	9.23	1.16	2.48	1.01	0.47	0.40	3.92	*	0.40	4.46	0.22	0.19
55 to 64 years	9.31	1.30	2.71	1.10	0.21	0.52	2.88	*	0.42	5.02	0.28	0.20
65 years and over	9.76	1.43	3.06	0.89	0.12	0.31	0.43	*	0.46	6.88	0.36	0.28

*Data not shown where base is less than 800,000

SOURCE: Adapted from "Table 3. Average Hours per Day Spent in Primary Activities for the Total Population, by Age, Sex, Race, Hispanic or Latino Ethnicity, and Educational Attainment, 2003 Annual Averages," in *American Time-Use Survey*, U.S. Department of Labor, Bureau of Labor Statistics, 2004, http://www.bls.gov/news.release/pdf/atus.pdf (accessed September 16, 2004)

CHAPTER 3
THE CHILDREN OF AMERICA

Since the mid-1960s, the proportion of children as part of the total U.S. population has decreased. The percentage of the population under age eighteen peaked in 1960 at 36% and began a decline to 26% by 1990. While the seventy-two million children under age eighteen still represented 26% of the population in 2000, the U.S. Census Bureau projected that by 2020 only 24% of the population would be children under age eighteen (*America's Children in Brief: Key Indicators of Well-Being, 2004*, Federal Interagency Forum on Child and Family Statistics, 2004). As the child population decreased through lower birth rates, the number of Americans over the age of sixty-five began to claim an increasing percentage of the overall population.

DIVERSITY OF CHILDREN

Census data show that white, non-Hispanic children steadily declined as a percentage of the child population from 74% in 1980 to 63% in 1999. That decline was projected to continue to 53% by 2020. In a reverse trend, Hispanic children, who were 9% of the child population in 1980, were projected to rise to 24% by 2020 (*America's Children in Brief: Key Indicators of Well-Being, 2004*).

The distribution of children by race and ethnicity varied widely by relationship to the householder in Census 2000. Although 15% percent of all children were identified as African-American, they represented 32% of all grandchildren, 35% of all foster children, and 29% of all children who were other relatives of the householder. This data suggested that African-American children were more likely to live in extended family households. Twenty-eight percent of Hispanic children age fifteen to seventeen were householders or spouses, a statistic that the Census Bureau suggested may have indicated early marriage patterns. (See Table 3.1.)

Children with disabilities posed unique challenges for families. While 5.7% of all children counted in 2000 had disabilities, they represented 22.4% of all foster children. The most significant proportion of children with disabilities (4.5%) had difficulty learning, remembering, or concentrating. Just over 1% of children had multiple disabilities. (See Table 3.1.)

LIVING ARRANGEMENTS OF CHILDREN

Family structure has been associated with the economic, parental, and community resources available to children, as well as their overall well-being. On average, living with two married parents has been associated with more favorable outcomes for children. Not surprisingly, the increasing number of divorces, marital separations, and out-of-wedlock births significantly reshaped the living arrangements of American children. In 2003 children under eighteen were considerably more likely to live with only one parent than children of just one or two prior generations.

A 2003 report from the U.S. Census Bureau provided a statistical snapshot of American households with children under the age of eighteen. In 2002 69% of children lived with two parents, 23% lived with only their mother, and 5% lived with only their father. Another 4% lived with neither parent. When children lived in households without either parent, 44% lived with a grandparent. (See Table 3.2.)

Many children lived with a parent who was cohabiting with an unmarried partner. While 23% of children lived with a single mother compared to 5% who lived with a single father, children in a single-father household were three times more likely to share the home with the parent's cohabiting partner. (See Figure 3.1.) Almost half of African-American children (48%) lived with a single mother, compared with 25% of Hispanic children and 16% of non-Hispanic white children. Of children who lived with a cohabiting parent, non-Hispanic white children more frequently experienced a cohabiting mother while Hispanic children more often experienced a cohabiting father. (See Figure 3.1.)

TABLE 3.1

Characteristics of children under 18 years by relationship to householder, 2000

Characteristic	Total	Son or daughter	Grandchild	Householder/ spouse[1]	Other relatives[2]	Foster child	Other nonrelatives[3]
Total, under 18 years	71,843,425	64,651,959	4,388,908	64,314	1,464,848	291,507	981,889
Percent	100.0	100.0	100.0	100.0	100.0	100.0	100.0
Race and Hispanic or Latino origin							
White alone	68.8	70.9	48.6	62.2	39.1	47.8	66.5
Black or African American alone	14.8	13.3	32.3	14.8	28.8	35.3	13.1
American Indian and Alaska Native alone	1.1	1.0	2.1	1.5	1.9	3.1	1.5
Asian alone	3.4	3.4	2.4	2.6	4.8	1.1	2.4
Native Hawaiian and Other Pacific Islander alone	0.2	0.1	0.3	0.2	0.5	0.3	0.2
Some other race alone	7.7	7.2	8.9	14.5	19.9	7.4	11.6
Two or more races	4.1	4.0	5.4	4.3	5.0	5.1	4.8
Hispanic or Latino (of any race)	17.0	16.1	21.1	28.4	38.4	17.2	24.2
White alone, not Hispanic or Latino	61.1	63.6	39.0	50.6	23.8	40.8	56.1
Nativity							
Native	95.6	95.9	97.2	80.4	79.3	97.3	89.3
Foreign born	4.4	4.1	2.8	19.6	20.7	2.7	10.7
Living arrangement[4]							
Living in married couple family group	68.0	74.7	10.8	(X)	5.5	(X)	(X)
Living in mother only family group	20.9	20.0	39.9	(X)	21.6	(X)	(X)
Living in father only family group	5.8	5.4	13.8	(X)	6.0	(X)	(X)
Living with neither parent	5.4	(X)	35.5	100.0	67.0	100.0	100.0
Child in unmarried partner household[5]	5.7	5.3	2.7	(X)	6.1	9.4	46.0
Educational attainment of the householder							
Less than high school	19.9	17.8	40.3	68.8	40.6	24.0	28.5
High school graduate (includes equivalency)	27.0	26.8	29.2	21.4	27.4	28.6	32.9
Some college	29.2	29.9	22.0	8.7	22.9	32.4	27.0
Bachelor's degree or more	23.9	25.5	8.5	1.1	9.1	15.0	11.6
Employment status of the householder							
In labor force	83.8	86.1	55.6	62.0	70.4	70.9	81.8
Employed[6]	95.8	96.0	94.8	86.1	92.4	95.8	94.3
Unemployed[6]	4.2	4.0	5.2	13.9	7.6	4.2	5.7
Not in labor force	16.2	13.9	44.4	38.0	29.6	29.1	18.2
Poverty status in 1999[7]							
In poverty	16.0	15.5	20.6	51.1	24.7	(X)	(X)
Not in poverty	84.0	84.5	79.4	48.9	75.3	(X)	(X)
Tenure of householder							
Owns home	66.8	67.1	70.2	26.4	51.8	71.7	52.5
Rents home	33.3	32.9	29.8	73.6	48.2	28.3	47.5
Total, 3 to 17 years	60,518,194	54,932,195	3,201,260	64,314	1,217,977	243,341	859,107
Percent	100.0	100.0	100.0	100.0	100.0	100.0	
School enrollment							
Enrolled in school[8]	90.8	91.4	86.4	53.4	83.4	90.8	82.6
Nursery school, preschool, or kindergarten	15.0	15.0	19.3	(X)	11.2	15.4	11.5
Public school[9]	68.0	66.8	77.4	(X)	83.7	84.9	80.2
Elementary (grades 1–8)	55.1	55.6	52.8	1.8	47.0	55.9	47.3
Public school[9]	89.1	88.7	92.9	94.8	95.0	96.3	95.4
High school (grades 9–12)	20.6	20.8	14.2	47.7	24.9	19.4	23.4
Public school[9]	90.9	90.6	93.7	92.2	95.1	95.9	94.8
Not enrolled in school	9.2	8.6	13.6	46.6	16.6	9.2	17.4

Some children lived in households maintained by people other than their parents. Foster children fit this grouping because they were not related to the householder. Figure 3.2 shows that some areas of the country, particularly the South, had higher incidents of children who were not a son or daughter of the householder in 2000. Marital difficulties, economic issues, or parents absent due to illness, military service, or prison sentences may have placed children in the homes of relatives. Some cultural traditions favored living in an extended family arrangement. Coastal areas, such as California, Florida, and Hawaii, with large numbers of immigrants have been characterized by above-average proportions of children who were not sons or daughters of the householder. Often relatives or friends already living in the United States provided housing to immigrant families until they could establish themselves.

Not all children were part of a household in Census 2000. The Census Bureau reported that, of the 71,843,425 under age eighteen, more than three hundred thousand lived in group quarters. This included correctional institutions, hospitals, residential treatment facilities, group homes, and schools for the disabled. Also counted in this category were children who, along with one or both parents, were part of the growing homeless population.

Children of Foreign-Born Householders

Census Bureau data revealed that in 2002 there were fourteen million children, or 20% of all children, living in a house-

TABLE 3.1

Characteristics of children under 18 years by relationship to householder, 2000 [CONTINUED]

Characteristic	Total	Son or daughter	Grandchild	Householder/ spouse[1]	Other relatives[2]	Foster child	Other nonrelatives[3]
Total, 5 to 17 years	52,826,320	48,097,684	2,602,671	64,314	1,078,672	213,519	769,460
Percent	100.0	100.0	100.0	100.0	100.0	100.0	100.0
Residence in 1995							
Same house in 1995	52.9	53.8	55.8	23.6	34.2	25.6	20.9
Different house in 1995	47.1	46.2	44.2	76.4	65.8	74.4	79.1
Language spoken at home							
English only	81.6	81.9	84.2	67.8	60.5	88.9	79.2
Language other than English	18.4	18.1	15.8	32.2	39.5	11.1	20.8
Disability status							
Severe hearing or vision impairment	1.0	1.0	1.3	2.2	1.3	2.7	1.4
Condition limiting basic activities	1.0	1.0	1.5	3.8	1.4	3.2	1.5
Difficulty learning, remembering or concentrating	4.5	4.3	5.9	4.6	5.4	20.6	5.9
Difficulty dressing, bathing or getting around inside the house	0.9	0.8	1.3	1.7	1.3	4.6	1.1
With any disability	5.7	5.5	7.6	8.8	7.1	22.4	7.6
With multiple disabilities[10]	1.2	1.1	1.7	2.4	1.5	5.5	1.5

X Not applicable.
[1]Refers to householders and spouses who are aged 15 to 17 years.
[2]Other relatives include brother/sister, nephew/niece, cousin, brother/sister-in-law, son/daughter-in-law, and the category "other relative." An example in the latter category would be great-grandchild.
[3]Other nonrelatives include roomer/boarder, housemate/roommate, unmarried partners, and the category "other nonrelative." An example in the latter category would be a child of an unmarried partner or roommate, but not a related child of the householder.
[4]Determined by relationship to householder or to reference person in a related subfamily. Universe excludes children aged 15 to 17 who are householders, reference persons of subfamilies, and their spouses.
[5]Excludes children aged 15 to 17 who are the householder or unmarried partner in an unmarried-partner household.
[6]Percent based on householders who were in the labor force.
[7]Poverty universe excludes children unrelated to the householder (foster children and other nonrelatives).
[8]Enrolled in school includes children enrolled in college, not shown separately.
[9]Percent based on those enrolled in grade category.
[10]Includes children aged 5 to 17 with any combination of two or more disabilities.

SOURCE: Terry Lugaila and Julia Overturf, "Table 3. Characteristics of Children under 18 Years by Relationship to Householder, 2000," in *Children and the Households They Live In, 2000,* Current Population Reports, CENSR-14, U.S. Department of Commerce, Economics and Statistics Administration, U.S. Census Bureau, February 2004, http://www.census.gov/prod/2004pubs/censr-14.pdf (accessed July 19, 2004)

hold with at least one foreign-born parent present. While children with foreign-born parents might need additional resources at school and at home in order to progress successfully in school, they were more likely to have the advantage of living in a two-parent family. Eighty-one percent of children living with foreign-born parents were living with two parents, compared to 69% of children living with native parents.

Stepchildren

Many divorced parents eventually remarried, and their children became part of stepfamilies, or blended families. The most common stepfamily consisted of children living with a biological mother and a stepfather, with no other children present. The frequency of this arrangement was attributable to the large number of divorced women who gained custody of their children. Another type of stepfamily consisted of at least one stepchild and one biological child of the couple. According to the U.S. Census Bureau, approximately 15% of all children lived in stepfamilies and were included in the Census 2000 count of children in two-parent families.

Children and Grandparents

Grandparents have long played a significant role in the lives of many children. Grandparents provide an important resource to struggling parents by assisting with child care and often contributing to the family income. In 2002 5.6 million children were living in households with a grandparent present. The majority of these children (3.7 million) resided in the grandparent's home. In 65% of these cases, at least one parent was also present in the household. One-third of children with a coresident grandparent lived with one or both parents as the householder. (See Table 3.3.)

In *Coresident Grandparents and Their Grandchildren: Grandparent-Maintained Families,* Lynne M. Casper and Kenneth R. Bryson of the Census Bureau reported on the rising trend of grandparents raising grandchildren. They noted that in 1970 3.2% of children under age eighteen lived in family households maintained by a grandparent. By 2002, 5.1% of children lived in grandparent-headed households. Grandparents had responsibility for more than one million children without a parent present in the home. Other Census data showed that children living in grandparent-maintained homes without a parent present were more likely to live in poverty and receive public assistance. Thirty-six percent of these children lacked health insurance. (See Figure 3.3.) According to Casper and Bryson, some researchers

TABLE 3.2

Children by age and family structure, March 2002[1]

(In thousands)

Characteristic	Total under 18 years Number	90-percent confidence interval	Under 1 year	1–2 years	3–5 years	6–8 years	9–11 years	12–14 years	15–17 years	Total under 6 years	Total 6–11 years
All children	72,321	689	3,917	7,917	11,528	11,954	12,669	12,492	11,842	23,363	24,623
Two parents	49,666	600	2,778	5,552	8,028	8,307	8,615	8,521	7,864	16,358	16,922
Child of householder	48,843	596	2,710	5,410	7,890	8,191	8,490	8,388	7,766	16,009	16,680
Grandchild of householder	476	64	56	107	89	71	60	64	30	251	131
Other relative of householder	315	52	12	32	46	42	61	59	63	91	102
Nonrelative of householder	32	17	—	4	3	4	4	11	6	7	8
Householder has an unmarried partner—parent is not the householder or partner[2]	13	11	—	1	—	—	5	6	—	2	5
Mother only	16,473	368	832	1,723	2,584	2,724	3,032	2,865	2,714	5,139	5,755
Child of householder	13,747	338	568	1,274	2,071	2,286	2,641	2,474	2,434	3,913	4,927
Grandchild of householder	1,657	120	215	355	366	246	191	180	104	936	438
Other relative of householder	524	68	36	61	59	72	74	120	103	155	146
Nonrelative of householder	545	69	13	34	88	120	125	92	73	135	245
Mother is householder in an unmarried partner household[2]	1,430	111	121	234	254	242	258	165	155	608	500
Mother is partner in an unmarried partner household[2]	369	57	4	10	52	93	89	67	55	65	182
Children under 15 years	13,759	338	832	1,723	2,584	2,724	3,032	2,865	(X)	5,139	5,756
In a POSSLQ household[3]	1,562	116	129	256	337	350	313	177	(X)	722	663
Father only	3,297	169	233	402	506	464	544	551	598	1,141	1,007
Child of householder	2,851	157	193	340	449	371	479	482	537	982	850
Grandchild of householder	275	49	33	42	47	50	38	44	22	121	87
Other relative of householder	92	28	5	12	6	15	15	15	24	23	30
Nonrelative of householder	78	26	2	8	5	28	12	9	15	14	40
Father is householder in an unmarried partner household[2]	1,022	94	139	212	222	119	131	110	88	574	250
Father is partner in an unmarried partner household[2]	59	23	1	2	2	26	11	6	10	6	36
Children under 15 years	2,699	153	233	402	506	464	544	551	(X)	1,141	1,008
In a POSSLQ household[3]	904	89	144	213	214	137	115	80	(X)	572	252
Neither parent	2,885	158	75	240	410	460	479	555	667	725	939
Grandchild of householder	1,273	105	26	113	196	224	238	243	233	335	462
Other relative of householder	802	84	24	67	101	97	127	160	226	192	224
Foster child	235	45	5	18	38	47	34	49	43	62	81
Nonrelative of householder	575	71	20	41	76	91	80	104	164	137	171
Householder has an unmarried partner[2]	216	43	9	13	32	36	40	43	43	54	76
Children under 15 years	2,218	139	75	240	410	460	479	555	(X)	725	939
In a POSSLQ household[3]	186	40	6	19	38	41	43	40	(X)	62	83

— Represents zero or rounds to zero.
X Not applicable.
[1]All people under age 18, excluding those living in group quarters, householders, subfamily reference people, and their spouses.
[2]If the parent is either the householder with an unmarried partner in the household or the unmarried partner of the householder, they are cohabiting based on this direct measure. Cohabiting couples where neither partner is the householder are not identified.
[3]POSSLQ (Persons of the Opposite Sex Sharing Living Quarters) is defined by the presence of only two people over age 15 in the household who are opposite sex, not related, and not married. There can be any number of people under age 15 in the household. The universe of children under age 15 is shown as the denominator for POSSLQ measurement.
Note: Data based on the Annual Demographic Supplement to the March 2002 Current Population Survey.

SOURCE: Jason Fields, "Table 1. Children by Age and Family Structure, March 2002," in *Children's Living Arrangements and Characteristics, March 2002*, Current Population Reports, P20-547, U.S. Department of Commerce, Economics and Statistics Administration, U.S. Census Bureau, June 2003, http://www.census.gov/prod/2003pubs/p20-547.pdf (accessed July 19, 2004).

attributed the growing trend in coresident grandparent/grandchildren families to the continuing incidence of divorce, the rise in single-parent households, parental substance abuse, teen pregnancy, AIDS, child abuse and neglect, and other similar factors.

ADOPTED AND FOSTER CHILDREN

Many American families who wanted to adopt a child considered two groups of available children:

• Children, primarily infants, whose parents voluntarily gave them up for adoption. The parents generally worked through private adoption agencies or made private placements with adoptive families. The number of these adoptees was not tracked. Another source was children from other countries.

• Children who had been placed in foster care based on court determination that they were abused or neglect-

FIGURE 3.1

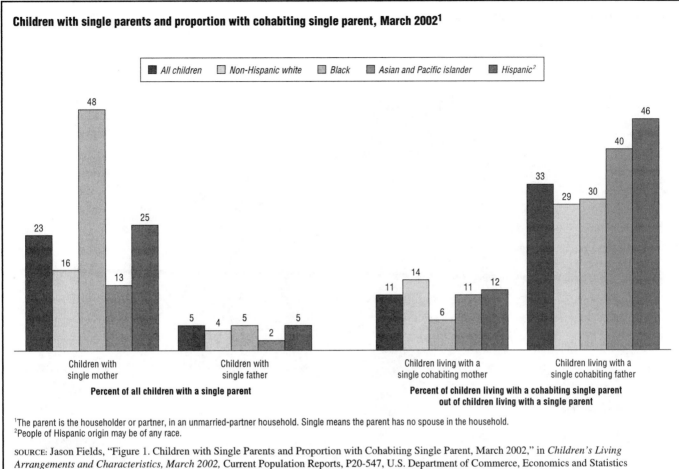

Children with single parents and proportion with cohabiting single parent, March 2002¹

Legend: ■ All children □ Non-Hispanic white □ Black ■ Asian and Pacific islander ■ Hispanic²

Percent of all children with a single parent

Children with single mother: 23, 16, 48, 13, 25
Children with single father: 5, 4, 5, 2, 5

Percent of children living with a cohabiting single parent out of children living with a single parent

Children living with a single cohabiting mother: 11, 14, 6, 11, 12
Children living with a single cohabiting father: 33, 29, 30, 40, 46

¹The parent is the householder or partner, in an unmarried-partner household. Single means the parent has no spouse in the household.
²People of Hispanic origin may be of any race.

SOURCE: Jason Fields, "Figure 1. Children with Single Parents and Proportion with Cohabiting Single Parent, March 2002," in *Children's Living Arrangements and Characteristics, March 2002,* Current Population Reports, P20-547, U.S. Department of Commerce, Economics and Statistics Administration, U.S. Census Bureau, June 2003, http://www.census.gov/prod/2003pubs/p20-547.pdf (accessed July 19, 2004)

ed, and for whom placement with adoptive families would serve the children's best interests

Adopted Children

A number of laws have been enacted to make it easier for families to adopt children.

- The 1993 Family and Medical Leave Act (PL 103–3) enabled parents to take time off work to adopt a child without losing their jobs or health insurance.

- The Interethnic Adoption Provisions of the Small Business Job Protection Act of 1996 amended the Multiethnic Placement Act of 1994 (PL 103–382) to ensure adoption processes were free from discrimination and delays based on the race, culture, and ethnicity of the child or the prospective parents.

- The Intercountry Adoption Act of 2000 (PL 106–279) facilitated immigration of foreign adopted children and placed requirements on states for supportive services.

- The Child Citizenship Act of 2000 (PL 106–395) provided automatic citizenship to both biological and adopted children of U.S. citizens who were born abroad and did not obtain citizenship at birth.

- The Economic Growth and Tax Relief Reconciliation Act of 2001 (PL 107–16) permanently extended the adoption credit implemented in 1996 and increased the maximum credit from $5,000 to $10,000 per eligible child.

- The Adoption Promotion Act of 2003 (PL 108–145) reauthorized an adoption incentive program and provided additional incentives for adoption of children with special needs, including older children (age nine and up), from foster care.

The National Adoption Information Clearinghouse (NAIC) estimated the 2004 cost of adoption from foster care at $0–$2,500. The cost of domestic adoption of a healthy infant ranged from $5,000 to $40,000, depending on the type of agency used and adoption circumstances. NAIC reported that fees to adopt a child from a foreign country ranged from $7,000 to $30,000, with additional fees possible depending on the country.

Intercountry Adoption

Many American families have chosen to adopt children from other countries. Because these foreign-born children required visas to enter the United States, the U.S.

FIGURE 3.2

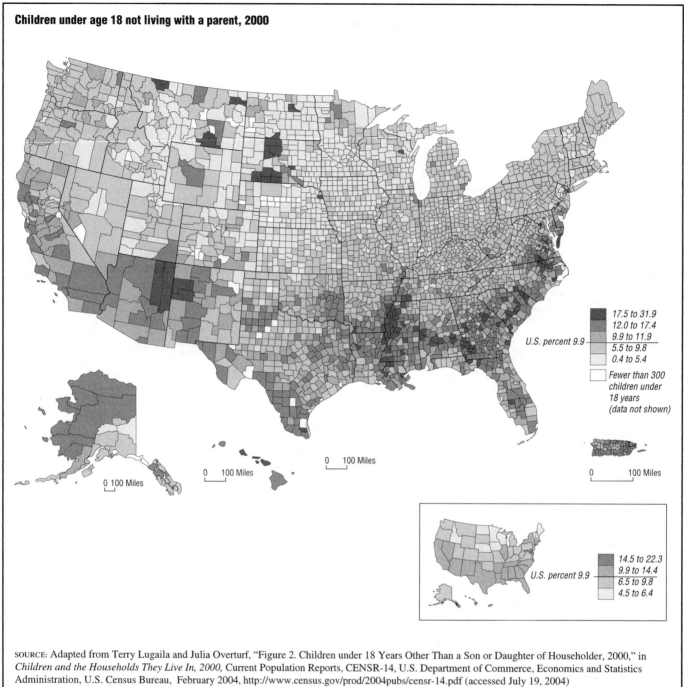

Children under age 18 not living with a parent, 2000

17.5 to 31.9
12.0 to 17.4
9.9 to 11.9
5.5 to 9.8
0.4 to 5.4

U.S. percent 9.9

Fewer than 300 children under 18 years (data not shown)

0 100 Miles

14.5 to 22.3
9.9 to 14.4
6.5 to 9.8
4.5 to 6.4

U.S. percent 9.9

SOURCE: Adapted from Terry Lugaila and Julia Overturf, "Figure 2. Children under 18 Years Other Than a Son or Daughter of Householder, 2000," in *Children and the Households They Live In, 2000,* Current Population Reports, CENSR-14, U.S. Department of Commerce, Economics and Statistics Administration, U.S. Census Bureau, February 2004, http://www.census.gov/prod/2004pubs/censr-14.pdf (accessed July 19, 2004)

Department of State maintains current records of the number of foreign adoptees. Foreign adoptions nearly tripled in the decade following 1993. That year, American families welcomed 7,377 foreign children. By 2003, the number of foreign adoptions had risen to 21,616 children. During that period China, Russia, South Korea, and Guatemala were the leading countries of origin for foreign adoptees.

Children in Foster Care

Foster care is an integral part of the child welfare system, designed to provide temporary respite and some stability for children whose families had difficulties parenting

or are no longer able to care for them. Some children remain in foster care until their parents resolve their problems. Other children cannot safely return home, and arrangements for their long-term welfare are necessary.

In the 2003 *Foster Care National Statistics,* the U.S. Department of Health and Human Services reported that an estimated 542,000 children were in foster care on September 30, 2001. The report compared data for 1998 and 2001 to identify trends. The gender mix of children in foster care remained stable during the period with 52% male and 48% female. The percentage of African-American children in foster care dropped from 44% in 1998 to 38%

TABLE 3.3

Characteristics of children who co-reside with grandparents, by presence of parents, March 2002[1]

(in thousands)

Characteristic	Total	Total with grand-parents	Total in grand-parent's household	With grandparents present — Grandparent is householder — Parent Present — Total	G'mother and g'father	G'mother only	G'father only	Grandparent is householder — No parents present — Total	G'mother and g'father	G'mother only	G'father only	Grandparent is not householder — Parent is householder — Total	G'mother and g'father	G'mother only	G'father only	Parent is not householder
Total	72,321	5,601	3,683	2,409	1,204	1,021	184	1,274	614	591	69	1,801	258	1,231	312	118
Age of child																
Under 6 years old	23,363	2,339	1,644	1,309	721	506	82	335	171	138	26	635	109	393	133	61
6 to 11 years old	24,623	1,770	1,118	656	307	293	56	462	240	201	21	619	90	428	101	33
12 to 17 years old	24,335	1,493	920	444	175	223	46	476	202	252	22	547	59	410	78	25
Race and ethnicity of child[2]																
White	56,276	3,674	2,418	1,701	947	601	153	717	429	245	43	1,177	180	784	213	81
Non-Hispanic	44,235	2,408	1,671	1,130	624	405	101	541	332	169	40	707	88	481	138	30
Black	11,646	1,445	1,077	576	178	381	17	501	153	327	21	339	27	253	59	29
Asian and Pacific Islander	3,223	361	89	67	44	16	7	22	19	3	—	262	48	176	38	9
Hispanic (of any race)	12,817	1,341	787	591	328	210	53	196	101	87	8	504	93	324	87	51
Presence of parents																
Two parents	49,666	1,706	477	477	255	155	67	(X)	(X)	(X)	(X)	1,217	164	840	213	12
Mother only	16,473	2,249	1,658	1,658	807	753	98	(X)	(X)	(X)	(X)	503	74	337	92	89
Father only	3,297	373	275	275	142	114	19	(X)	(X)	(X)	(X)	81	21	53	7	7
Neither parent	2,885	1,273	1,274	(X)	(X)	(X)	(X)	1,274	614	591	69	(X)	(X)	(X)	(X)	—
Family income																
Under $15,000	9,516	611	508	178	33	132	13	330	59	256	15	88	—	78	10	14
$15,000 to $29,999	12,094	995	704	389	111	254	24	315	138	154	23	270	28	190	52	21
$30,000 to $49,999	15,140	1,278	911	626	249	307	70	285	161	113	11	330	66	217	47	37
$50,000 to $74,999	14,414	1,190	718	556	298	218	40	162	119	38	54	456	61	305	90	16
$75,000 and over	21,157	1,527	840	659	513	110	36	181	137	30	14	657	103	441	113	30
Poverty status																
Below 100 percent of poverty	12,239	988	743	362	106	217	39	381	98	270	13	217	24	158	35	28
100 to 199 percent of poverty	15,686	1,512	1,088	696	287	357	52	392	174	192	26	382	59	256	67	42
200 percent of poverty and above	44,396	3,101	1,851	1,350	810	447	93	501	342	129	30	1,203	176	817	210	48
Health insurance coverage																
Covered by health insurance	63,907	4,293	2,637	1,856	914	802	140	817	378	394	45	1,539	213	1,053	273	81
Not covered by health insurance	8,414	1,309	1,008	551	289	219	43	457	236	197	24	262	46	177	39	38
Household receives public assistance																
Receives assistance	3,372	506	417	202	94	98	10	215	59	146	10	60	2	46	12	28
Does not receive assistance	68,949	5,096	3,265	2,206	1,110	923	173	1,059	555	445	59	1,741	256	1,185	300	92

TABLE 3.3

Characteristics of children who co-reside with grandparents, by presence of parents, March 2002[1] [CONTINUED]

(in thousands)

Characteristic	Total	Total with grandparents	Total in grandparent's household	With grandparents present												
				Grandparent is householder								Grandparent is not householder				
				Parent Present				No parents present				Parent is householder				Parent is not householder
				Total	Grandmother and grandfather	Grandmother only	Grandfather only	Total	Grandmother and grandfather	Grandmother only	Grandfather only	Total	Grandmother and grandfather	Grandmother only	Grandfather only	
Household receives food stamps																
Receives food stamps	7,873	908	702	467	174	252	41	235	48	178	9	159	9	128	22	45
Does not receive food stamps	64,448	4,694	2,980	1,942	1,029	770	143	1,038	565	413	60	1,642	249	1,103	290	73
Household tenure																
Owns/buying	48,542	4,091	2,723	1,818	1,019	647	152	905	528	329	48	1,304	202	870	232	64
Rents	22,512	1,448	925	564	165	368	31	361	84	257	20	474	51	349	74	49
No cash rent	1,266	62	34	27	20	6	1	7	2	5	—	22	5	11	6	5
Type of residence[3]																
Central city, in MSA	20,971	2,042	1,376	893	346	487	60	483	189	279	15	602	104	409	89	63
Outside central city, in MSA	38,194	2,641	1,577	1,098	647	367	84	479	260	186	33	1,022	137	708	177	42
Outside MSA	13,155	919	727	417	211	167	39	310	165	125	20	178	17	114	47	15

— Represents zero or rounds to zero.

X Not applicable.

[1] All people under age 18, excluding group quarters, householders, subfamily reference people, and their spouses.

[2] Data are not shown separately for the American Indian and Alaska Native population because of the small sample size in the Current Population Survey in March 2002.

[3] "MSA" refers to Metropolitan Statistical Area.

Note: Data based on the Annual Demographic Supplement to the March 2002 Current Population Survey.

SOURCE: Jason Fields, "Table 3. Characteristics of Children Who Co-Reside with Grandparents by Presence of Parents, March 2002," in *Children's Living Arrangements and Characteristics: March 2002*, Current Population Reports, P20-547, U.S. Department of Commerce, Economics and Statistics Administration, U.S. Census Bureau, June 2003, http://www.census.gov/prod/2003pubs/p20-547.pdf (accessed July 19, 2004)

FIGURE 3.3

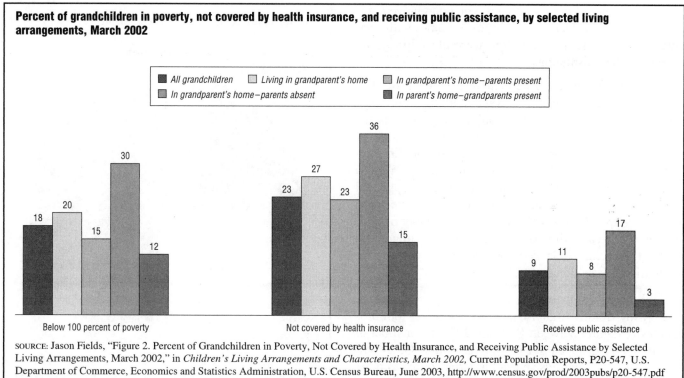

Percent of grandchildren in poverty, not covered by health insurance, and receiving public assistance, by selected living arrangements, March 2002

Legend:
- ■ All grandchildren
- □ Living in grandparent's home
- ■ In grandparent's home–parents present
- ■ In grandparent's home–parents absent
- ■ In parent's home–grandparents present

Below 100 percent of poverty: 18, 20, 15, 30, 12

Not covered by health insurance: 23, 27, 23, 36, 15

Receives public assistance: 9, 11, 8, 17, 3

SOURCE: Jason Fields, "Figure 2. Percent of Grandchildren in Poverty, Not Covered by Health Insurance, and Receiving Public Assistance by Selected Living Arrangements, March 2002," in *Children's Living Arrangements and Characteristics, March 2002,* Current Population Reports, P20-547, U.S. Department of Commerce, Economics and Statistics Administration, U.S. Census Bureau, June 2003, http://www.census.gov/prod/2003pubs/p20-547.pdf (accessed July 19, 2004)

FIGURE 3.4

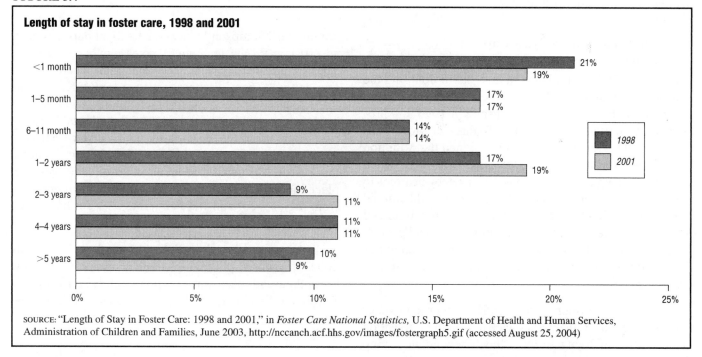

Length of stay in foster care, 1998 and 2001

Length of stay	1998	2001
<1 month	21%	19%
1–5 month	17%	17%
6–11 month	14%	14%
1–2 years	17%	19%
2–3 years	9%	11%
4–4 years	11%	11%
>5 years	10%	9%

SOURCE: "Length of Stay in Foster Care: 1998 and 2001," in *Foster Care National Statistics,* U.S. Department of Health and Human Services, Administration of Children and Families, June 2003, http://nccanch.acf.hhs.gov/images/fostergraph5.gif (accessed August 25, 2004)

in 2001. The percentage of other races increased slightly, to 37% white and 8% listed as other races. Seventeen percent of children in foster care were Hispanic.

The age of children entering and exiting the foster care system remained unchanged between 1998 and 2001. The median age of entry was 8.7 years and the median age of exit was 10.2 years. However, the median age of all chil-

dren in the system rose from 9.5 years in 1998 to 10.6 years in 2001. The length of time children stayed in foster care also remained relatively stable with 19% of children remaining from one to two years in 2001. (See Figure 3.4.)

The distribution of children in the various types of placement settings remained relatively unchanged, although fewer children were placed with relatives in

2001 than in 1998. Almost half of all foster children (48%) were placed in foster homes with nonrelative families. Another 24% were placed in foster homes with relatives. Most of the other children were placed in group homes or other institutions. (See Figure 3.5.)

The primary goal for permanent placement of children in foster care was to return the child to his/her parents (referred to as "reunification"). Adoption was the second choice, followed by living with a relative or guardian, long-term foster care, or emancipation. Emancipation laws vary from state to state but generally allow a teenager to petition a court for the termination of parental rights and full independence. The most dramatic trend from 1998 to 2001 was a decrease in the number of children in foster care with no permanent placement goal. In 2001 11% of children lacked a permanent placement goal, a significant reduction from 23% in 1998.

While the number of children leaving foster care to live with relatives/guardians or adoptive families increased slightly between 1998 and 2001, the number of reunifications dropped five percentage points. Other outcomes, such as runaways and children transferred to other agencies, decreased one percentage point. Not all outcomes were successful. A median of 10.3% of children who entered foster care in 2001 reentered the system within twelve months of discharge.

Children Adopted from Foster Care

In 1997 the Clinton administration launched the "Adoption 2002" initiative with the goal of doubling the number of foster children adopted each year—from approximately twenty-seven thousand in 1996 to a projected fifty-four thousand in 2002. To this end, on November 19, 1997, President Bill Clinton signed the Adoption and Safe Families Act of 1997 (PL 105–89), which required, among other provisions, permanency hearings to be held no later than twelve months after a child entered foster care. The federal government offered financial incentives to states to increase adoption rates and provided technical assistance to states, courts, and communities in an effort to place children in adoptive homes within a shorter time frame.

Current or former foster youths sixteen and older could obtain government assistance during their transition to independent living through the Independent Living Program. This program provided grants to states for education and employment aid, training in daily living skills, and individual and group counseling.

CHILDREN WAITING TO BE ADOPTED. In fiscal year 1998, 36,000 children were adopted from the public foster care system and 117,000 foster children awaited adoption. With more than 129,000 children in foster care waiting to be adopted in 2004, Health & Human Services Secretary

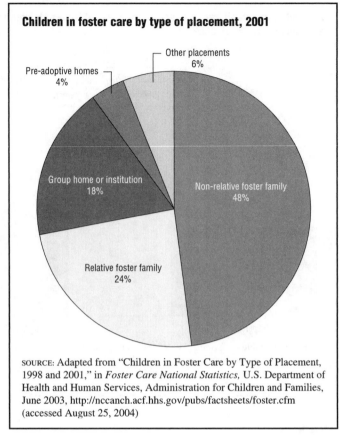

FIGURE 3.5

Children in foster care by type of placement, 2001

Other placements
6%

Pre-adoptive homes
4%

Group home or institution
18%

Non-relative foster family
48%

Relative foster family
24%

SOURCE: Adapted from "Children in Foster Care by Type of Placement, 1998 and 2001," in *Foster Care National Statistics*, U.S. Department of Health and Human Services, Administration for Children and Families, June 2003, http://nccanch.acf.hhs.gov/pubs/factsheets/foster.cfm (accessed August 25, 2004)

Tommy G. Thompson launched a national public service advertising (PSA) campaign to increase public awareness. The new ads were part of a five-year, multifaceted initiative called "The Collaboration to AdoptUSKids." The PSAs focused on adoption of older children (ages eight to seventeen) who comprised 53% of the adoptable foster care population. Of these children, 44% were African-American. In announcing this campaign, Thompson noted that research showed that foster children who were not placed in permanent homes were less likely to graduate from high school and were at greater risk for homelessness, jail time, and reliance on welfare.

A Web site, www.AdoptUSKids, was launched in July 2002. It featured photographs and biographies of some seven thousand foster care children available for adoption. Within the first year, nearly three thousand children featured on the site were placed with adoptive families.

CHILDREN IN SCHOOL

The Census Bureau estimated that there were 36.8 million children of elementary school age in 2003, a decrease of 274,000 children from 2000. Utah and Alaska had the highest proportion of their population in the five to thirteen age group (15% each). Texas, Arizona, California, and Idaho followed with 14% each. Nationally, children age five to thirteen averaged 13% of the population.

TABLE 3.4

Number and percentage of homeschooled children, 1999 and 2003

	Homeschooled students			
	1999		2003	
School enrollment status	Number	Percent	Number	Percent
Total	**850,000**	**100.0**	**1,096,000**	**100.0**
Homeschooled only	697,000	82.0	898,000	82.0
Enrolled in school part time	153,000	18.0	198,000	18.0
Enrolled in school for less than 9 hours a week	107,000	12.6	137,000	12.5
Enrolled in school for 9 to 25 hours a week	46,000	5.4	61,000	5.6

SOURCE: "Table 1. Number and Percentage Distribution of Homeschooled Students, Ages 5 through 17 in Kindergarten through 12th Grades, by School Enrollment Status, 1999 and 2003," in *1.1 Million Home-schooled Students in the United States in 2003*, NCES 2004-115, U.S. Department of Education, National Center for Education Statistics, July 2004, http://nces.ed.gov/pubs2004/2004115.pdf (accessed August 9, 2004)

The American Housing Survey 2003 revealed that 25.7% of the 105,842 occupied housing units in the nation were home to children aged five to fifteen. In 82% of these households, children attended K–12 public schools while 10% were enrolled in K–12 private schools. Another 1% of children in this age group were home-schooled.

A variety of school choice options—magnet schools, charter and contract schools, vouchers, alternative schools, and home-schooling—have been introduced since 1980 in an effort to reform education for American children. The choice to educate children at home required the greatest commitment of time and effort on the part of parents. According to a 2003 report by the National Center for Educational Statistics, about 1.1 million children were home-schooled in 2003. The report revealed that between 1999 and 2003 the percentage of school-age children being educated at home grew from 1.7% to 2.2%. While the majority of these students received all of their education at home, 18% spent twenty-five hours per week or less enrolled in school. (See Table 3.4.) In an article titled "Why Johnny Learns at Home" in the August 16, 2004, edition of *Publishers Weekly,* home-school media consultant Zan Tyler projected that "the growth of home-schooling will continue between 7% and 15% annually." The article cited "conservative estimates" of the number of home-schooled children at two million.

The leading reason (31%) for parents' choice of home-schooling was concern about the environment in other school options. Another 30% of parents chose home-schooling for religious reasons. Other reasons, such as family unity and individualized teaching prompted another 9% of parents to elect home-schooling.

WORKING PARENTS AND CHILD CARE

Since the 1970s, one of the most dramatic changes in the structure of the American family has been the increased employment of mothers outside the home. According to the sixth annual interagency report *America's Children: Key National Indicators of Well-Being, 2002,* the share of all children with at least one parent working full-time increased from 70% in 1980 to 80% in 2000. Reflecting a tight economy and company downsizing efforts, the share of all children with at least one parent working full-time dropped to 78% in 2002. For children living in two-parent households, 89% had at least one parent working in 2002, compared to 80% in 1980. Forty-nine percent of single mothers and 70% of single fathers were working in 2002. (See Figure 3.6.)

Despite the growing number of women in the workforce, since 1994 the number of children in two-parent families with a stay-at-home mother and working father increased steadily. In 2002 about eleven million children, or 25% of children under age fifteen living with two married parents, had full-time stay-at-home mothers. About 189,000 similarly situated children had stay-at-home fathers and full-time working mothers in 2002. The number of fathers who remained at home to care for the family while their wives worked increased erratically between 1994 and 2004. (See Figure 3.7.)

As more and more mothers held paying jobs, the issue of child care became a great concern, not only for parents but also for policymakers. The implementation of welfare-reform legislation, which required welfare recipients to work, further pushed the problem of available child care to the forefront. While only one-third of children with single mothers saw their mothers employed full-time in 1980, that share increased to almost half of children with single mothers by 2002. (See Figure 3.6.)

For both single parents and two-parent working couples, child care presented significant challenges. Among preschool age children, 48% of 0–2 year olds and 25% of 3–6 year olds received total parental care from stay-at-home mothers or fathers in 2001. Some two-parent working couples worked different shifts to allow one parent to be at home with the children. In *America's Children 2004* the Federal Interagency Forum on Child and Family Statistics compares the type of care received by children age zero to two and three to six (not yet in kindergarten) in 2001. For infants and toddlers (age zero to two) the distribution was almost 50–50 parental care and nonparental care. More than half of the older children were in center-based care such as daycare centers, pre-kindergartens, nursery schools, Head Start programs, and other early childhood education programs.

Once children started school, parents were still concerned about before and after school care. Almost half of children in kindergarten through third grade (K–3) and children in fourth through eighth grade (4–8) were cared for outside of school hours by a parent. Twenty-five percent of children in grades 4–8 were responsible for themselves before and after school while parents worked.

FIGURE 3.6

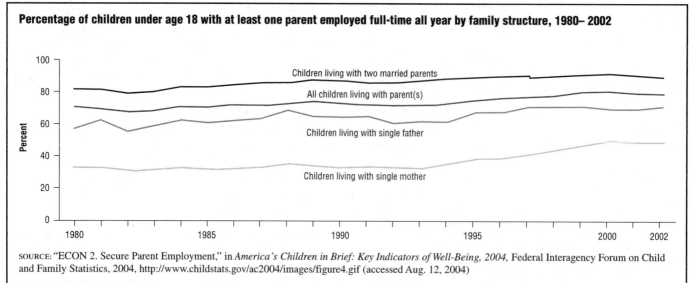

Percentage of children under age 18 with at least one parent employed full-time all year by family structure, 1980– 2002

SOURCE: "ECON 2. Secure Parent Employment," in *America's Children in Brief: Key Indicators of Well-Being, 2004,* Federal Interagency Forum on Child and Family Statistics, 2004, http://www.childstats.gov/ac2004/images/figure4.gif (accessed Aug. 12, 2004)

FIGURE 3.7

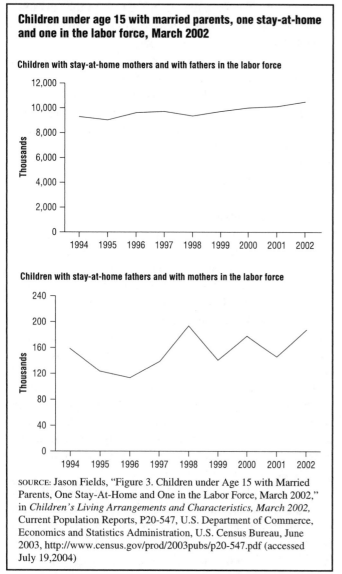

Children under age 15 with married parents, one stay-at-home and one in the labor force, March 2002

Children with stay-at-home mothers and with fathers in the labor force

Children with stay-at-home fathers and with mothers in the labor force

SOURCE: Jason Fields, "Figure 3. Children under Age 15 with Married Parents, One Stay-At-Home and One in the Labor Force, March 2002," in *Children's Living Arrangements and Characteristics, March 2002,* Current Population Reports, P20-547, U.S. Department of Commerce, Economics and Statistics Administration, U.S. Census Bureau, June 2003, http://www.census.gov/prod/2003pubs/p20-547.pdf (accessed July 19,2004)

Nearly half of school-age children participated in some type of after-school activities that provided alternate supervision. Sports attracted 28% of K–3-grade children and 38% of 4–8-grade children. Another 18% of K–3- and 26% of 4–8-grade children were involved in religious activities. In addition, parents reported their children took part in after-school arts activities, clubs, academic programs, community service, and scouting.

Child Care for the Working Poor

Since the 1930s, the federal government has subsidized child care for low-income families. Government-funded programs such as Head Start, which began as a nutritional and health program for poor children in the 1960s, offered educational readiness to prepare children for school as part of the child-care program. The Child Care and Development Fund (CCDF), authorized by the Personal Responsibility and Work Opportunity Reconciliation Act of 1996 (PL 104–193), helped low-income families and those leaving the welfare rolls to obtain child care so they could pursue employment, job training, or education.

Some Employers Address Child-Care Problems

In the United States, employer-sponsored child-care benefits have been rare, although the trend toward on-site child care has increased. Some employers offer child-care reimbursement accounts funded with employee pretax contributions. Employees in medium and large establishments were more likely than those in smaller establishments to receive child-care benefits.

In 2002 a new Child Care Assistance Tax Credit became available to employers. Employers who provided child-care resources or facilities for employees could take a tax credit of up to $150,000 for actual expenses of the benefits provided. In a 2003 Bureau of Labor Statistics survey of private industry employers, 5% of workers had access to employer sponsored on-site or off-site child care. Full-time employees earning $15 per hour or higher were more likely to have this option than part-time and lower paid workers. Just 3% of workers earning less than $15 per hour had employer provided child care, compared to 8% of higher paid workers. Employer sponsored child care was available to nearly four times as many workers in white-collar occupations (7%) as blue-collar occupations (2%). Companies with a hundred or more employees were more likely than smaller companies to provide child care. (See Table 3.5.)

Income Tax Credit

The Internal Revenue Service offered some assistance to working parents through the Dependent Care Tax Credit (DCTC). This credit applied not only to care for children under age thirteen but also to costs of care for other dependents, such as a spouse or parent who was physically or mentally incapable of self-care. The maximum credit for the 2003 tax year was $3,000 for one child and $6,000 for two children. Some states offered tax credits as well. Those who made too little money to pay income tax, however, were not eligible to file for this income tax credit.

THE ECONOMIC SITUATION OF CHILDREN

Children living in single-mother households represented 22.8% of all children living in families. Yet they also represented 51.7% of children living below poverty level, 62.3% of children receiving public assistance, and 61.1% of children receiving food stamps. By contrast, the 68.7% of children who lived with two parents represented just 31.8% of children living below poverty level. The percentage of children of single fathers living below poverty level was quite similar to their representation in the total population of children. (See Table 3.6.)

Children in Poverty

In *America's Children 2004* the Federal Interagency Forum on Child and Family Statistics reported that the poverty rate for children living with families rose from 15.8% in 2001 to 16.3% in 2002. This marked the first statistically significant increase since the child poverty rate peaked at 22% in 1993. The U.S. Department of Agriculture reported in *Household Food Security in the United States, 2002* that over thirteen million children under age eighteen (18.8% of all children) lived in food insecure households, and 567,000 of these children went hungry during the year.

Teens in the Workforce

By the time they were teenagers, many children begin to seek some type of work experience. Census figures show that of the twelve million minors age fifteen to seventeen in 2002, 25% were counted in the labor force.

TABLE 3.5

Employer assistance for child care, 2003

Characteristics	Total	Employer provided funds	On-site and off-site child care	Child care resource and referral services
			Employer assistance for child care	
All employees	18	3	5	10
Worker characteristics:				
White-collar occupations	26	5	7	15
Blue-collar occupations	10	1	2	6
Service occupations	10	2	4	5
Full time	21	4	5	12
Part time	11	2	4	5
Union	25	3	7	15
Nonunion	18	3	5	10
Average wage less than $15 per hour	11	2	3	5
Average wage $15 per hour or higher	31	5	8	18
Establishment characteristics:				
Goods-producing	16	3	2	11
Service-producing	19	3	6	10
1–99 workers	7	2	2	3
100 workers or more	32	5	8	19
Geographic areas:				
Metropolitan areas	21	4	5	12
Nonmetropolitan areas	5	2	2	2
New England	22	4	8	12
Middle Atlantic	24	2	6	14
East North Central	21	3	6	11
West North Central	17	3	6	8
South Atlantic	15	4	3	9
East South Central	16	4	4	7
West South Central	14	2	3	8
Mountain	19	2	5	12
Pacific	17	4	3	10

SOURCE: Adapted from "Table 4. Percentage of Workers with Access to Selected Benefits, by Selected Characteristics, Private Industry, National Compensation Survey, March 2003," in *Employee Benefits in Private Industry, 2003*, U.S. Department of Labor, Bureau of Labor Statistics, September 2003, http://www.bls.gov/ncs/ebs/sp/ebnr0008.pdf (accessed August 25, 2004)

While most of these working youths held part-time jobs, 7% worked full-time and 21% were unemployed. The high unemployment rate for teens who had been in the workforce, compared to a 5.8% unemployment rate for adults in 2002, reflected the need for additional training and skills as well as a shortage of part-time jobs. Teens living in inner city metropolitan areas experienced 24.7% unemployment while about 20% of their counterparts in suburban, small-town, and rural areas were unemployed. While African-American teens had the second-lowest workforce participation rate at 17%—the rate for Asian and Pacific Islander teens stood at 16.7%—they also experienced the highest rate of unemployment at 39.7%. (See Table 3.7.)

Contrary to the image of children in poor or single-parent families forced to go to work to help support the family, children in two-parent families were more likely to be in the workforce than children in single-parent families in 2002, according to the same Census report. Additionally, the

TABLE 3.6

Children's economic situation by family structure, March 2002[1]

Characteristic	Total	Two parents	Mother only	Father only	Neither parent
			Number		
Total	**72,321**	**49,666**	**16,473**	**3,297**	**2,885**
Family income					
Under $15,000	9,516	1,993	5,706	559	1,257
$15,000 to $29,999	12,094	5,705	4,933	939	516
$30,000 to $49,999	15,140	10,360	3,328	963	489
$50,000 to $74,999	14,414	12,160	1,493	455	307
$75,000 and over	21,157	19,447	1,013	380	316
Poverty status					
Below 100 percent of poverty	12,239	3,895	6,326	638	1,380
100 to 199 percent of poverty	15,686	9,147	4,949	935	655
200 percent of poverty and above	44,396	36,623	5,199	1,723	851
Household receives public assistance					
Receives assistance	3,372	776	2,101	154	340
Does not receive assistance	68,949	48,889	14,372	3,143	2,545
Household receives food stamps					
Receives food stamps	7,873	2,213	4,813	418	430
Does not receive food stamps	64,448	47,453	11,660	2,879	2,455
Household tenure					
Owns/buying	48,542	38,362	6,547	1,808	1,825
Rents	22,512	10,366	9,689	1,444	1,012
No cash rent	1,266	938	237	44	48
			Percent		
Total	**100.0**	**68.7**	**22.8**	**4.6**	**4.0**
Family income					
Under $15,000	100.0	20.9	60.0	5.9	13.2
$15,000 to $29,999	100.0	47.2	40.8	7.8	4.3
$30,000 to $49,999	100.0	68.4	22.0	6.4	3.2
$50,000 to $74,999	100.0	84.4	10.4	3.2	2.1
$75,000 and over	100.0	91.9	4.8	1.8	1.5
Poverty status					
Below 100 percent of poverty	100.0	31.8	51.7	5.2	11.3
100 to 199 percent of poverty	100.0	58.3	31.6	6.0	4.2
200 percent of poverty and above	100.0	82.5	11.7	3.9	1.9
Household receives public assistance					
Receives assistance	100.0	23.0	62.3	4.6	10.1
Does not receive assistance	100.0	70.9	20.8	4.6	3.7
Household receives food stamps					
Receives food stamps	100.0	28.1	61.1	5.3	5.5
Does not receive food stamps	100.0	73.6	18.1	4.5	3.8
Household tenure					
Owns/buying	100.0	79.0	13.5	3.7	3.8
Rents	100.0	46.0	43.0	6.4	4.5
No cash rent	100.0	74.1	18.7	3.5	3.8

— Represents zero or rounds to zero.
[1]All people under age 18, excluding group quarters, householders, subfamily reference people, and their spouses.

SOURCE: Jason Fields, "Table 7. Children's Economic Situation by Family Structure, March 2002," in *Children's Living Arrangements and Characteristics, March 2002,* Current Population Reports, P20-547, U.S. Department of Commerce, Economics and Statistics Administration, U.S. Census Bureau, June 2003, http://www.census.gov/prod/2003pubs/p20-547.pdf (accessed July 19, 2004)

percentage of children in the workforce increased with the level of education of their parents and family income. Only 17% of children in families with incomes under $15,000 were counted in the workforce, compared to 28% of children whose families had incomes of $50,000 or more.

COST OF RAISING A CHILD

Each year the U.S. Department of Agriculture (USDA) provided estimates of annual family expenditures on children from their birth through age seventeen. These estimates were used by states to determine child support guidelines and foster care payments, by courts to determine compensation in personal injury and wrongful death cases, and for public education of anyone considering when or whether to have a child. Estimates are tied to family income. In 2003 the average household in the lowest income group spent 28% of their before-tax annual income on a child, while those in the highest income group spent 14%. In actual dollars, however, the highest income group spent twice the amount spent by the lowest income group. Such studies

TABLE 3.7

Children ages 15–17 years by their labor force status and selected characteristics, March 2002[1]

(In thousands)

| | | | In the labor force | | | | | |
| | | | Total | | Employed[2] | | Unemployed | |
Characteristic	Total	Not in labor force	Number	Percent in the labor force	Full time	Part time	Total	Unemployment rate[4]
Children 15–17 years	11,842	8,853	2,989	25.2	208	2,158	623	20.8
Age of child								
15 years old	3,976	3,606	370	9.3	31	245	94	25.4
16 years old	3,988	2,945	1,042	26.1	61	740	241	23.1
17 years old	3,878	2,302	1,576	40.6	116	1,173	287	18.2
Sex of child								
Male	6,110	4,638	1,472	24.1	129	1,003	340	23.1
Female	5,732	4,214	1,518	26.5	79	1,156	283	18.6
Race and ethnicity of child[3]								
White	9,298	6,746	2,553	27.5	176	1,906	471	18.4
Non-Hispanic	7,679	5,441	2,237	29.1	115	1,726	396	17.7
Black	1,796	1,490	305	17.0	24	160	121	39.7
Asian and Pacific Islander	570	475	95	16.7	6	74	15	15.8
Hispanic (of any race)	1,730	1,400	330	19.1	67	183	80	24.2
Presence of parents								
Two parents	7,864	5,819	2,046	26.0	98	1,597	351	17.2
Mother only	2,714	2,096	618	22.8	41	395	182	29.4
Father only	598	456	142	23.7	11	92	39	27.5
Neither parent	667	482	184	27.6	58	75	51	27.7
Education of parent								
Less than high school	1,704	1,352	352	20.7	56	197	99	28.1
High school degree	3,486	2,608	878	25.2	38	635	205	23.3
Some college	3,115	2,256	860	27.6	35	655	170	19.8
Bachelor's degree or more	2,871	2,155	716	24.9	21	597	98	13.7
No parents present	667	482	184	27.6	58	75	51	27.7
Family income								
Under $15,000	1,263	1,056	205	16.2	32	101	72	35.1
$15,000 to $29,999	1,705	1,364	341	20.0	17	209	115	33.7
$30,000 to $49,999	2,514	1,881	633	25.2	54	429	150	23.7
$50,000 to $74,999	2,342	1,688	653	27.9	46	477	130	19.9
$75,000 and over	4,019	2,862	1,157	28.8	58	943	156	13.5
Type of residence[5]								
Central city, in MSA	3,183	2,518	665	20.9	64	437	164	24.7
Outside central city, in MSA	6,372	4,657	1,715	26.9	104	1,275	336	19.6
Outside MSA	2,288	1,678	610	26.7	40	447	123	20.2

[1]The universe for this table is children age 15 to 17 years. Only the population 15 and over have labor force data recorded for them in the CPS. Children under age 15, householders, subfamily reference people, their spouses, and those in group quarters are excluded from this table.
[2]Full-time employment is 35 hours or more of work in the previous week. Part-time employment is less than 35 hours of work in the previous week.
[3]Data are not shown separately for the American Indian and Alaska Native population because of the small sample size in the Current Population Survey in March 2002.
[4]The unemployment rate is the percent unemployed of the population in the labor force.
[5]"MSA" refers to Metropolitan Statistical Area.
Note: Data based on the Annual Demographic Supplement to the March 2002 Current Population Survey.

SOURCE: Jason Fields, "Table 6. Children Age 15–17 Years by Their Labor Force Status and Selected Characteristics, March 2002," in *Children's Living Arrangements and Characteristics, March 2002,* Current Population Reports, P20-547, U.S. Department of Commerce, Economics and Statistics Administration, U.S. Census Bureau, June 2003, http://www.census.gov/prod/2003pubs/p20-547.pdf (accessed July 19, 2004)

demonstrated a fact of life for families—no matter what the income bracket, it was expensive to raise a child.

At all income levels, housing was the greatest child-rearing expense. In the average middle-income family, housing accounted for 34% of expenses for a child in 2003. Food was the second-largest expense across all income levels. (See Figure 3.8.)

Children's needs became more expensive as they grew older. At all income levels food, transportation, clothing, and health expenses related to child-rearing increased as the child grew. Figure 3.9 depicts the shifting distribution of annual child-rearing expenses for a middle income, husband-wife family as a child grew from birth through age seventeen. Food became a greater proportion of expense between the ages of six and eleven. Child-care expenses decreased significantly at age six when the child entered school. The hours spent in school reduced the number of hours of costly daycare required for working parents.

FIGURE 3.8

Expenditures on a child from birth through age 17 as a percentage of total child-rearing expenditures, 2003*

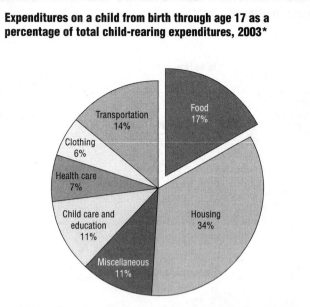

*U.S. average for the younger child in middle-income, husband-wife families with two children.

SOURCE: Mark Lino, "Figure 2. Expenditure Shares on a Child from Birth through Age 17 as a Percentage of Total Child-Rearing Expenditures, 2003," in *Expenditures on Children by Families, 2003* U.S. Department of Agriculture, Center for Nutrition Policy and Promotion, 2003, http://www.usda.gov/cnpp/FENR/FENRV16N1/fenrv16n1p31.pdf (accessed August 5, 2004)

TABLE 3.8

Family expenditures on a child, by lower income single-parent and husband-wife households, 2003*

Age of child	Single-parent households	Husband-wife households
0–2	$5,700	$6,820
3–5	6,440	6,970
6–8	7,230	7,040
9–11	6,710	6,990
12–14	7,210	7,840
15–17	7,960	7,770
Total (0–17)	**$123,750**	**$130,290**

*Estimates are for the younger child in two-child families in the overall United States.

SOURCE: Mark Lino, "Table 1. Family Expenditures on a Child, by Lower Income Single-Parent and Husband-Wife Households, 2003," in *Expenditures on Children by Families, 2003,* U.S. Department of Agriculture, Center for Nutrition Policy and Promotion, 2003, http://www.usda.gov/cnpp/FENR/FENRV16N1/fenrv16n1p31.pdf (accessed August 5, 2004)

Where the family lived in 2003 influenced the cost of raising a child. Expenses were highest in urban areas of the West and the Northeast, which had the highest housing costs. Average child-rearing expenses were lowest in the urban Midwest and rural areas where housing and overall cost of living were lower. (See Figure 3.10.)

The impact of child-rearing expenses was greater for single-parent families. Table 3.8 compares expenses for average single-parent and husband-wife families with

annual before-tax incomes less than $40,700. About 83% of single-parent households and 33% of husband-wife households fell in this income group in the 2003 USDA study *Expenditures in Children by Families.* Single-parent families, with an average annual income of $17,000, had significantly lower financial resources than husband-wife families who averaged $25,400 per year in income. Yet child-rearing costs did not vary significantly between the two types of families. As a result, child-rearing expenses consumed a greater portion of the annual income of single-parent families.

A college education was often the largest expense faced by parents after children pass age seventeen. Using information from the College Board's *Trends in College Pricing 2003,* the USDA estimated average total charges for tuition and fees and room and board during the 2003–04 school year were $9,929 at four-year public institutions and $23,443 at four-year private schools.

FIGURE 3.9

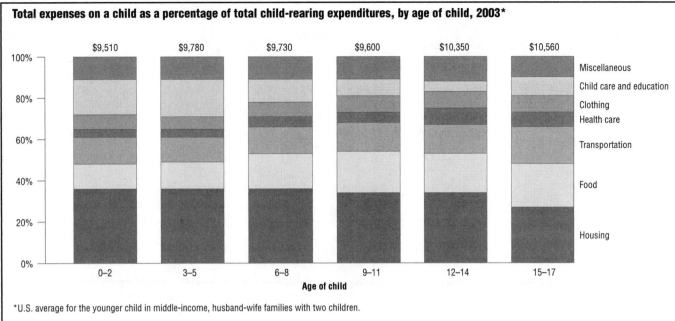

Total expenses on a child as a percentage of total child-rearing expenditures, by age of child, 2003*

*U.S. average for the younger child in middle-income, husband-wife families with two children.

SOURCE: Mark Lino, "Figure 3. Total Expenses and Expenditures Shares on a Child (as a Percentage of Total Child-Rearing Expenditures), by Age of Child, 2003," in *Expenditures on Children by Families, 2003,* U.S. Department of Agriculture, Center for Nutrition Policy and Promotion, 2003, http://www.usda.gov/cnpp/FENR/FENRV16N1/fenrv16n1p31.pdf (accessed August 5, 2004)

FIGURE 3.10

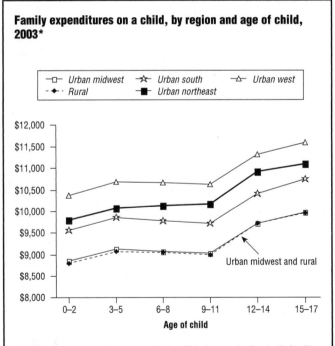

Family expenditures on a child, by region and age of child, 2003*

* Regional averages for the younger child in middle-income, husband-wife families with two children.

SOURCE: Mark Lino, "Figure 4. Family Expenditures on a Child, by Region and Age of Child, 2003," in *Expenditures on Children by Families, 2003"* U.S. Department of Agriculture, Center for Nutrition Policy and Promotion, 2003, http://www.usda.gov/cnpp/FENR/FENRV16N1/fenrv16n1p31.pdf (accessed August 5, 2004)

CHAPTER 4
SOCIAL ISSUES AFFECTING AMERICA'S CHILDREN

In proclaiming November 24 through November 30, 2002, National Family Week, President George W. Bush noted that earlier in the year he signed bipartisan legislation:

> to expand the Promoting Safe and Stable Families Program, which provides States with vital resources to help families stay together and to promote adoption. The program seeks to prevent child abuse and neglect, avoid removing children from their homes, support family reunification services, and help those children who are unable to return home by providing crucial adoption and post-adoptive services.

AMERICA'S CHILDREN: INDICATORS OF WELL-BEING

The well-being of America's children improved in many respects during the early years of the twenty-first century, according to the seventh annual Federal Interagency Forum on Child and Family Statistics report, *America's Children: Key National Indicators of Well-Being, 2003*. Teenage pregnancies reached a record low and teen violence dropped dramatically over the past decade. The proportion of children ages three to five enrolled in primary education rose nineteen percentage points, and high school completion rates improved slightly. Infant and childhood death rates continued to decline, adolescent smoking decreased, and fewer children were exposed to the hazards of secondhand smoke. On the other hand, more children were overweight, the incidence of low birth weight infants increased, the number of children living in crowded housing conditions increased, and fewer children had at least one parent with full-time employment.

The Children's Defense Fund offered a different perspective in *The State of America's Children 2004*. The organization reported that one in six children in the United States continued to live in poverty and one in eight—9.3 million—children had no health insurance. An estimated three million children were suspected victims of child abuse and neglect. Only 31% of fourth graders read at or above grade level and almost one in ten teens aged sixteen to nineteen was a school dropout. Eight children or teenagers died from gunfire every day.

CHILD POVERTY

Poverty was associated with a number of serious problems for children, including inadequate health care and lower educational achievement. In 2003 children were 25.4% of the total population but 35.9% of people in poverty, according to U.S. Census figures. Since the early 1980s, the poverty rates for adults aged sixty-five and over nearly matched those for adults aged eighteen to sixty-four, demonstrating great improvement in the well-being of the elderly population. In 1974 children, for the first time, replaced the elderly as the poorest age group. As poverty rates for people aged sixty-five and over continued to decline, the poverty rate for children continued to climb to a 1993 peak of about 22%. The child poverty rate then began a steady decline but leveled off at about 16% in 1999. It began to rise again in 2002. The 2003 child poverty rate of 17.6% represented almost a full percentage point increase over the 16.7% rate in 2002.

In 2003 10% of all families lived in poverty. Families with no "breadwinner," or person who provided primary financial support through steady employment, were most likely to suffer poverty. Such families headed by a female householder had the highest poverty rate at 70.8%. Married-couple families with one or more workers had the lowest poverty rate at 5%. (See Figure 4.1.)

Lower Educational Achievement

"Low-income students' achievement 30 to 37 points below peers" headlined the front page of the August 7, 2004, edition of *Rocky Mountain News* in Denver, Colorado. Across the nation, results of standardized reading and math tests reveal that children in poverty lag behind their classmates in educational achievement.

FIGURE 4.1

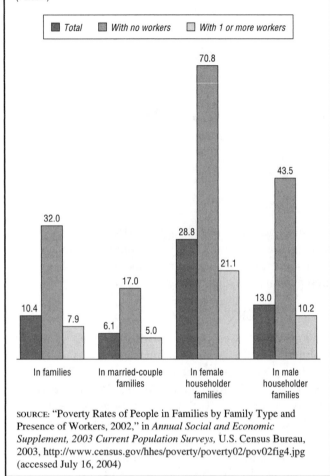

Poverty rates of people in families by family type and presence of workers, 2002

(Percent)

■ Total ■ With no workers ☐ With 1 or more workers

SOURCE: "Poverty Rates of People in Families by Family Type and Presence of Workers, 2002," in *Annual Social and Economic Supplement, 2003 Current Population Surveys,* U.S. Census Bureau, 2003, http://www.census.gov/hhes/poverty/poverty02/pov02fig4.jpg (accessed July 16, 2004)

For purposes of comparison, the National Assessment of Educational Progress (NAEP) exam defined low-income students as those eligible for the federal free lunch and reduced-price lunch program. In the 2003–04 school year, a child in a family of three was eligible for reduced-price lunches if the family's annual income was $28,231 or less. A child in a family of three earning $19,838 or less per year was eligible for free lunches.

Average 2003 national NAEP math scores for all students were higher than in any previous assessment years. Low-income students on average, however, continued to score lower than other students. At the fourth grade level low-income students averaged twenty-two points lower. At the eighth grade level the gap widened with low-income students scoring an average of twenty-eight points lower than other students. (See Figure 4.2.)

Average NAEP reading scores for all students declined slightly from 2002 to 2003. As with math scores, reading scores revealed that low-income students continued to lag behind their classmates. At the fourth grade

level low-income students averaged scores twenty-eight points lower than other students. The gap narrowed slightly at the eighth grade level to a twenty-four-point difference in average scores. (See Figure 4.3.)

CHILDREN'S HEALTH

Health Insurance

While medical science has made great advancements in health care in recent years, the cost of treatment and the price of health insurance escalated. "The cost of family health insurance is rapidly approaching the gross earnings of a full-time minimum wage worker," said Drew Altman, President and CEO of the Kaiser Family Foundation at the September 2004 release of the organization's Annual Employer Health Benefits Survey. "If these trends continue, workers and employers will find it increasingly difficult to pay for family health coverage and every year the share of Americans who have employer-sponsored health coverage will fall."

Children with health insurance could receive preventive health care, treatment for recurring illnesses such as ear infections and asthma, and treatment when they were sick. The social and economic changes that affected children during the last decades of the twentieth century made access to health care even more essential. Changes in family composition and economic conditions put many children in situations that often required health services—hunger, poor housing conditions, violence, and neglect. Children living with two married parents were more likely to have health insurance (91.3%) compared to children living with their mother only (85.8%) or father only (82.2%), Census data revealed. Only 59.3% of children living with neither parent had health insurance. (See Table 4.1.)

From 1987 to 1996 the number of American children without health insurance climbed from 8.2 million to 10.6 million, the highest levels ever recorded by the U.S. Census Bureau. That trend began to reverse in 1999, when the number of uninsured children dropped to 9.1 million. By 2000 8.5 million children were uninsured and that number remained the same through 2002. While 11.6% of all children were without health insurance in 2002, 20.1% of children in poverty had no insurance. A much higher proportion of Hispanic children (22.7%) lacked insurance than children of other racial or ethnic groups. (See Figure 4.4.)

CHILDREN IN LOW-INCOME WORKING FAMILIES. Census Bureau records revealed that, of children with insurance, nearly one in four was covered by Medicaid. Most uninsured children came from low-income working families that were not eligible for public assistance because the family earned too much to qualify for Medicaid. In most cases the parents worked for small companies that did not offer health insurance. When these companies

FIGURE 4.2

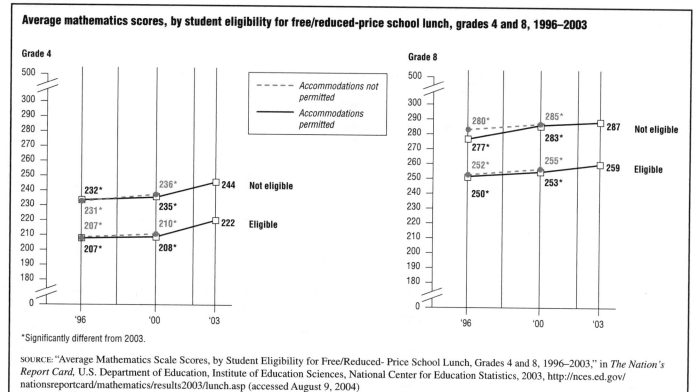

Average mathematics scores, by student eligibility for free/reduced-price school lunch, grades 4 and 8, 1996–2003

*Significantly different from 2003.

SOURCE: "Average Mathematics Scale Scores, by Student Eligibility for Free/Reduced- Price School Lunch, Grades 4 and 8, 1996–2003," in *The Nation's Report Card,* U.S. Department of Education, Institute of Education Sciences, National Center for Education Statistics, 2003, http://nces.ed.gov/nationsreportcard/mathematics/results2003/lunch.asp (accessed August 9, 2004)

FIGURE 4.3

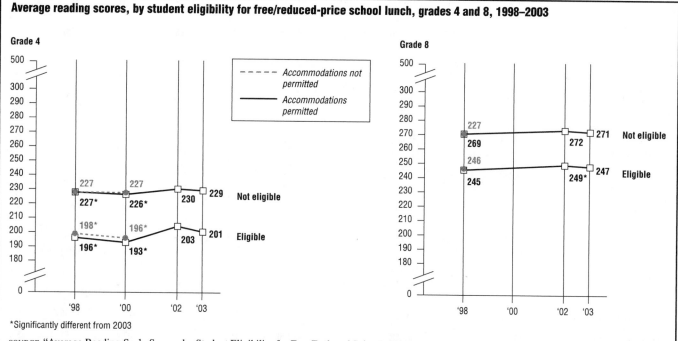

Average reading scores, by student eligibility for free/reduced-price school lunch, grades 4 and 8, 1998–2003

*Significantly different from 2003

SOURCE: "Average Reading Scale Scores, by Student Eligibility for Free/Reduced-Price School Lunch, Grades 4 and 8, 1998–2003," in *The Nation's Report Card,* U.S. Department of Education, Institute of Education Sciences, National Center for Education Statistics, 2003, http://nces.ed.gov/nationsreportcard/reading/results2003/lunch.asp (accessed August 9, 2004)

did offer insurance plans, the cost to employees was often too much for low-income workers. According to the National Academy of Sciences and its Institute of Medicine, even with insurance, low-income families had a number of additional barriers to overcome, such as difficulty in scheduling appointments, cultural differences with medical providers, or a lack of services easily accessible from where they lived.

TABLE 4.1

Children's health insurance coverage by presence of parents and selected characteristics, March 2002[1]

(In thousands and percent)

Characteristic	All children Total	All children Percent covered by health insurance	Two parents Total	Two parents Percent covered by health insurance	Mother only Total	Mother only Percent covered by health insurance	Father only Total	Father only Percent covered by health insurance	Neither parent Total	Neither parent Percent covered by health insurance
Total	**72,321**	**88.4**	**49,666**	**91.3**	**16,473**	**85.8**	**3,297**	**82.2**	**2,885**	**59.3**
Age of child										
Under 6 years	23,363	89.3	16,358	92.0	5,139	86.3	1,141	81.4	725	62.3
6–11 years	24,623	88.8	16,922	91.2	5,755	87.1	1,007	83.5	939	61.4
12–17 years	24,335	87.1	16,386	90.8	5,579	84.0	1,149	81.7	1,222	55.8
Race and ethnicity of child[2]										
White	56,276	89.0	41,944	91.5	10,052	85.2	2,548	83.8	1,732	60.5
Non-Hispanic	44,235	92.7	34,011	94.7	7,124	88.4	1,926	88.0	1,174	67.4
Black	1,646	86.2	4,481	91.5	5,605	87.8	605	77.4	956	57.3
Asian and Pacific islander	3,223	88.4	2,637	90.6	419	85.0	65	78.5	102	50.0
Hispanic (of any race)	12,817	76.0	8,338	77.9	3,212	78.1	641	71.3	626	45.5
Presence of siblings										
None	14,693	86.4	7,937	91.5	4,667	83.1	1,271	81.8	818	61.7
One sibling	28,498	90.9	20,931	92.9	5,915	87.8	1,177	82.1	475	63.2
Two siblings	18,436	88.6	13,209	91.1	3,772	87.6	591	81.7	863	59.2
Three siblings	6,965	85.1	4,943	88.8	1,358	82.9	211	83.4	454	51.8
Four siblings	2,132	84.1	1,480	84.9	492	86.4	24	100.0	137	64.2
Five or more siblings	1,596	78.9	1,167	81.8	268	78.7	23	91.3	138	52.2
Unmarried-partner household[3]										
Parent is not householder or partner	69,441	88.6	49,666	91.3	14,674	86.1	2,216	83.5	2,885	59.3
Parent is householder or partner	2,880	81.9	(X)	(X)	1,799	83.4	1,081	79.5	(X)	(X)
Parent is householder	2,452	82.7	(X)	(X)	1,430	85.0	1,022	79.5	(X)	(X)
Parent is partner	428	77.8	(X)	(X)	369	77.5	59	79.7	(X)	(X)
POSSLQ household[4]										
Not a POSSLQ household	57,826	89.0	41,802	91.3	12,197	86.3	1,795	83.8	2,033	61.3
POSSLQ household	2,652	81.7	(X)	(X)	1,562	85.4	904	79.4	186	60.8
Out of universe – child 15 to 17 years old	1,842	86.9	7,864	91.3	2,714	83.8	598	81.4	667	52.5
Education of parent										
Less than high school	10,900	75.4	6,526	73.5	3,642	79.6	732	70.9	(X)	(X)
High school degree	20,871	89.0	13,573	90.8	5,969	86.1	1,329	83.7	(X)	(X)
Some college	19,315	92.2	13,552	94.2	4,925	87.7	838	86.2	(X)	(X)
Bachelor's degree or more	18,351	95.9	16,015	96.5	1,938	91.6	398	89.4	(X)	(X)
No parents present	2,885	59.3	(X)	(X)	(X)	(X)	(X)	(X)	2,885	59.3
Marital status of parent										
Married spouse present	49,666	91.3	49,666	91.3	(X)	(X)	(X)	(X)	(X)	(X)
Married spouse absent	951	75.9	(X)	(X)	787	75.5	164	78.0	(X)	(X)
Widowed	857	79.8	(X)	(X)	720	80.8	137	73.7	(X)	(X)
Divorced	6,932	88.4	(X)	(X)	5,593	88.8	1,339	86.9	(X)	(X)
Separated	2,918	83.8	(X)	(X)	2,500	84.0	418	83.0	(X)	(X)
Never married	8,111	84.6	(X)	(X)	6,872	85.8	1,239	78.4	(X)	(X)
No parent present	2,885	59.3	(X)	(X)	(X)	(X)	(X)	(X)	2,885	59.3
Family income										
Under $15,000	9,516	78.6	1,993	73.0	5,706	84.5	559	74.2	1,257	62.3
$15,000 to $29,999	12,094	81.8	5,705	80.9	4,933	85.9	939	78.0	516	60.1
$30,000 to $49,999	15,140	86.5	10,360	87.8	3,328	87.7	963	84.2	489	55.6
$50,000 to $74,999	14,414	92.5	12,160	94.1	1,493	87.6	455	90.1	307	54.4
$75,000 and over	21,157	95.1	19,447	96.4	1,013	83.9	380	90.0	316	57.0
Poverty status										
Below 100 percent of poverty	12,239	78.0	3,895	75.1	6,326	84.0	638	74.1	1,380	60.9
100 to 199 percent of poverty	15,686	82.5	9,147	83.3	4,949	85.3	935	78.1	655	56.5
200 percent of poverty and above	44,396	93.3	36,623	95.0	5,199	88.5	1,723	87.4	851	58.6
Household receives public assistance										
Receives assistance	3,372	96.5	776	98.2	2,101	98.5	154	92.2	340	82.6
Does not receive assistance	68,949	88.0	48,889	91.2	14,372	83.9	3,143	81.7	2,545	56.2

STATE CHILDREN'S HEALTH INSURANCE PROGRAM (SCHIP). In an effort to improve access to health-care coverage for uninsured children from low-income families who were ineligible for Medicaid, Congress initiated the State Children's Health Insurance Program (SCHIP) as part of the Balanced Budget Act of 1997 (PL 105–33). Each state developed its own eligibility rules for federally assisted insurance programs designed to support working

TABLE 4.1

Children's health insurance coverage by presence of parents and selected characteristics, March 2002[1] [CONTINUED]

(In thousands and percent)

Characteristic	All children		Two parents		Mother only		Father only		Neither parent	
	Total	Percent covered by health insurance	Total	Percent covered by health insurance	Total	Percent covered by health insurance	Total	Percent covered by health insurance	Total	Percent covered by health insurance
Household tenure										
Owns/buying	48,542	90.5	38,362	93.3	6,547	84.5	1,808	85.2	1,825	59.6
Rents	22,512	83.6	10,366	83.9	9,689	86.7	1,444	78.9	1,012	58.4
No cash rent	1,266	89.6	938	93.1	237	84.0	44	68.2	48	66.7
Type of residence[5]										
Central city, in MSA	20,971	85.6	12,202	88.6	6,621	85.8	1,105	77.6	1,044	57.9
Outside central city, in MSA	38,194	89.9	28,540	92.8	6,944	85.3	1,477	83.6	1,234	55.9
Outside MSA	13,155	88.4	8,924	90.4	2,908	87.0	716	86.3	608	68.6

X Not applicable.

[1]All people under age 18, excluding group quarters, householders, subfamily reference people, and their spouses.
[2]Data are not shown separately for the American Indian and Alaska Native population because of the small sample size in the Current Population Survey in March 2001.
[3]If the parent is either the householder with an unmarried partner in the household, or the unmarried partner of the householder, they are cohabiting based on this direct measure. Cohabiting couples where neither partner is the householder are not identified.
[4]POSSLQ (Persons of the Opposite Sex Sharing Living Quarters) is defined by the presence of only two people over age 15 in the household who are opposite sex, not related, and not married. There can be any number of people under age 15 in the household. The universe of children under age 15 is shown as the denominator for POSSLQ measurement.
[5]"MSA" refers to Metropolitan Statistical Area.

SOURCE: Jason Fields, "Table 9. Children's Health Insurance Coverage by Presence of Parents and Selected Characteristics, March 2002," in *Children's Living Arrangements and Characteristics, March 2002,* Current Population Reports, P20-547, U.S. Department of Commerce, Economics and Statistics Administration, U.S. Census Bureau, June 2003, http://www.census.gov/prod/2003pubs/p20-547.pdf (accessed July 19, 2004)

families and low-income families alike by providing health insurance to their children. By 2004 in most states, uninsured children eighteen years old and younger whose families earned up to $34,100 a year (for a family of four) were eligible. The programs covered doctor visits, prescription medicines, hospitalizations, and much more. Most states also covered the cost of dental care, eye care, and medical equipment. To encourage parents of uninsured children to enroll in the state programs, the U.S. Department of Health and Human Services (HHS) began a national campaign to link families with the free or low-cost programs. Diverse business and organizational partners were enlisted to support a promotional effort called *Insure Kids Now!*

Overweight and Inactive Children

In 2002 a report issued by the office of the U.S. Surgeon General noted a number of risk factors for overweight children. These included high cholesterol and high blood pressure, both of which were linked to heart disease; type 2 diabetes; and poor self-esteem and depression. In addition, statistics showed that overweight children would almost inevitably carry that weight into adulthood. The Centers for Disease Control and Prevention (CDC) reported in 2003 that approximately 15% of all U.S. children and adolescents were overweight in 1999–2000. This was roughly triple the level of those overweight among children and adolescents in the late 1970s.

Sandy Proctor, coordinator of the Kansas State University Expanded Food and Nutrition Education Program, cited a variety of causes for the increase in overweight children, including reduced physical activity and poor eating habits. She noted that fewer children walked to school while television, video games, and computers offered popular but sedentary after-school entertainment. Children often had less freedom to play outside without supervision due to parents' fears of child abduction. Compounding these issues were funding constraints that forced many schools to reduce or eliminate physical education programs.

ROLE OF SCHOOLS IN CHILDREN'S WEIGHT PROBLEMS. Changes in eating habits also contributed to weight gains. Many working parents and busy families abandoned home-cooked family meals and relied more on prepared and fast foods, which typically had high fat and salt content. Food choices available in schools followed the taste patterns of students. In an October 2003 article for *Education Week on the Web,* Darcia Harris Bowman reported the lucrative practice of school districts signing exclusive vending contracts with soft drink companies. Such contracts generated an estimated $54 million annually for Texas public schools, according to one survey. Subsequently, Texas became one of the first states to limit children's access to "foods of minimum nutritional value" in elementary and middle schools.

In its *Youth Risk Behavior Surveillance—United States, 2003* the Centers for Disease Control and Prevention (CDC) found that 15% of all high school students were at risk of becoming overweight in 2003, while another 14% were actually overweight. Nearly twice as many male students as female students were in the over-

FIGURE 4.4

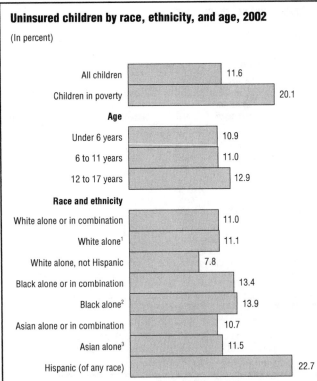

Uninsured children by race, ethnicity, and age, 2002

(In percent)

All children	11.6
Children in poverty	20.1
Age	
Under 6 years	10.9
6 to 11 years	11.0
12 to 17 years	12.9
Race and ethnicity	
White alone or in combination	11.0
White alone[1]	11.1
White alone, not Hispanic	7.8
Black alone or in combination	13.4
Black alone[2]	13.9
Asian alone or in combination	10.7
Asian alone[3]	11.5
Hispanic (of any race)	22.7

[1]The 2003 CPS asked respondents to choose one or more races. White alone refers to people who reported White and did not report any other race category. The use of this single-race population does not imply that it is the preferred method of presenting or analyzing data. The Census Bureau uses a variety of approaches. Information on people who reported more than one race, such as "White and American Indian and Alaska Native" or "Asian and Black or African American," is available from Census 2000 through American FactFinder. About 2.6 percent of people reported more than one race in 2000.
[2]Black alone refers to people who reported Black or African American and did not report any other race category.
[3]Asian alone refers to people who reported Asian and did not report any other race category.

SOURCE: Robert J. Mills and Shailesh Bhandari, "Figure 4. Uninsured Children by Race, Ethnicity, and Age, 2002," in *Health Insurance Coverage in the United States: 2002*, Current Population Reports, P60-223, U. S. Department of Commerce, Economics and Statistics Administration, U.S. Census Bureau, September 2003, http://www.census.gov/prod/2003pubs/p60-223.pdf (accessed September 7, 2004)

weight category. More than one-third of African-American female students and two-fifths of Hispanic male students were at risk or actually overweight, while white, non-Hispanic female students had the lowest proportion of being at risk or overweight. (See Table 4.2.)

According to the same 2003 report, less than one-third of high school students participated in daily physical education at school. (See Table 4.3.) By comparison, 38% of all high school students watched three or more hours of television per school day. The number of African-American students watching three or more hours of television was more than double that of white students. (See Table 4.4.)

UNHEALTHY ATTITUDES TOWARD WEIGHT AMONG FEMALE STUDENTS. In a paradoxical turn, as overweight rates for Americans climbed, many "waiflike," extremely thin women were featured in television, video, and fash-

ion media aimed at youth. In their quest for acceptance and popularity, many adolescent and teenage females measured themselves by pop culture icons and felt fat, even if they were of normal weight for their height and build. The 2003 CDC report revealed that 36.1% of female high school students described themselves as overweight, and 59.3% of female students reported that they were trying to lose weight. By contrast, 23.5% of male students saw themselves as overweight and 29.6% were trying to slim down. (See Table 4.5.)

Female teens were also more likely than males to engage in unhealthy behaviors in an attempt to lose weight. Twice as many female as male students had gone without eating for twenty-four hours or more, the CDC report found. Use of diet pills, powders, or liquids, without the advice of a doctor, increased with age among female students. About 9% of ninth-grade females tried these weight loss or weight prevention products compared to about 13% of eleventh- and twelfth-grade females. Among female students at all grade levels, more than 8% reported vomiting or taking laxatives to lose weight or prevent weight gain. (See Table 4.6.) In some cases females developed distorted self-images that led to a serious eating disorder called anorexia nervosa, defined as a refusal to maintain a minimally normal body weight. The American Psychiatric Association estimated that from .5% to 1% of women between ages fifteen and thirty suffered from anorexia.

TEEN SEXUALITY

By the late twentieth century, American teens were more sexually active than previous generations. While sexual activity was rare in young teens, it increased as teens grew older. By the age of seventeen, most teens reported at least one sexual experience. Concurrent with sexual activity were risks of sexually transmitted diseases (STDs), pregnancy, and dropping out of school.

Sexual Risk Behaviors

The 2003 *Youth Risk Behavior Survey* from the CDC found that 46.7% of teens in grades nine through twelve reported they had ever had sexual intercourse. Just 4.2% of all female students and 10.4% of male students reported their first sexual intercourse occurred before age thirteen. African-American teens were most sexually active. Compared to less than half of all teens who had ever had sexual intercourse, 60.9% of African-American females and 73.8% of males reported having ever had sexual intercourse. While 17.5% of all male teenagers reported they had four or more sexual partners during their lifetime, 41.7% of African-American males claimed four or more partners. (See Table 4.7.)

Risks of pregnancy and acquiring STDs were clearly on the minds of many teens. Almost two-thirds of high

TABLE 4.2

Percentage of high school students who were at risk for becoming or were overweight, 2003[1,2]

Category	At risk for becoming overweight			Overweight		
	Female %	Male %	Total %	Female %	Male %	Total %
Race/ethnicity						
White	13.8	14.3	**14.1**	7.8	16.2	**12.2**
Black	21.2	15.5	**18.3**	15.6	19.5	**17.6**
Hispanic	15.7	19.0	**17.3**	11.8	21.7	**16.8**
Grade						
9	15.6	15.3	**15.4**	11.2	19.0	**15.3**
10	15.3	14.7	**15.0**	9.3	17.9	**13.7**
11	16.9	16.6	**16.8**	8.6	17.0	**12.9**
12	13.2	15.6	**14.4**	8.0	14.7	**11.4**
Total	**15.3**	**15.5**	**15.4**	**9.4**	**17.4**	**13.5**

[1]Students who were ≥85th percentile but <95th percentile for body mass index, by age and sex, based on reference data.
[2]Students who were ≥95th percentile for body mass index, by age and sex, based on reference data.

SOURCE: "Table 58. Percentage of High School Students Who Were at Risk for Becoming or Were Overweight, by Sex, Race/Ethnicity, and Grade," in *Youth Risk Behavior Surveillance—United States, 2003,* Morbidity and Mortality Weekly Report, vol. 53, no. SS-2, Department of Health and Human Services, Centers for Disease Control and Prevention, May 21, 2004, http://www.cdc.gov/mmwr/PDF/SS/SS5302.pdf (accessed July 27, 2004)

TABLE 4.3

Percentage of high school students who attended physical education class daily, 2003

Category	Attended PE class daily*					
	Female %	CI (±)	Male %	CI (±)	Total %	CI (±)
Race/Ethnicity						
White**	23.1	7.3	26.8	7.1	**24.9**	7.0
Black**	29.0	7.5	37.1	6.0	**33.0**	6.3
Hispanic	34.0	8.5	39.5	9.0	**36.7**	8.0
Grade						
9	38.0	9.7	37.7	8.5	**37.9**	8.6
10	29.1	8.8	33.5	7.9	**31.3**	8.0
11	19.2	4.8	26.0	5.0	**22.6**	4.6
12	15.2	4.0	21.4	4.9	**18.2**	4.0
Total	**26.4**	6.1	**30.5**	5.7	**28.4**	5.7

*5 days in an average week when they were in school

SOURCE: Adapted from "Table 54. Percentage of High School Students Who Were Enrolled in Physical Education (PE), Attended PE Class Daily, and Spent > 20 Minutes Exercising or Playing Sports during an Average PE Class, by Sex, Race/Ethnicity, and Grade," in *Youth Risk Behavior Surveillance—United States, 2003*, Morbidity and Mortality Weekly Report, vol. 53, no. SS-2, Department of Health and Human Services, Centers for Disease Control and Prevention, May 21, 2004, http://www.cdc.gov/mmwr /PDF/SS/SS5302.pdf (accessed July 27, 2004)

TABLE 4.4

Percentage of high school students who watched 3 or more hours of television per day, 2003

Category	Watched ≥3 hours/day of TV		
	Female %	Male %	Total %
Race/ethnicity			
White	26.8	31.7	**29.3**
Black	70.0	64.3	**67.2**
Hispanic	45.1	46.8	**45.9**
Grade			
9	41.2	46.5	**44.0**
10	39.0	42.9	**41.0**
11	34.7	34.1	**34.4**
12	31.3	29.9	**30.6**
Total	**37.0**	**39.3**	**38.2**

SOURCE: Adapted from "Table 56. Percentage of High School Students Who Did Strengthening Exercises, Played on One or More Sports Teams, and Who Watched >3 Hours/Day of Television, by Sex, Race/Ethnicity, and Grade," in *Youth Risk Behavior Surveillance—United States, 2003,* Morbidity and Mortality Weekly Report, vol. 53, no. SS-2, Department of Health and Human Services, Centers for Disease Control and Prevention, May 21, 2004, http://www.cdc.gov/mmwr/PDF/SS/SS5302.pdf (accessed July 27, 2004)

school students reported having used condoms the last time they had sexual intercourse. More than one-fifth of female students reported using birth control pills.

Noncoital Behaviors

The growing perception among young people that noncoital behaviors (avoiding the actual physical union of male and female genitalia) were not "sex" placed more teens at risk. A study by the Urban Institute, a nonprofit policy research organization based in Washington, D.C., showed that while 55% of teenage males stated they had had vaginal sex, two-thirds had experienced oral or anal sex or had been masturbated by a female.

Researchers and public health experts found that many young people perceived these noncoital behaviors as something other than sex—and sometimes even believed they were being sexually abstinent while participating in noncoital sexual behavior. While noncoital behaviors avoided the risk of pregnancy, teens engaged in these behaviors remained at risk for exposure to sexually transmitted diseases.

TABLE 4.5

Percentage of high school students who described themselves as overweight and who were trying to lose weight, 2003

	Described themselves as overweight			Were trying to lose weight		
	Female	Male	Total	Female	Male	Total
Category	%	%	%	%	%	%
Race/ethnicity						
White	38.5	23.5	**30.8**	62.6	27.9	**44.8**
Black	26.4	17.9	**22.3**	46.7	22.7	**34.7**
Hispanic	36.1	27.1	**31.6**	61.7	37.4	**49.4**
Grade						
9	33.1	22.6	**27.7**	54.1	31.2	**42.2**
10	36.1	23.2	**29.6**	62.2	28.3	**45.1**
11	36.9	24.3	**30.5**	60.4	28.3	**44.1**
12	38.7	24.1	**31.4**	61.7	28.0	**44.6**
Total	**36.1**	**23.5**	**29.6**	**59.3**	**29.1**	**43.8**

SOURCE: "Table 60. Percentage of High School Students Who Described Themselves as Slightly or Very Overweight and Who Were Trying to Lose Weight, by Sex, Race/Ethnicity, and Grade," in *Youth Risk Behavior Surveillance—United States, 2003,* Morbidity and Mortality Weekly Report, vol. 53, no. SS-2, Department of Health and Human Services, Centers for Disease Control and Prevention, May 21, 2004, http://www.cdc.gov/mmwr/PDF/SS/SS5302.pdf (accessed July 27, 2004)

TABLE 4.6

Percentage of high school students who engaged in unhealthy behaviors associated with weight control, 2003[1]

	Went without eating for ≥24 hours to lose weight or to keep from gaining weight			Took diet pills, powders, or liquids to lose weight or to keep from gaining weight[2]			Vomited or took laxatives to lose weight or to keep from gaining weight		
	Female	Male	Total	Female	Male	Total	Female	Male	Total
Category	%	%	%	%	%	%	%	%	%
Race/ethnicity									
White	18.4	7.1	**12.5**	13.0	6.8	**9.8**	8.5	2.7	**5.5**
Black	14.5	10.5	**12.5**	5.1	4.9	**5.0**	5.6	5.0	**5.3**
Hispanic	18.2	9.2	**13.7**	11.7	9.2	**10.5**	9.7	5.1	**7.4**
Grade									
9	18.8	10.7	**14.6**	9.2	7.0	**8.0**	7.9	4.6	**6.2**
10	18.5	7.0	**12.7**	10.9	5.8	**8.3**	9.3	3.5	**6.4**
11	19.6	8.2	**13.8**	12.6	7.7	**10.1**	8.8	2.6	**5.7**
12	15.7	6.9	**11.2**	13.0	8.5	**10.8**	7.3	3.8	**5.5**
Total	**18.3**	**8.5**	**13.3**	**11.3**	**7.1**	**9.2**	**8.4**	**3.7**	**6.0**

[1]During the 30 days preceding the survey.
[2]Without a doctor's advice.

SOURCE: "Table 64. Percentage of High School Students Who Engaged in Unhealthy Behaviors Associated with Weight Control, by Sex, Race/Ethnicity, and Grade," in *Youth Risk Behavior Surveillance—United States, 2003,* Morbidity and Mortality Weekly Report, vol. 53, no. SS-2, Department of Health and Human Services, Centers for Disease Control and Prevention, May 21, 2004, http://www.cdc.gov/mmwr/PDF/SS/SS5302.pdf (accessed July 27, 2004)

TEEN PREGNANCY AND BIRTHS

The National Center for Health Statistics (NCHS) tracks vital statistics in the United States. It found that between 1990 and 2002 the birth rate for all women under age thirty declined. For teenagers age fifteen to seventeen the rate dropped by nearly 40%, to 23.2 births per one thousand women. For older teens age eighteen to nineteen the birth rate declined by 18%, to 72.8 per one thousand women. (See Figure 4.5.) Other data from the Federal Interagency Forum on Child and Family Statistics revealed that reduced adolescent birth rates were most significant among African-American teens. The 1991 rate of 86 per one thousand for African-American females age fifteen to seventeen declined to just 41 per one thousand in 2002.

Some analysts ascribed the declining pregnancy trend to the increasing use of birth control methods, especially longer-lasting contraceptives such as Norplant and Depo-Provera. The increasing use of condoms due to fear of contracting AIDS and other sexually transmitted diseases was also thought to contribute to the lower pregnancy rate. Other analysts, however, credited an increase in the practice of abstinence.

Many public-health experts believed that the factors that predisposed adolescents to drug use were the same ones that predisposed them to teen pregnancy—poverty, family dysfunction, child abuse, and early education difficulties.

Of concern for all births was the increase in low birth weight babies (5.5 pounds or less). According to the CDC, at 7.0% in 1990, the incidence of low birth weight babies

TABLE 4.7

Percentage of high school students who engaged in sexual behaviors, 2003

Category	Ever had sexual intercourse			Had first sexual intercourse before age 13 years			Had ≥4 sex partners during lifetime		
	Female	Male	Total	Female	Male	Total	Female	Male	Total
	%	%	%	%	%	%	%	%	%
Race/ethnicity									
White	43.0	40.5	**41.8**	3.4	5.0	**4.2**	10.1	11.5	**10.8**
Black	60.9	73.8	**67.3**	6.9	31.8	**19.0**	16.3	41.7	**28.8**
Hispanic	46.4	56.8	**51.4**	5.2	11.6	**8.3**	11.2	20.5	**15.7**
Grade									
9	27.9	37.3	**32.8**	5.3	13.2	**9.3**	6.4	14.2	**10.4**
10	43.1	45.1	**44.1**	5.7	11.2	**8.5**	8.8	16.4	**12.6**
11	53.1	53.4	**53.2**	3.2	7.5	**5.4**	13.4	18.6	**16.0**
12	62.3	60.7	**61.6**	1.9	8.8	**5.5**	17.9	22.2	**20.3**
Total	**45.3**	**48.0**	**46.7**	**4.2**	**10.4**	**7.4**	**11.2**	**17.5**	**14.4**

SOURCE: "Table 42. Percentage of High School Students Who Engaged in Sexual Behaviors, by Sex, Race/Ethnicity, and Grade," in *Youth Risk Behavior Surveillance—United States, 2003,* Morbidity and Mortality Weekly Report, vol. 53, no. SS-2, Department of Health and Human Services, Centers for Disease Control and Prevention, May 21, 2004, http://www.cdc.gov/mmwr/PDF/SS/SS5302.pdf (accessed July 27, 2004)

FIGURE 4.5

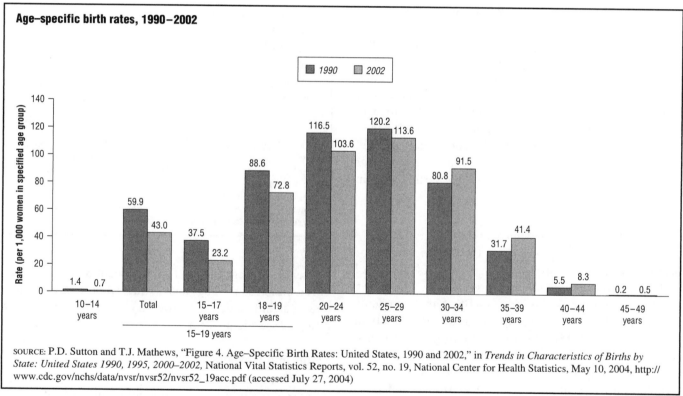

Age–specific birth rates, 1990–2002

SOURCE: P.D. Sutton and T.J. Mathews, "Figure 4. Age–Specific Birth Rates: United States, 1990 and 2002," in *Trends in Characteristics of Births by State: United States 1990, 1995, 2000–2002,* National Vital Statistics Reports, vol. 52, no. 19, National Center for Health Statistics, May 10, 2004, http://www.cdc.gov/nchs/data/nvsr/nvsr52/nvsr52_19acc.pdf (accessed July 27, 2004)

rose to 7.8% in 2002. This was not an issue specific only to teenage mothers. Besides prenatal care concerns, medical experts noted the increase in higher-order multiple births (greater than twins), which tended to lower the birth weight of all the infants.

YOUTH RISK BEHAVIORS

In 2003 the CDC reported that the leading causes of disease and death among adults were cardiovascular disease (39.4%) and cancer (23.5%). Among youth and young adults aged ten to twenty-four, almost three-quarters of all deaths resulted from just four causes: motor-vehicle crashes (32.3%), other unintentional injuries (11.7%), homicide (15.1%), and suicide (11.7%).

As early as 1991 the CDC identified six priority health-risk behaviors that were linked to disease and death among **all** age groups:

1) Behaviors that contribute to unintentional injuries and violence

2) Tobacco use

3) Alcohol and other drug use

4) Sexual behaviors that contribute to unintended pregnancy and sexually transmitted diseases (STDs)

5) Unhealthy dietary behaviors

6) Physical inactivity and overweight

The CDC determined that health-risk behaviors were often established during youth and continued into adulthood. Furthermore, the CDC concluded that these behaviors were interrelated and preventable. As educational initiatives were developed to help youth change these behaviors, the CDC established methods, such as the *Youth Risk Behavior Survey* (YRBS), to monitor progress. This school-based, biennial survey tracked health-risk behaviors of students in grades nine through twelve.

Risk-Behavior for Leading Causes of Death among Youth

Results of the 2003 survey demonstrated that, during the thirty days preceding the survey, numerous high school students engaged in behaviors that increased their likelihood of death from one of the four causes: motor-vehicle crashes, other unintentional injuries, homicide, and suicide. In addition, many students had developed health-risk behaviors that, if continued, could contribute to cardiovascular disease and cancer in their adult years. For example, 22% of high school students had smoked cigarettes, 78% had not eaten five or more servings per day of fruits and vegetables, 33% had participated in insufficient physical activity, and 14% were overweight.

Motor Vehicles, Seatbelts, and Alcohol

Motor-vehicle crashes were the leading cause of death in the ten to twenty-four age group in 2003. Alcohol and failure to use seatbelts were significant contributing factors. According to the 2003 YRBS, female students appeared to be less likely to ignore seat belt safety than male students. While 17.6% of ninth-grade females reported that they never or rarely used seatbelts when riding as a passenger in a car, just 10.9% of twelfth-grade females said they did not buckle up. Among male students, however, 22.9% of ninth graders and 21.1% of twelfth graders rarely or never wore seat belts as a passenger. Drinking and driving habits also differed among male and female students surveyed. Female students were more likely to ride with a driver who had been drinking alcohol (31.1%) than to drive a vehicle after drinking (8.9%). An average 15% of male students admitted they had driven a car after drinking.

A related study by the HHS revealed that youth and young adults in the seventeen to twenty-four age range were most likely to drive a motor vehicle while under the

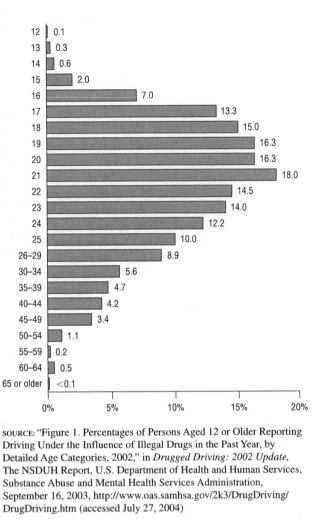

SOURCE: "Figure 1. Percentages of Persons Aged 12 or Older Reporting Driving Under the Influence of Illegal Drugs in the Past Year, by Detailed Age Categories, 2002," in *Drugged Driving: 2002 Update*, The NSDUH Report, U.S. Department of Health and Human Services, Substance Abuse and Mental Health Services Administration, September 16, 2003, http://www.oas.samhsa.gov/2k3/DrugDriving/DrugDriving.htm (accessed July 27, 2004)

influence of illegal drugs. Seven percent of sixteen-year-olds reported using drugs and driving, while 18% of twenty-one-year-olds did, which was the highest out of all age groups. (See Figure 4.6.)

Fights and Weapons

Fighting and carrying weapons increased risks of unintentional injuries and homicides among students. In the 2003 YRBS, an average 25% of female students and 40.5% of male students reported they had been in one or more fights in the twelve months preceding the survey. As students matured, the number involved in fights decreased. While 31.9% of ninth-grade females and 44.8% of ninth-grade males reported being in fights, by twelfth grade only 17.7% of females and 35% of males were involved in fights. Injuries resulted from fights for 2.6% of female students and 5.7% of male students. Carrying a weapon was more common among male students (26.9%) than female students (6.7%). More specifically, only 1.6% of female students reported carrying a gun compared to 10.2% of male students. As students matured, carrying weapons became less frequent for female students but slightly more frequent for male students.

Tobacco, Alcohol, and Drugs

The YRBS revealed reductions in use of tobacco and alcohol among youth. The percentage of students who reported current cigarette smoking had dropped from a high of 36% in 1997 to 22% in 2003. There was little difference in cigarette use between male and female students. In the thirty days prior to the survey, 21.9% of female students and 21.8% of male students had smoked one or more cigarettes. While 75% of high school students had tried alcohol, 44.9% had one or more alcoholic drinks within the thirty days preceding the survey, and 28.3% had five or more drinks in a row during the same period. Just over 40% of students reported they had tried marijuana, while 22.4% reported current marijuana use.

Although 8.7% of all students reported they had tried some form of cocaine (including powder, "crack", or "freebase") at least once, only 4.1% reported current use. Just over 3% of students reported they had used a needle to inject illegal drugs. When asked about use of inhalants (sniffing glue, breathing paint, or breathing the contents of aerosol spray cans), 12.1% of students had experimented at least once and 3.9% reported current use. Just over 6% of students also reported they had used illegal steroids. Just over 3% of students had tried heroin at least once, 7.6% had tried methamphetamines, and 11.1% had tried ecstasy.

More than one-fourth of high school students experimented with drinking alcohol and close to one-fifth smoked at least one cigarette before age thirteen. Marijuana may have been less easily obtained, yet 10% of students tried that substance at young ages. A greater percentage of male than female students reported they had tried each of these substances prior to age thirteen.

Teen Suicide

The YRBS also studied depression among teens. Abandoning usual activities due to feeling sad or hopeless almost every day for two or more weeks was more common among female students (35.5%) than male students (21.9%). But when it came to seriously considering a suicide attempt or actually making a suicide plan, the gap between male and female narrowed, with 18.9% of girls and 14.1% of boys reported having made a suicide plan in the twelve months prior to responding to the YRBS. While the percentage of males who made a suicide plan was fairly constant at all grade levels, the proportion of female students who planned suicide declined steadily from 20.9% of ninth graders to 16.2% of twelfth graders. The decrease in actual suicide attempts by grade level was

even more dramatic for female students. Among ninth-grade females 14.7% had attempted suicide during the twelve months preceding the survey compared to 6.9% of twelfth-grade females. About one-fourth of the suicide attempts reported by female students required medical attention. Less than half the percentage of male students (5.4%) attempted suicide compared to female students (11.5%) and the decrease in attempts by grade level was far less significant.

National Health Objectives

In January 2000 the HHS released a statement of national health objectives called *Healthy People 2010.* This comprehensive set of disease prevention and health promotion objectives was designed to guide the nation's health achievement over the first decade of the new century. Created by scientists both inside and outside of government, it identified a wide range of public health priorities and specific, measurable objectives. The results from the 2003 YRBS were measured against the *Healthy People 2010* goals for youth. Some objectives had much room for improvement, such as the 28.4% of teens who participated in daily school physical education compared to the 2010 target of 50%. The proportion of teens who said they rode with a driver who had been drinking alcohol had decreased to 30.2%, nearly matching the 30% target for 2010. Physical fighting among teens had also dropped to within one percentage point of the target.

CHILD VICTIMS OF ABUSE AND NEGLECT

According to the HHS report *Child Maltreatment 2002,* an estimated 896,000 children were victims of maltreatment in 2002. More than half of the reports alleging maltreatment of a child came from professionals—education, legal and law enforcement, social services, and medical personnel. The remainder of reports came from family members, neighbors, and other sources, including 9.6% from anonymous sources. Another 0.7% of reports came from alleged victims themselves.

Reports of alleged maltreatment were investigated by Child Protective Services to determine the validity of the allegation and a course of action. The HHS report tracks the number of reported cases assessed and the number in which children were determined to be victims from 1990–2002. During that period the number of children assessed rose 21.3%, while the number of children determined to be victims dropped 7.3%. The rate of all children who received an assessment or investigation increased from 36.1 per one thousand children in 1990 to 43.8 per one thousand children in 2002. Of reports alleging child maltreatment received in 2002, 60.5% were determined to be unsubstantiated.

The youngest children had the highest rate of victimization, according to the HHS report. Children under one year in age were most frequently victims of maltreatment (9.6%). From that age the victimization rate declined gradually from 6.2% for one-year-olds to 5.4% for ten-year-olds.

Half of all child victims were white (54.2%). (See Figure 4.7.) However, the Department of Health and Human Services reported that, when compared to the total number of children of the same race in the United States, American Indian or Alaska Native children had the highest rate of victimization (21.7 per one thousand children of the same race). African-American children were close behind at a rate of 20.2 per one thousand children of the same race. Asian and Pacific Islander children had the lowest rate at 3.7 per one thousand.

Parents as Perpetrators

Perhaps the most disturbing aspect of child maltreatment was that more than 80% of perpetrators were parents, the HHS data revealed. Other relatives (6.6%) and unmarried partners of the parent (2.9%) were also perpetrators of abuse. Less than 1.5% of perpetrators were foster parents, daycare providers, or staff of residential facilities. An "other" category, which included camp counselors and school employees, accounted for 4.7% of perpetrators. Among the perpetrators, 58% were women. While parents were the primary perpetrators of all maltreatment, they were responsible for less than 3% of sexual abuse cases. Other relatives were responsible for 29% of sexual abuse, and nearly one-quarter of sexual abusers were nonrelatives and persons not in caregiving roles with the child.

Reports on child maltreatment grouped cases into six types: physical abuse, neglect, medical neglect, sexual abuse, psychological maltreatment, and other abuse. Figure 4.8 depicts five-year patterns of the six types of abuse. Clearly neglect (including medical neglect) was the most frequent type of child abuse, accounting for 60.5% of cases. Both physical abuse and sexual abuse cases showed some slight decreases since 1998.

Children were found to be victims of maltreatment in approximately 28% of cases investigated, the HHS report asserted. About one-fifth of child victims were placed in foster care. Other cases received a variety of support and monitoring services.

Child Fatalities

Child fatalities were the most tragic results of maltreatment. An estimated fourteen hundred children died from abuse or neglect in 2002. The overall child fatality rate due to abuse or neglect was two per one hundred thousand children—an increase from 1.84 per one hundred thousand in 2000. Three-quarters of these children were younger than four years of age. (See Figure 4.9.) Infant boys had a higher death rate (nineteen per one hun-

dred thousand boys of the same age) than infant girls (twelve per one hundred thousand). Consistent with the high rate of neglect among all maltreatment cases, one-third of all child fatalities were attributed to neglect. (See Figure 4.10.)

SCHOOL VIOLENCE

Indicators of School Crime and Safety, 2002, a joint report by the U.S. Departments of Education and Justice, revealed a 46% drop in violent crime victimization rates in schools from 1991 to 2000. According to the report, students were twice as likely to become victims of serious violent crime away from school than at school. However, violence, theft, bullying, drugs, and firearms continued to be problems in many schools.

Other data, reported in the CDC's *Youth Risk Behavior Survey* (YRBS), found that between 1999 and 2001 the percentage of students who reported being bullied at school rose from 5% to 8%. In 2001 the greatest number of students (14%) reported bullying occurred in sixth grade. Bullying incidents declined to about 2% by twelfth grade. (See Figure 4.11.)

Eight percent of female high school students and 17.1% of male students reported being in a fight on school property in 2003, according to YRBS data. Fighting was more prevalent among ninth graders and decreased significantly in tenth through twelfth grades. About 5% of all high school students reported one or more days in which they did not go to school because of safety concerns. Almost 30% of all students reported having had property stolen or deliberately damaged at school. (See Table 4.8.)

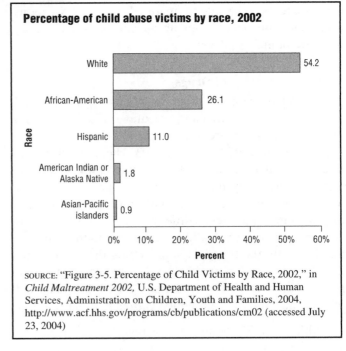

FIGURE 4.7

Percentage of child abuse victims by race, 2002

SOURCE: "Figure 3-5. Percentage of Child Victims by Race, 2002," in *Child Maltreatment 2002,* U.S. Department of Health and Human Services, Administration on Children, Youth and Families, 2004, http://www.acf.hhs.gov/programs/cb/publications/cm02 (accessed July 23, 2004)

FIGURE 4.8

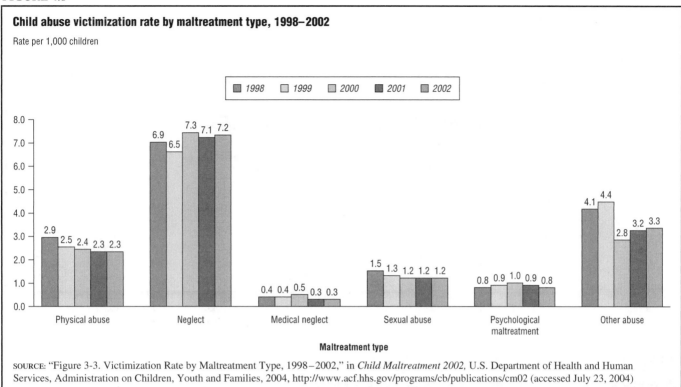

Child abuse victimization rate by maltreatment type, 1998–2002

Rate per 1,000 children

Legend: 1998, 1999, 2000, 2001, 2002

Physical abuse: 2.9, 2.5, 2.4, 2.3, 2.3
Neglect: 6.9, 6.5, 7.3, 7.1, 7.2
Medical neglect: 0.4, 0.4, 0.5, 0.3, 0.3
Sexual abuse: 1.5, 1.3, 1.2, 1.2, 1.2
Psychological maltreatment: 0.8, 0.9, 1.0, 0.9, 0.8
Other abuse: 4.1, 4.4, 2.8, 3.2, 3.3

Maltreatment type

SOURCE: "Figure 3-3. Victimization Rate by Maltreatment Type, 1998–2002," in *Child Maltreatment 2002,* U.S. Department of Health and Human Services, Administration on Children, Youth and Families, 2004, http://www.acf.hhs.gov/programs/cb/publications/cm02 (accessed July 23, 2004)

Weapons in Schools

In the YRBS report, 6.1% percent of all high school students reported carrying a weapon on school property, and 9.2% said they had been threatened or injured with a weapon on school property. Male students in ninth grade were more likely to have been injured or threatened with a weapon (15.4%), while more than 10% of eleventh- and twelfth-grade males carried weapons. (See Table 4.9.)

Among high school students, 5.8% reported that they had used marijuana on school property. In addition, more than one-fourth of all high school students said they had been offered, sold, or given an illegal drug on school property during the past year. Hispanic male students had the highest rates in each category, both for marijuana use on school property (10.4%) and if they had been offered, sold, or given an illegal drug on school property (40.6%). (See Table 4.10.)

Violence against Teachers

Indicators of School Crime and Safety, 2002 also considered the safety of teachers. In the 1999–2000 school year, 305,000 (9%) of all elementary and secondary school teachers were threatened with injury by a student, and 135,000 (4%) were physically attacked by a student. From 1996 through 2000, teachers were victims of more than one million thefts and 599,000 violent crimes (rape or sexual assault, robbery, aggravated assault, and simple assault) at school. In 2001 forty-nine senior and junior high teachers per one thousand were victims of violent crimes at school—mostly simple assaults—compared to

FIGURE 4.9

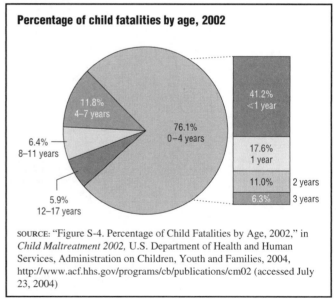

Percentage of child fatalities by age, 2002

76.1% 0–4 years
11.8% 4–7 years
6.4% 8–11 years
5.9% 12–17 years

41.2% <1 year
17.6% 1 year
11.0% 2 years
6.3% 3 years

SOURCE: "Figure S-4. Percentage of Child Fatalities by Age, 2002," in *Child Maltreatment 2002,* U.S. Department of Health and Human Services, Administration on Children, Youth and Families, 2004, http://www.acf.hhs.gov/programs/cb/publications/cm02 (accessed July 23, 2004)

fifteen elementary teachers per one thousand. Urban teachers were twice as likely as rural teachers to be victims of violence at school—thirty-six per one thousand compared to seventeen per one thousand.

Other Factors Contributing to Violence

In a 2000 report titled *Youth Gangs in Schools* from the Office of Juvenile Justice and Delinquency Prevention of the U.S. Department of Justice, one-half of teens surveyed said there were guns in their homes and about half

FIGURE 4.10

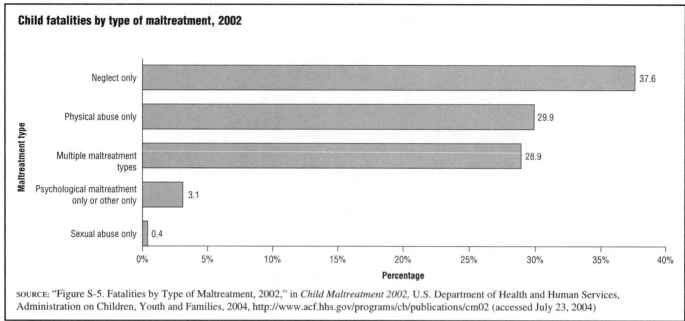

Child fatalities by type of maltreatment, 2002

SOURCE: "Figure S-5. Fatalities by Type of Maltreatment, 2002," in *Child Maltreatment 2002,* U.S. Department of Health and Human Services, Administration on Children, Youth and Families, 2004, http://www.acf.hhs.gov/programs/cb/publications/cm02 (accessed July 23, 2004)

FIGURE 4.11

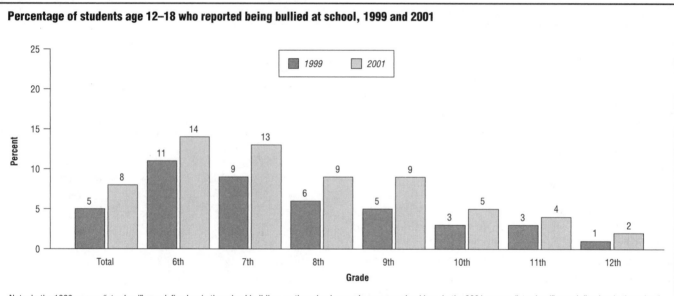

Percentage of students age 12–18 who reported being bullied at school, 1999 and 2001

Note: In the 1999 survey, "at school" was defined as in the school building, on the school grounds, or on a school bus. In the 2001 survey, "at school" was defined as in the school building, on school property, on a school bus, or going to and from school.

SOURCE: "Figure 6.2. Percentage of Students Age 12–18 Who Reported Being Bullied at School during the Previous 6 Months, by Grade, 1999 and 2001," in *Indicators of School Crime and Safety, 2003,* U.S. Department of Education, Institute of Education Sciences, National Center for Education Statistics, Bureau of Justice Statistics, Office of Justice Programs, 2004, http://nces.ed.gov/pubs2004/2004004.pdf (accessed August 10, 2004)

said it was at least somewhat important to know how to shoot a gun. Six percent of teens surveyed said it was very or somewhat important to belong to a gang or "posse." Thirty-seven percent of students reported there was a gang presence at their school.

Decline in Juvenile Violence

The level of juvenile violence in America during the 1980s and early 1990s caused predictions of a national crisis of violent youth. According to a 2002 report by the Urban Institute, the number of juvenile arrests for violent crimes—murder, rape, robbery, and aggravated assault—rose 64% between 1980 and 1994. The tide turned in 1994, and by 2000 arrests for violent crimes by all age groups had declined significantly. Arrests for murder declined most significantly for the under-eighteen age group (71%) and the eighteen to twenty-four age group (41%).

TABLE 4.8

Percentage of high school students who were in a physical fight on school property[1], who did not go to school because they felt unsafe at school or on their way to and from school[2], and who had their property stolen or damaged on school property, 2003[3]

Category	Engaged in a physical fight on school property			Did not go to school because of safety concerns			Property stolen or deliberately damaged on school property		
	Female %	Male %	Total %	Female %	Male %	Total %	Female %	Male %	Total %
Race/ethnicity									
White	5.3	14.3	**10.0**	2.9	3.3	**3.1**	25.6	30.6	**28.2**
Black	12.6	21.5	**17.1**	9.0	7.9	**8.4**	27.0	33.9	**30.4**
Hispanic	13.8	19.3	**16.7**	10.0	8.9	**9.4**	27.6	37.0	**32.3**
Grade									
9	12.2	23.3	**18.0**	6.6	7.1	**6.9**	31.9	37.4	**34.8**
10	7.3	18.1	**12.8**	5.1	5.3	**5.2**	26.6	34.3	**30.5**
11	6.4	14.2	**10.4**	4.6	4.3	**4.5**	23.9	30.5	**27.2**
12	4.7	9.6	**7.3**	3.9	3.8	**3.8**	20.2	27.9	**24.2**
Total	**8.0**	**17.1**	**12.8**	**5.3**	**5.5**	**5.4**	**26.2**	**33.1**	**29.8**

[1]One or more times during the 12 months preceding the survey.
[2]On ≥1 of the 30 days preceding the survey.
[3]For example, car, clothing, or books.

SOURCE: Adapted from "Table 14. Percentage of High School Students Who Were in a Physical Fight on School Property, Who Did Not Go to School Because They Felt Unsafe at School or on Their Way to and from School, and Who Had Their Property Stolen or Damaged on School Property, by Sex, Race/Ethnicity, and Grade," in *Youth Risk Behavior Surveillance—United States, 2003,* Morbidity and Mortality Weekly Report, vol. 53, no. SS-2, Department of Health and Human Services, Centers for Disease Control and Prevention, May 21, 2004, http://www.cdc.gov/mmwr/PDF/SS/SS5302.pdf (accessed July 27, 2004)

Juvenile violent crimes declined more than crimes by young adults and older adults. Between 1994 and 2000 juvenile arrests for all types of offenses dropped 13%. Juvenile arrests for violent crimes dropped 34%, and arrests for property violations decreased 31%. During that same period, however, juvenile arrests for driving under the influence rose 54%, violation of liquor laws rose 33%, and drug abuse violations rose 29%.

The Centers for Disease Control and Prevention (CDC) reported that in 2002 more than 877,700 young people ages ten to twenty-four were injured from violent acts. Approximately one in thirteen required hospitaliza-tion. Homicide was the second-leading cause of death among young people ages ten to twenty-four overall. In 2001, 5,486 young people ages ten to twenty-four were murdered—an average of fifteen each day—and 79% were killed with firearms.

The CDC identified youth violence as a complex public health problem, describing it as widespread and highly visible, but preventable. The May 2002 *World Report on Violence and Health* [serial online] noted that, in addition to causing injury and death, youth violence undermined communities by increasing the cost of health care, reducing productivity, decreasing property values, and disrupting social services.

TABLE 4.9

Percentage of high school students who carried a weapon on school property and were threatened or injured with a weapon on school property, 2003 [1,2,3]

Category	Carries a weapon on school property			Threatened or injured with a weapon on school property		
	Female %	Male %	Total %	Female %	Male %	Total %
Race/ethnicity						
White	2.2	8.5	**5.5**	5.8	9.6	**7.8**
Black	5.5	8.4	**6.9**	7.5	14.3	**10.9**
Hispanic	4.2	7.7	**6.0**	6.9	11.9	**9.4**
Grade						
9	3.8	6.6	**5.3**	8.3	15.4	**12.1**
10	3.0	8.9	**6.0**	7.0	11.3	**9.2**
11	2.7	10.3	**6.6**	5.4	9.2	**7.3**
12	2.5	10.2	**6.4**	3.9	8.5	**6.3**
Total	**3.1**	**8.9**	**6.1**	**6.5**	**11.6**	**9.2**

[1]On ≥1 of the 30 days preceding the survey.
[2]For example, a gun, knife, or club.
[3]One or more times during the 12 months preceding the survey.

SOURCE: Adapted from "Table 12. Percentage of High School Students Who Carried a Weapon on School Property and Were Threatened or Injured with a Weapon on School Property, by Sex, Race/Ethnicity, and Grade," in *Youth Risk Behavior Surveillance—United States, 2003,* Morbidity and Mortality Weekly Report, vol. 53, no. SS-2, Department of Health and Human Services, Centers for Disease Control and Prevention, May 21, 2004, http://www.cdc.gov/mmwr/PDF/SS/SS5302.pdf (accessed July 27, 2004)

TABLE 4.10

Percentage of high school students who engaged in drug-related behaviors on school property, 2003

Category	Marijuana use on school property [1]			Offered, sold, or given an illegal drug on school property [2]		
	Female %	Male %	Total %	Female %	Male %	Total %
Race/ethnicity						
White	3.1	5.8	**4.5**	24.5	30.2	**27.5**
Black	3.6	9.7	**6.6**	18.3	27.7	**23.1**
Hispanic	6.0	10.4	**8.2**	32.5	40.6	**36.5**
Grade						
9	5.1	8.1	**6.6**	26.7	32.1	**29.5**
10	3.0	7.2	**5.2**	26.5	31.9	**29.2**
11	3.3	7.9	**5.6**	26.1	33.5	**29.9**
12	2.6	7.1	**5.0**	19.6	29.7	**24.9**
Total	**3.7**	**7.6**	**5.8**	**25.0**	**31.9**	**28.7**

[1]Used marijuana one or more times during the 30 days preceding the survey.
[2]During the 12 months preceding the survey.

SOURCE: Adapted from "Table 40. Percentage of High School Students Who Engaged in Drug-Related Behaviors on School Property, by Sex, Race/Ethnicity, and Grade," in *Youth Risk Behavior Surveillance—United States, 2003,* Morbidity and Mortality Weekly Report, vol. 53, no. SS-2, Department of Health and Human Services, Centers for Disease Control and Prevention, May 21, 2004, http://www.cdc.gov/mmwr/PDF/SS/SS5302.pdf (accessed July 27, 2004)

CHAPTER 5

POVERTY, HEALTH CARE, HOMELESSNESS, HOUSING, AND EMPLOYMENT

POVERTY

The U.S. Census Bureau first began tracking poverty data in America in 1959. The following year it counted 39.9 million Americans, or about 22.2% of the population, living below the poverty level. Changes in the definition of poverty levels over the years make pre-1980 comparisons difficult, but the percentage fell to 12.3% in the mid-1970s and fluctuated over the next two decades, hitting 14% in 1985. In 2001 the poverty rate stood at 11.7% and rose to 12.1% in 2002 and 12.5% in 2003. While the poverty rates for adults and senior citizens hovered around 10–11%, the poverty rate for children under age eighteen rose almost a full percentage point from 16.7% to 17.6% between 2002 and 2003. (See Table 5.1.)

Minorities in America have historically experienced higher rates of poverty. In 1959 the poverty rate for African-Americans was 55%, compared to 18% for whites. The African-American poverty rate tumbled in the 1960s and made another significant decline during the 1990s. In 2001, however, the poverty rate for African-Americans was 22.7% and 21.4% for Hispanics, while the rates for Asian and Pacific Islanders, white, and non-Hispanic white populations were at or below 10%. In 2002 and 2003 the African-American poverty rate stabilized at 24.4%. Similar poverty rates were recorded for Native Americans (23.2%) and Hispanics (22.5%). (See Table 5.1.)

Between 1980 and 2003 the Census Bureau's poverty threshold for a family of four increased 125%. The Census Bureau poverty threshold for 2003 was $18,660 for a family of four that included two children. (See Figure 5.1.)

Working Poor Families

Having a job did not necessarily shield a family from poverty. In 2001 about 6.8 million people were classified as working poor. They represented 4.9% of the workforce, an increase from 4.7% in 2000.

TABLE 5.1

Poverty rates, 2002–03

(Percent)

	2002	2003
National	12.1	12.5
Children under 18	16.7	17.6
Adults 18–64	10.8	10.8
Adults over 65	10.2	10.2
White, non-Hispanic	8.2	8.2
African-American	24.4	24.4
Asian	10.1	11.8
Native American	23.2	23.2
Hispanic	22.5	22.5
Foreign-born citizens	10.0	10.0
Foreign-born noncitizens	21.7	21.7

SOURCE: Adapted from *Income, Poverty, and Health Insurance Coverage in the United States: 2003,* P60-226, U.S. Department of Commerce, Economics and Statistics Administration, U.S. Census Bureau, August 2004, http://www.census.gov/prod/2004pubs/p60-226.pdf (accessed September 13, 2004)

Often lacking job skills and adequate child care and health care, the working poor faced problems such as low-wage jobs (43.8%), reduced hours of work (1.7%), and periods of unemployment (10.4%), according to 2004 data from the U.S. Department of Agriculture. (See Figure 5.2.) Only 2.6% of those who worked full-time year-round were below the poverty level, but 11.8% of those who either worked part-time, seasonally, or intermittently fell below the poverty mark.

Food Stamps

The Food Stamp Program was established in 1964 as part of the Lyndon Johnson administration's "War on Poverty." The program helps needy families and individuals pay for enough food to live on. The U.S. Department of Agriculture reported that in an average month in 2002, 8.2 million households received food stamp benefits. Fifty-four percent of these households included children,

FIGURE 5.1

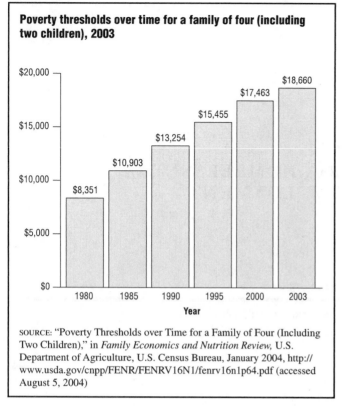

Poverty thresholds over time for a family of four (including two children), 2003

SOURCE: "Poverty Thresholds over Time for a Family of Four (Including Two Children)," in *Family Economics and Nutrition Review,* U.S. Department of Agriculture, U.S. Census Bureau, January 2004, http://www.usda.gov/cnpp/FENR/FENRV16N1/fenrv16n1p64.pdf (accessed August 5, 2004)

FIGURE 5.2

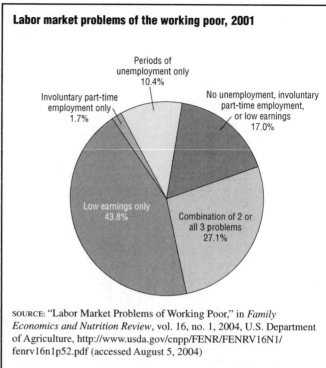

Labor market problems of the working poor, 2001

SOURCE: "Labor Market Problems of Working Poor," in *Family Economics and Nutrition Review,* vol. 16, no. 1, 2004, U.S. Department of Agriculture, http://www.usda.gov/cnpp/FENR/FENRV16N1/fenrv16n1p52.pdf (accessed August 5, 2004)

and most were headed by a single female. Nineteen percent of households receiving food stamps were elderly people, most living alone. Twenty-seven percent of food stamp households were persons with disabilities, and more than half lived alone. The average monthly food stamp benefit in 2002 was $173.00. A household with children (average 3.3 people) received $254.00, compared to a two-person household with one or both persons disabled receiving $64.00 per month.

Increased Requests for Food Assistance in Cities

In *The U.S. Conference of Mayors—Sodexho Hunger and Homelessness Survey 2003*, an average of 39% of adults who requested food assistance were employed. Working parents in Charleston, South Carolina, had difficulty getting to the Food Stamp Office during business hours. San Antonio, Texas, reported a 30% child poverty rate and noted that many clients lost their food stamp eligibility due to welfare reform but were unable to provide adequate food for their families. In Portland, Oregon, 55% of households served with emergency food included children. The Greater Boston Food Bank reported a 50% increase in requests for milk, cereal, and nutritious snacks for children. Louisville, Kentucky, reported a 20% increase in distribution of baby formula.

Thirteen percent of requests for food assistance recorded in the survey came from the elderly. Many cities reported the elderly and disabled on fixed incomes struggled with the rising cost of prescription medications and

rising utility bills. The increase in senior citizen requests for assistance in Louisville, Kentucky, was proportional to the financial cuts in Medicare and Medicaid. Food resources were an issue for grandparents in Philadelphia, Pennsylvania, who were taking care of grandchildren while trying to remain healthy themselves. An estimated 14% of requests for emergency food went unmet. In addition to lack of agency resources, cities reported that some families were too proud to ask for help and some frail elderly people were unable to get to food pantries.

Low-Income, Female-Headed Families

In 1947 the median family income was $3,031. The median income for a similarly situated family in 2001 was $51,407. The value of a dollar, however, changed over the years with inflation. For a more equitable comparison, Table 5.2 shows actual dollars converted to "constant" dollars (adjusted for inflation). The $3,031 family income from 1947 would be worth $20,402 in 2001 dollars. In 1947 the median family income for a female householder with no husband present was 72% of that earned by the average family, but declined by 1950 to 58%. The decline in family income for female-headed families continued downward to a low of 48% of average family income in 1990. In a slight upturn, however, female-headed families had median 2001 income equal to 50% of the average family income.

Health Insurance Challenges

The availability of affordable health insurance became a serious national concern as costs of health care rose in the

TABLE 5.2

Median family income by race and type of family, 1947–2001

| | Median income in current dollars | | | | | | Median income in constant (2001) dollars | | | | | |
| | | | | Married-couple families | | Female house-holder, no husband present | | | | Married-couple families | | Female house-holder, no husband present |
Year	All famlies[1]	White	Black[2]	Total	Wife in paid labor force		All famlies[1]	White	Black[2]	Total	Wife in paid labor force	
1947	3,031	3,157	1,614	3,109	(NA)	2,172	20,402	21,250	10,864	20,927	(NA)	14,620
1948	3,187	3,310	1,768	3,272	(NA)	2,064	19,846	20,612	11,009	20,375	(NA)	12,853
1949	3,107	3,232	1,650	3,195	3,857	2,103	19,584	20,372	10,400	20,139	24,311	13,256
1950	3,319	3,445	1,869	3,446	4,003	1,922	20,668	21,452	11,638	21,458	24,927	11,968
1951	3,709	3,859	2,032	3,837	4,631	2,220	21,391	22,256	11,719	22,129	26,709	12,803
1952	3,890	4,114	2,338	4,061	4,900	2,235	22,040	23,310	13,247	23,009	27,763	12,663
1953	4,242	4,398	2,466	4,371	5,405	2,455	23,825	24,702	13,850	24,550	30,357	13,789
1954	4,167	4,338	2,416	4,333	5,336	2,294	23,252	24,206	13,481	24,179	29,775	12,801
1955	4,418	4,613	2,544	4,599	5,622	2,471	24,706	25,797	14,227	25,718	31,439	13,818
1956	4,780	5,002	2,632	4,973	5,957	2,754	26,387	27,613	14,530	27,453	32,885	15,203
1957	4,966	5,168	2,763	5,157	6,141	2,763	26,506	27,584	14,747	27,525	32,777	14,747
1958	5,087	5,300	2,715	5,315	6,214	2,741	26,387	27,492	14,083	27,570	32,233	14,218
1959	5,417	5,643	2,915	5,662	6,705	2,764	27,930	29,095	15,030	29,193	34,571	14,251
1960	5,620	5,835	3,230	5,873	6,900	2,968	28,464	29,553	16,359	29,746	34,947	15,032
1961	5,735	5,981	3,191	6,037	7,188	2,993	28,764	29,998	16,005	30,279	36,052	15,012
1962	5,956	6,237	3,328	6,263	7,461	3,131	29,585	30,981	16,531	31,110	37,061	15,552
1963	6,249	6,548	3,465	6,593	7,789	3,211	30,627	32,093	16,982	32,313	38,175	15,738
1964	6,569	6,858	3,838	6,932	8,170	3,458	31,773	33,171	18,564	33,529	39,516	16,726
1965	6,957	7,251	3,993	7,265	8,597	3,532	33,152	34,553	19,028	34,620	40,967	16,831
1966	7,532	7,825	4,691	7,838	9,246	4,010	34,861	36,217	21,712	36,277	42,794	18,560
1967	7,933	8,234	4,875	8,441	9,956	4,294	35,629	36,981	21,895	37,911	44,715	19,286
1968	8,632	8,937	5,360	9,144	10,686	4,477	37,275	38,592	23,146	39,486	46,145	19,333
1969	9,433	9,794	5,999	10,001	11,629	4,822	39,034	40,528	24,824	41,385	48,121	19,954
1970	9,867	10,236	6,279	10,516	12,276	5,093	38,954	40,411	24,789	41,516	48,465	20,107
1971	10,285	10,672	6,440	10,990	12,853	5,114	38,878	40,341	24,344	41,543	48,585	19,331
1972	11,116	11,549	6,864	11,903	13,897	5,342	40,764	42,352	25,171	43,650	50,962	19,590
1973	12,051	12,595	7,269	13,028	15,237	5,797	41,590	43,467	25,086	44,961	52,585	20,006
1974	12,902	13,408	8,006	13,923	16,221	6,488	40,513	42,102	25,139	43,719	50,935	20,373
1975	13,719	14,268	8,779	14,867	17,237	6,844	39,784	41,376	25,458	43,113	49,985	19,847
1976	14,958	15,537	9,242	16,203	18,731	7,211	41,023	42,611	25,347	44,438	51,371	19,777
1977	16,009	16,740	9,563	17,616	20,268	7,765	41,271	43,156	24,653	45,414	52,251	20,018
1978	17,640	18,368	10,879	19,340	22,109	8,537	43,601	45,400	26,890	47,803	54,647	21,101
1979	19,587	20,439	11,574	21,429	24,861	9,880	44,255	46,180	26,151	48,417	56,171	22,323
1980	21,023	21,904	12,674	23,141	26,879	10,408	42,776	44,569	25,788	47,086	54,691	21,177
1981	22,388	23,517	13,266	25,065	29,247	10,960	41,642	43,742	24,675	46,622	54,400	20,386
1982	23,433	24,603	13,598	26,019	30,342	11,484	41,151	43,206	23,880	45,693	53,285	20,167
1983	24,580	25,757	14,506	27,286	32,107	11,789	41,444	43,428	24,458	46,006	54,135	19,877
1984	26,433	27,686	15,431	29,612	34,668	12,803	42,858	44,890	25,020	48,012	56,210	20,759
1985	27,735	29,152	16,786	31,100	36,431	13,660	43,518	45,742	26,339	48,798	57,163	21,434
1986	29,458	30,809	17,604	32,805	38,346	13,647	45,393	47,475	27,127	50,551	59,089	21,029
1987	30,970	32,385	18,406	34,879	40,751	14,683	46,151	48,259	27,428	51,976	60,726	21,880
1988	32,191	33,915	19,329	36,389	42,709	15,346	46,285	48,763	27,792	52,321	61,408	22,065
1989	34,213	35,975	20,209	38,547	45,266	16,442	47,166	49,595	27,860	53,141	62,404	22,667
1990	35,353	36,915	21,423	39,895	46,777	16,932	46,429	48,480	28,135	52,394	61,432	22,237
1991	35,939	37,783	21,548	40,995	48,169	16,692	45,551	47,888	27,311	51,959	61,052	21,156
1992	36,573	38,670	21,103	41,890	49,775	17,025	45,221	47,814	26,093	51,795	61,544	21,051
1993	36,959	39,300	21,542	43,005	51,204	17,443	44,586	47,410	25,987	51,880	61,771	21,043
1994	38,782	40,884	24,698	44,959	53,309	18,236	45,820	48,304	29,180	53,118	62,984	21,546
1995	40,611	42,646	25,970	47,062	55,823	19,691	46,843	49,191	29,956	54,284	64,390	22,713
1996	42,300	44,756	26,522	49,707	58,381	19,911	47,516	50,275	29,792	55,836	65,580	22,366
1997	44,568	46,754	28,602	51,591	60,669	21,023	49,017	51,421	31,457	56,741	66,726	23,122
1998	46,737	49,023	29,404	54,180	63,751	22,163	50,689	53,168	31,890	58,761	69,142	24,037
1999	48,950	51,224	31,778	56,676	66,529	23,732	51,996	54,411	33,755	60,202	70,668	25,209
2000	50,890	53,256	34,192	59,184	69,463	25,794	52,310	54,742	35,146	60,836	71,402	26,514
2000	50,732	53,029	33,676	59,099	69,235	25,716	52,148	54,509	34,616	60,748	71,167	26,434
2001	51,407	54,067	33,598	60,335	70,834	25,745	51,407	54,067	33,598	60,335	70,834	25,745

NA Not available.

[1]Includes other races not shown separately.

[2]1947–1966, Black and other races.

SOURCE: Adapted from "No. HS-25. Money Income of Families—Median Income in Current and Constant (2001) Dollars by Race and Type of Family, 1947–2001," *Statistical Abstract of the United States, 2003,* U.S. Census Bureau, September 30, 2002, http://www.census.gov/statab/hist/HS-25.pdf (accessed August 2, 2004)

FIGURE 5.3

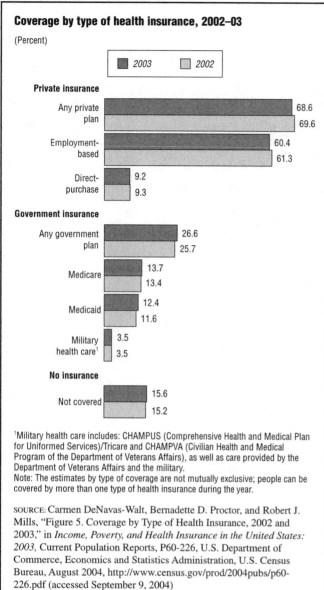

Coverage by type of health insurance, 2002–03

(Percent)

Legend: 2003 | 2002

Private insurance

Any private plan
- 68.6 (2003)
- 69.6 (2002)

Employment-based
- 60.4 (2003)
- 61.3 (2002)

Direct-purchase
- 9.2 (2003)
- 9.3 (2002)

Government insurance

Any government plan
- 26.6 (2003)
- 25.7 (2002)

Medicare
- 13.7 (2003)
- 13.4 (2002)

Medicaid
- 12.4 (2003)
- 11.6 (2002)

Military health care[1]
- 3.5 (2003)
- 3.5 (2002)

No insurance

Not covered
- 15.6 (2003)
- 15.2 (2002)

[1]Military health care includes: CHAMPUS (Comprehensive Health and Medical Plan for Uniformed Services)/Tricare and CHAMPVA (Civilian Health and Medical Program of the Department of Veterans Affairs), as well as care provided by the Department of Veterans Affairs and the military.
Note: The estimates by type of coverage are not mutually exclusive; people can be covered by more than one type of health insurance during the year.

SOURCE: Carmen DeNavas-Walt, Bernadette D. Proctor, and Robert J. Mills, "Figure 5. Coverage by Type of Health Insurance, 2002 and 2003," in *Income, Poverty, and Health Insurance in the United States: 2003,* Current Population Reports, P60-226, U.S. Department of Commerce, Economics and Statistics Administration, U.S. Census Bureau, August 2004, http://www.census.gov/prod/2004pubs/p60-226.pdf (accessed September 9, 2004)

1990s. The percentage of the nation's population without coverage grew from 15.2% in 2002 to 15.6% in 2003. Among people who were employed in 2003, 60.4% had some type of employment-based health insurance, but this figure was a decrease from 60.3% in 2002. For people in poverty who could least afford medical expenses, obtaining adequate health coverage was a significant challenge. The percentage of people on government insurance plans rose from 25.7% in 2002 to 26.6% in 2003. (See Figure 5.3.)

"Since 2000, the cost of health insurance has risen 59%, while workers' wages have increased only 12%," said Jon Gabel of the Health Research and Educational Trust in September 2004. "Since 2001, employee contributions increased 57% for single coverage and 49% for family coverage, while workers' wages have increased only 12%. This is why fewer small employers are offering coverage, and why fewer workers are taking up coverage."

While the number of people with health insurance grew by one million from 2002 to 2003, the number of uninsured increased by 1.4 million. The largest increase among Americans without insurance was primarily among white, non-Hispanic residents.

OBESITY—A TWENTY-FIRST CENTURY EPIDEMIC

As a society we can no longer afford to make poor health choices such as being physically inactive and eating an unhealthy diet; these choices have led to a tremendous obesity epidemic.

Vice Admiral Richard H. Carmona, MD, MPH, FACS, U.S. Surgeon General

The Centers for Disease Control and Prevention (CDC) reported in 2004 that chronic diseases accounted for seven of every ten deaths in the United States and more than 75% of medical care expenses. The CDC noted that many of these chronic diseases were preventable. Physical inactivity and unhealthy eating were identified as contributing factors to obesity, cancer, cardiovascular disease, and diabetes. Together these two behaviors were responsible for at least four hundred thousand deaths each year. Only tobacco use caused more preventable deaths. Among other factors, the CDC cited the increase in food portions as a major factor in unhealthy eating choices. The standard size soft drink, for example, long established as eight ounces, grew to a twelve-ounce size. Many restaurants promoted even larger sixteen- and twenty-ounce sizes.

Weight gain among Americans was noted as early as 1976, according to CDC data. Its 2000 data revealed that nearly 59% of Americans, both adults and children, were obese. Figure 5.4 provides a visual image of the growth of the obesity epidemic by state from 1991 to 2002.

Responsibility for America's Overweight Problems

In a 2003 survey Wirthlin Worldwide asked Americans to rank on a one to ten scale (one equaled "no responsibility" and ten equaled "total responsibility") how much responsibility various individuals and organizations should have for helping them to be healthy. When asked "Who is responsible for my health?" personal responsibility ranked highest at 8.2 on a 1-to-10 scale. Respondents, however, also wanted schools, the media, food and beverage companies, the government, and fast food restaurants to share the responsibility. (See Figure 5.5.) These views were more prevalent among lower income and less educated persons, who, the survey report noted, were often the most frequent customers for convenience foods and fast food restaurants.

Seventy-nine percent of Americans surveyed by Wirthlin Worldwide in 2003 said obesity was an extremely or very serious problem. When asked to rate factors that contributed to health, women ranked weight highest (7.7 on a 1–10 scale), while men identified quality of diet as

FIGURE 5.4

Obesity trends among adults, 1991–2002*

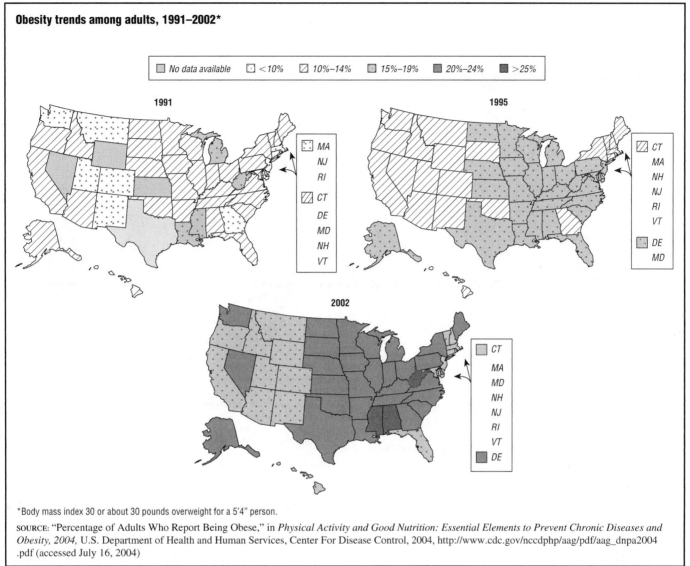

*Body mass index 30 or about 30 pounds overweight for a 5'4" person.

SOURCE: "Percentage of Adults Who Report Being Obese," in *Physical Activity and Good Nutrition: Essential Elements to Prevent Chronic Diseases and Obesity, 2004,* U.S. Department of Health and Human Services, Center For Disease Control, 2004, http://www.cdc.gov/nccdphp/aag/pdf/aag_dnpa2004.pdf (accessed July 16, 2004)

most important (7.2). Use of nutritional supplements was least important to both men and women.

The problem of obesity affected all ages, races, sexes, and socioeconomic levels. The CDC budgeted $34 million in 2003 and $39 million in 2004 to fund state initiatives to address problems of physical activity, poor nutrition, and obesity.

HOMELESSNESS

> Poor people are frequently unable to pay for housing, food, child care, health care, and education. Difficult choices must be made when limited resources cover only some of these necessities. Being poor means being an illness, an accident, or a paycheck away from living on the streets.
>
> "Why Are People Homeless?," The National Coalition for the Homeless, September 2002

The incidence of homelessness began to increase in the 1980s, and by the beginning of the twenty-first century

homeless people could be found on the streets of virtually every American city. The National Coalition for the Homeless identified two trends that were largely responsible for the rise in homelessness in the preceding twenty to twenty-five years: a growing shortage of affordable rental housing, and an increase in poverty. Between 1970 and 1982 demolition of many low-rent, single-room hotels in major cities contributed to the shortage of rental housing, according to *Homelessness in America* (Oryx Press, 1996), a publication of the National Coalition for the Homeless. New York City, for example, lost 87% of its $200 per month or less rooms that had housed low-income people, including many suffering from mental illness or substance abuse. Eroding employment opportunities and declining public assistance were identified as two factors contributing to the rise in poverty.

The U.S. Conference of Mayors (USCM) began studying the problems of hunger and homelessness in 1980. Their annual surveys of twenty-five major cities

FIGURE 5.5

FIGURE 5.6

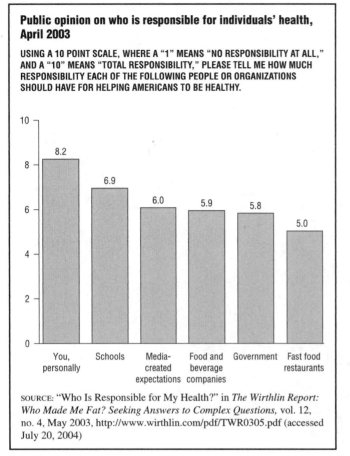

Public opinion on who is responsible for individuals' health, April 2003

USING A 10 POINT SCALE, WHERE A "1" MEANS "NO RESPONSIBILITY AT ALL," AND A "10" MEANS "TOTAL RESPONSIBILITY," PLEASE TELL ME HOW MUCH RESPONSIBILITY EACH OF THE FOLLOWING PEOPLE OR ORGANIZATIONS SHOULD HAVE FOR HELPING AMERICANS TO BE HEALTHY.

SOURCE: "Who Is Responsible for My Health?" in *The Wirthlin Report: Who Made Me Fat? Seeking Answers to Complex Questions,* vol. 12, no. 4, May 2003, http://www.wirthlin.com/pdf/TWR0305.pdf (accessed July 20, 2004)

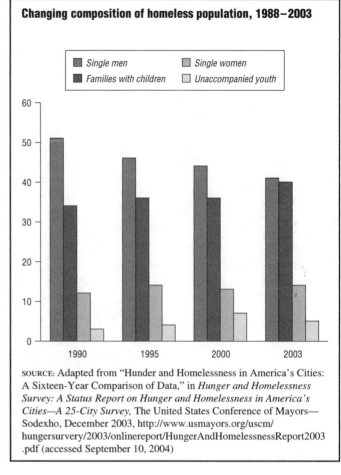

Changing composition of homeless population, 1988–2003

SOURCE: Adapted from "Hunder and Homelessness in America's Cities: A Sixteen-Year Comparison of Data," in *Hunger and Homelessness Survey: A Status Report on Hunger and Homelessness in America's Cities—A 25-City Survey,* The United States Conference of Mayors—Sodexho, December 2003, http://www.usmayors.org/uscm/hungersurvery/2003/onlinereport/HungerAndHomelessnessReport2003.pdf (accessed September 10, 2004)

produced sixteen years of comparative data published in annual reports. *The U.S. Conference of Mayors—Sodexho Hunger and Homelessness Survey 2003* indicated that while the federal definition of affordable housing was housing that cost 30% of a family's income, the average low-income family in cities surveyed by the U.S. Conference of Mayors spent 46% of their income on housing. In 2001 the National Low Income Housing Coalition estimated that in the median state a minimum-wage worker had to work eighty-nine hours each week (more than the equivalent of two full-time jobs) to afford a two-bedroom apartment at 30% of his or her income.

In 60% of cities included in the U.S. Conference of Mayors' 2003 survey, families might have to break up in order to be sheltered—some shelters, for example, took only women and children, forcing fathers to go to another shelter for men. In 48% of cities families might have to spend their daytime hours outside the shelter. Although the waiting time for public housing averaged twenty-four months in surveyed cities, people in shelters remained homeless an average of five months.

Locating the Homeless Population

Counting homeless people presents special challenges for the Census Bureau. Typically, shelters have been the source of data on the number of people without homes.

However, except in the coldest of weather, some homeless people avoid shelters in favor of more independent living in parks, under bridges, and in other remote locations. The Census Bureau reported that between 1990 and 2000 the number of people living in emergency and transitional shelters decreased 4.4%, from 178,638 to 170,706. In 2000 the Northeast claimed the largest proportion of the nation's shelter population (30.7%), while the Midwest had the least (16.7%). Nearly one-fifth (18.7%) of the population in emergency and transitional shelters lived in New York State.

Hunger and Homelessness in Major Cities

The U.S. Conference of Mayors' 2003 survey indicated that in the twenty-five major cities surveyed, requests for emergency food increased an average of 17% from the preceding year. Requests for emergency shelter increased an average of 13% from the preceding year. An estimated 59% of requests for food came from families with children.

USCM data provided a picture of the changing profile of the homeless population. As the proportion of single men dropped from 51% in 1990 to 41% in 2003, families with children rose from 34% to 40%. During that period the incidence of homeless single women and unaccompanied youth each rose two percentage points. (See Figure 5.6.) The same survey estimated that in 2003 nearly half

FIGURE 5.7

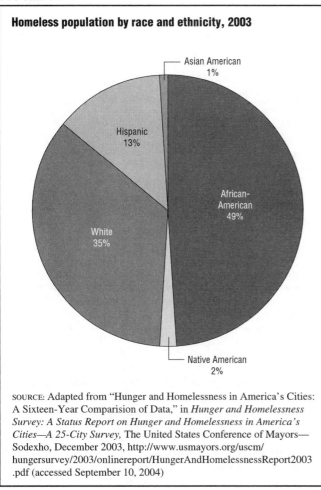

Homeless population by race and ethnicity, 2003

Asian American 1%

Hispanic 13%

African-American 49%

White 35%

Native American 2%

SOURCE: Adapted from "Hunger and Homelessness in America's Cities: A Sixteen-Year Comparision of Data," in *Hunger and Homelessness Survey: A Status Report on Hunger and Homelessness in America's Cities—A 25-City Survey,* The United States Conference of Mayors—Sodexho, December 2003, http://www.usmayors.org/uscm/hungersurvey/2003/onlinereport/HungerAndHomelessnessReport2003.pdf (accessed September 10, 2004)

of the homeless population was African-American, while 35% was white and 13% was Hispanic. (See Figure 5.7.)

Government Efforts to Address Homelessness

The first federal task force on homelessness was created in 1983 to provide information to local communities on how to obtain surplus federal property. The Homeless Eligibility Clarification Act of 1986 removed the requirement for a permanent address and other barriers to existing programs such as Supplemental Security Income, Aid to Families with Dependent Children, veterans' benefits, food stamps, and Medicaid. The Homeless Housing Act, passed that same year, also helped fund emergency shelters across the nation.

The 1987 Stewart B. McKinney Homeless Assistance Act required federal agencies to identify and make available surplus federal property, such as buildings and land, for use by states, local governments, and nonprofit agencies to assist homeless people. The Act and its subsequent amendments also provided community block grant programs for health care and mental health services to the homeless and amended the Food Stamp program to facilitate participation by homeless persons. The 1990 amendments specified in greater detail the obligations of states

and local educational agencies in assuring the access of homeless children and youth to public education.

The Bringing America Home Act (H.R. 2897) was introduced in 2003 during the 108th Congress. The comprehensive bill designed to end homelessness proposed, among other features, a requirement that use of any federal dollars for demolition of existing housing would require a replacement resulting in no net loss of housing units.

Homeless Crime Victims

Battered women who lived in poverty often face the choice between remaining in abusive relationships or becoming homeless. In 2001 the National Coalition Against Domestic Violence estimated that half of all women and children experiencing homelessness were fleeing from domestic violence. In its 2003 survey of hunger and homelessness, the U.S. Conference of Mayors reported that domestic violence was cited as the main cause of homelessness by 58% of responding cities.

On the streets homeless people were vulnerable to becoming victims of crimes such as theft and assault. A National Coalition for the Homeless study reported that between 1999 and 2003 the number of homeless people who died from violent attacks decreased from forty-eight to nine. However, the number of incidents of violent attacks against homeless people tripled from twenty to sixty-one. Such statistics were only an indication of the problem, though, since many more crimes were thought to be unreported.

Employed but Unable to Feed the Family

Many of the mayors who participated in the survey on homelessness reported that the strong economy of the late 1990s had not benefited the homeless in their city. They cited increasing housing costs, for example, which made it more difficult for the poor to afford housing. In 1999 every participating city reported a lack of affordable housing. Low-skill jobs, generally the only type of work for which many homeless people could qualify, were difficult to find. Welfare reform had also sparked an increase in the number of requests for emergency food assistance.

In 2004 the U.S. Department of Agriculture estimated the minimum cost of feeding a one-year-old child at $75 per month. By the time a child reached age nine, and on through the teenage years, the minimum monthly cost of feeding that child ranged from $120 to $130. The monthly minimum food costs for a family of four—two adults and two children—ranged from $422 to $488 depending on the ages of the children.

Unemployment

Many cities surveyed reported shelters were filled due to significant community job losses, low wages in the area, and lack of affordable housing. The U.S. Department of Labor's Bureau of Labor Statistics documented the increase in the nationwide unemployment picture from 2000 to 2003. Some of the hardest hit areas were Alaska, Washington, Oregon, Michigan, the District of Columbia, South Carolina, and Louisiana.

As unemployment rose, American workers were concerned about the loss of jobs to overseas locations where labor costs were cheaper. A Department of Labor report titled *Extended Mass Layoffs Associated with Domestic and Overseas Relocations for the First Quarter 2004* revealed 51% of mass layoffs were permanent closures of worksites affecting 10,019 workers. Just 2.5% of the 182,456 workers separated from nonseasonal jobs between January and March of 2004 were the result of relocating work overseas. One-third of layoffs related to movement of work occurred in the Midwest and another 31% were in the South.

HOUSING

Owning one's own home has long been a cornerstone of the American dream. In 1890 less than half of householders owned their homes. Home ownership dwindled slowly until 1920, when a robust economy spurred greater home buying. The Great Depression of the 1930s drove the rate of home ownership to the century's low of 43.6% in 1940. The post–World War II economic boom, favorable tax laws, easier financing, and a revived home-building industry started a home ownership explosion that exceeded 60% within two decades. By 2000 at least two out of three householders had attained the goal of home ownership. (See Figure 5.8.)

Despite the drive for home ownership, the Census Bureau reported that in 1940 45.3% of houses lacked completed plumbing facilities—indoor running water, sinks, bathtubs or showers, and toilets. By 2000 just 1.2% of housing units had incomplete plumbing. In 1960 many households lacked amenities considered essential in the twenty-first century. Twenty-two percent of homes did not have telephones in 1960 (and party lines far outnumbered private lines) compared to just 2.4% in 2000. In 1960 21.5% of households did not own or have access to a motor vehicle. In 2000 just 10.3% of households—primarily city dwellers who used public transportation—had no vehicle while, 17% of households had three or more.

According to the National Housing Institute, by 2004 the nation's poor faced the country's biggest job and housing crisis since the Great Depression. "Today, a worker making minimum wage cannot afford housing at fair market rent anywhere in the United States," said Donald Whitehead, executive director of the National Coalition for the Homeless (NCH) in late 2003.

Census 2000 recorded 115.9 million housing units—defined as a house, an apartment, a mobile home, a group

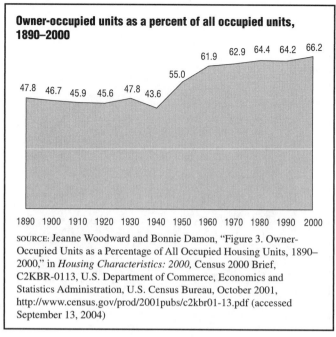

FIGURE 5.8

Owner-occupied units as a percent of all occupied units, 1890–2000

SOURCE: Jeanne Woodward and Bonnie Damon, "Figure 3. Owner-Occupied Units as a Percentage of All Occupied Housing Units, 1890–2000," in *Housing Characteristics: 2000,* Census 2000 Brief, C2KBR-0113, U.S. Department of Commerce, Economics and Statistics Administration, U.S. Census Bureau, October 2001, http://www.census.gov/prod/2001pubs/c2kbr01-13.pdf (accessed September 13, 2004)

of rooms, or a single room intended as separate living quarters—in the United States. Multifamily housing was more prevalent in the Northeast. Sixteen percent of housing structures had two to four units and 21% had five or more units. While single family detached homes were predominant in the Midwest, South, and West, the West nearly matched the Northeast with 20% multifamily housing with five or more units. The Northeast and the Midwest were characterized by older homes built before 1940, while more new home construction was found in the South and West. (See Table 5.3.)

The Mobile Home Phenomenon

Classified as "trailers" in 1950, mobile homes became the fastest-growing type of housing in the later decades of the twentieth century, according to Census Bureau data. They were less expensive than other types of housing, could be located on small, inexpensive lots in parks designed for mobile homes, and they could be moved to a new location. From 315,000 in 1950, the mobile home inventory grew to almost 8.8 million by 2000. During peak growth periods of the 1970s and 1980s, 2.5 million new mobile homes were added each decade. (See Figure 5.9.) By 1990 more than half of all mobile homes were located in the South, and mobile homes accounted for 11.6% of all housing in the South. Figure 5.10 illustrates the states with the highest concentration of mobile homes as a percentage of all housing in the state. By 2000 Florida had the most mobile homes at 849,000.

Crowded Housing

The Census Bureau reported that between 1990 and 2000 crowded housing rose from 4.9% of all occupied

TABLE 5.3

Structural characteristics of housing units, by region, 2000

Area	All housing units	Units in structure (percent)				Year structure built (percent)	
		1, detached or attached	2 to 4	5 or more	Mobile home	New homes (built 1995 to March 2000)	Old homes (built before 1940)
United States	115,904,641	65.8	9.1	17.3	7.6	9.7	15.0
Region							
Northeast	22,180,440	59.4	16.3	21.3	3.0	4.7	28.9
Midwest	26,963,635	70.9	9.0	14.5	5.4	8.4	21.2
South	42,382,546	66.5	6.2	15.4	11.6	12.7	7.2
West	24,378,020	64.9	7.5	20.0	7.1	10.5	9.1

SOURCE: Adapted from Robert Benefield and Robert Bonnette, "Table 4. Structural Characteristics for the United States and Regions, 2000," in *Structural and Occupancy Characteristics of Housing: 2000,* Census 2000 Brief, U.S. Department of Commerce, Economics and Statistics Administration, U.S. Census Bureau, November 2003, http://www.census.gov/prod/2003pubs/c2kbr-32.pdf (accessed July 23, 2004)

FIGURE 5.9

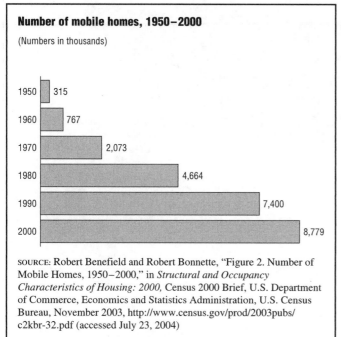

Number of mobile homes, 1950–2000

(Numbers in thousands)

Year	
1950	315
1960	767
1970	2,073
1980	4,664
1990	7,400
2000	8,779

SOURCE: Robert Benefield and Robert Bonnette, "Figure 2. Number of Mobile Homes, 1950–2000," in *Structural and Occupancy Characteristics of Housing: 2000,* Census 2000 Brief, U.S. Department of Commerce, Economics and Statistics Administration, U.S. Census Bureau, November 2003, http://www.census.gov/prod/2003pubs/c2kbr-32.pdf (accessed July 23, 2004)

units to 5.7%. Crowding, in Census terminology, is defined as more than one person per room. In California and Hawaii more than 15% of all housing units were deemed to be crowded in 2000. Crowded housing was most common in the Southwest, and in Alaska, Florida, and New York. (See Figure 5.11.)

In 2000 2.7 million households were classified "severely crowded," with more than 1.5 persons per room. Multifamily housing with five or more apartments or units was most likely to be "severely crowded." (See Figure 5.12.) Almost 36% of all severely crowded housing units were in California. The state had 1.7 million crowded and one million severely crowded households. People who rented were more likely to live in crowded or severely crowded conditions. While 3.1% of homeowners lived in crowded conditions, 11% of renters averaged more than one person per room. Just

1.2% of homeowners were severely crowded compared to 5.8% of renters.

Cost of Housing

The cost of housing, whether owned or rented, presents challenges to many families. Housing costs include utilities, fuel, water, garbage collection, and rent or mortgage payments plus real estate taxes and property insurance for those who own their homes. Table 5.4 and Table 5.5 compare median housing costs for renters and homeowners. Ranked from highest to lowest by state, New Jersey was the most expensive place for homeowners in 2003 at a median cost of $1,723 per month—43% over the national median monthly homeowner cost. The highest median monthly rental cost was $811 in Hawaii—25% over the national median monthly rental. For both home owners and renters West Virginia was the least expensive state in which to live.

EMPLOYMENT

In a 2001 address to the Council for Excellence in Government, Secretary of Labor Elaine Chao reported that the American workforce was strong. She noted, however, that workplaces had

> transformed overnight from physical plants and offices to mobile packages of twenty-first century technology and work trends that tell us old notions of the workforce cannot meet the needs and expectations of a new generation of workers. . . . Years ago, unemployment meant no jobs. Today, in many cases, unemployment means a disconnect between the new jobs our economy is producing—and the current skill levels of Americans in the workforce. The "skills gap" is too wide for too many Americans.

Chao went on to discuss future anticipated labor shortages. As the post–World War II "baby boom" generation moved into retirement, the number of people in the labor force was projected to decline substantially.

Growth in the Labor Force

Over the last four decades of the twentieth century, the massive numbers of baby boomers and women entering

FIGURE 5.10

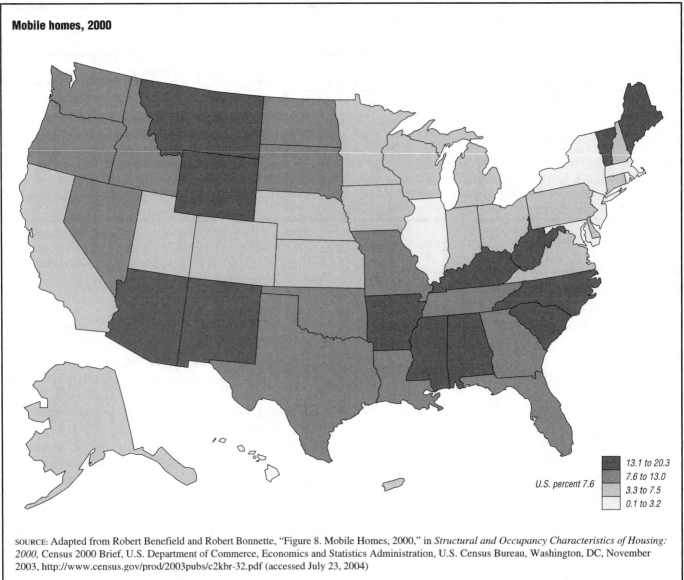

Mobile homes, 2000

■	13.1 to 20.3
■	7.6 to 13.0
■	3.3 to 7.5
□	0.1 to 3.2

U.S. percent 7.6

SOURCE: Adapted from Robert Benefield and Robert Bonnette, "Figure 8. Mobile Homes, 2000," in *Structural and Occupancy Characteristics of Housing: 2000,* Census 2000 Brief, U.S. Department of Commerce, Economics and Statistics Administration, U.S. Census Bureau, Washington, DC, November 2003, http://www.census.gov/prod/2003pubs/c2kbr-32.pdf (accessed July 23, 2004)

the workplace accounted for substantial growth in the American labor force. ("Labor force" includes persons who hold part- or full-time jobs and those who are unemployed but looking for work.) In 1999, 83.1% of the 71.3 million American families had at least one employed member; 93% of those families had at least one member who worked full-time (thirty-five hours or more). The Bureau of Labor Statistics reported that in October 2002 there were 143.1 million people in the civilian labor force, with 134.9 million employed and 8.2 million unemployed.

In a 2002 article for *Monthly Labor Review Online,* Abraham T. Mosisa reported that much of the rapidly changing ethnic and racial diversity of the workforce could be attributed to the increase in foreign-born workers. In 1960 one in seventeen workers was foreign born; in 2002 one in eight workers was born outside the United States. In 1960 three-fourths of foreign workers came from Europe, which dwindled to one out of every six for-

eign-born workers in 2002. Shifting immigration patterns brought more immigrants from Latin America and Asia. Foreign-born workers accounted for nearly half of the growth in the labor force between 1996 and 2000.

New Trend in Home Workers

Facilitated by advancing computer technology and Internet access, working from home emerged as a new trend in the 1990s. In 1960 the Census Bureau reported that 4.6 million people worked from home—half of them, however, operated family farms. The number of people working from home dropped more than 50% to a low of 2.1 million by 1980 as the number of family farmers dwindled. By 1990, however, 3.4 million people worked from home. Census Bureau demographer Phillip A. Salopek said in *Increase in At-Home Workers Reverses Earlier Trend* (March 1998) that "the decade of the 1980s marked a rebirth of work at home in the United States. It is noteworthy that this impressive growth occurred before the expansion of the Internet."

FIGURE 5.11

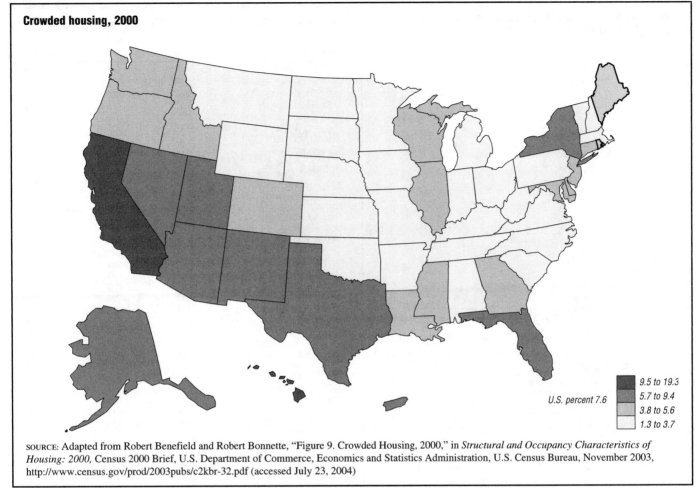

Crowded housing, 2000

U.S. percent 7.6

9.5 to 19.3
5.7 to 9.4
3.8 to 5.6
1.3 to 3.7

SOURCE: Adapted from Robert Benefield and Robert Bonnette, "Figure 9. Crowded Housing, 2000," in *Structural and Occupancy Characteristics of Housing: 2000,* Census 2000 Brief, U.S. Department of Commerce, Economics and Statistics Administration, U.S. Census Bureau, November 2003, http://www.census.gov/prod/2003pubs/c2kbr-32.pdf (accessed July 23, 2004)

By 2001 19.8 million people reported they worked at home at least once a week. Of these, 3.8 million people, including many self-employed persons, used their homes as their base of operation. Another three million employees of businesses regularly worked from home an average of eighteen hours per week.

Of the home workers in 2001, 30% (5.9 million) were self-employed. Thirty-three percent of men and 27% of women who worked at home were self-employed. Close to half of the self-employed people operated their businesses from their homes.

Parents Working at Home

Another one million people who were employees of businesses reported that they performed their work at home or used the home as a base of operation. Five percent said they sometimes worked at home in order to attend to family needs, and 2% worked from home to reduce commuting time or expense. Ten million employees of businesses also said they worked from home on an unpaid basis; half took work home to finish or catch up on assignments. (See Table 5.6.)

Norman Nie of the Stanford Institute predicted in 1999 that "by 2005, at least 25% of the American workforce will be telecommuters or home office workers." Nie said "telecommuting may be the first social transformation in centuries that pulls working fathers and mothers back into the home rather than pushing them out." The challenges of recruiting and retaining baby boomers during the latter part of the twentieth century prompted employers to offer family-friendly work schedules, including flexible work hours and options to work from home all or part of the time. In 2001 24.8% of women and 19.1% of men who worked from home at least part of the time had children under the age of six. (See Table 5.7.)

Of those who worked at home in 2001, three-quarters used telephones and computers to conduct business. The Internet or e-mail were used for business purposes by 62.5% of home workers. Just 40% of home workers used fax machines. (See Table 5.8.)

FIGURE 5.12

Percent of housing units that were crowded or severely crowded, by units in structure, 2000

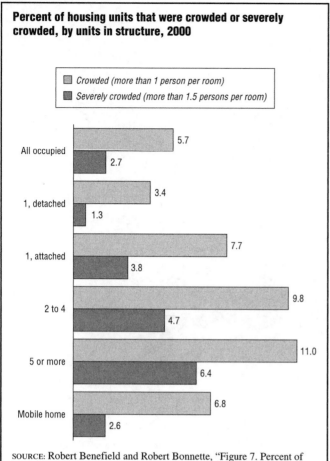

SOURCE: Robert Benefield and Robert Bonnette, "Figure 7. Percent of Housing Units That Were Crowded or Severely Crowded by Units in Structure. 2000," in *Structural and Occupancy Characteristics of Housing: 2000,* Census 2000 Brief, U.S. Department of Commerce, Economics and Statistics Administration, U.S. Census Bureau, November 2003, http://www.census.gov/prod/2003pubs/c2kbr-32.pdf (accessed July 23, 2004)

TABLE 5.4

Median monthly housing costs for renter-occupied units, 2003

Rank	State	Median	Lower bound	Upper bound
	United States	**646**	**644**	**648**
1	Hawaii	811	776	846
2	California	810	803	817
3	New Jersey	790	782	798
4	Massachusetts	774	759	789
5	Alaska	747	721	773
6	Nevada	735	719	752
7	Colorado	726	705	747
8	Maryland	723	698	748
9	Connecticut	721	709	733
10	New York	703	696	710
11	New Hampshire	701	683	719
12	Virginia	696	680	713
13	Washington	690	678	702
14	Florida	687	677	697
15	Georgia	672	660	684
16	Delaware	664	648	681
17	Illinois	660	652	668
18	District of Columbia	658	642	675
19	Arizona	641	626	656
20	Oregon	638	625	651
21	Minnesota	635	623	647
22	Utah	622	597	647
23	Texas	621	614	628
24	Rhode Island	602	589	615
25	North Carolina	588	578	598
26	Vermont	578	560	596
26	Wisconsin	578	566	590
28	Michigan	574	562	586
29	Pennsylvania	562	554	570
30	Indiana	559	544	574
31	South Carolina	558	543	573
32	Ohio	552	545	559
33	Kansas	548	522	574
34	Louisiana	539	526	552
34	Missouri	539	531	547
34	Tennessee	539	531	547
37	Nebraska	535	523	547
38	Idaho	534	518	551
39	Maine	527	512	542
40	Iowa	520	508	532
41	New Mexico	519	499	539
42	Oklahoma	514	504	524
43	Arkansas	501	481	521
44	Mississippi	487	472	502
45	Kentucky	484	474	494
46	Montana	479	467	491
47	Alabama	472	460	484
48	South Dakota	469	456	482
49	Wyoming	459	426	492
50	North Dakota	440	430	450
51	West Virginia	414	393	435

SOURCE: "Median Monthly Housing Costs for Renter-Occupied Units (in 2003 Inflation-Adjusted Dollars)," in *2003 American Community Survey,* U.S. Census Bureau, American Community Survey Office, 2004, http://www.census.gov/acs/www/Products/Ranking/2003/R16T040.htm (accessed September 13, 2004)

TABLE 5.5

Median monthly housing costs for specified owner-occupied units, 2003

Rank	State	Median	Lower bound	Upper bound
	United States	**1,204**	**1,200**	**1,208**
1	New Jersey	1,723	1,704	1,742
2	Hawaii	1,666	1,458	1,874
3	California	1,660	1,647	1,673
4	Connecticut	1,598	1,570	1,626
5	Massachusetts	1,571	1,548	1,594
6	District of Columbia	1,482	1,422	1,542
7	New York	1,474	1,451	1,497
8	New Hampshire	1,420	1,397	1,443
9	Maryland	1,395	1,378	1,412
10	Rhode Island	1,381	1,359	1,403
11	Washington	1,380	1,361	1,399
12	Alaska	1,374	1,347	1,401
13	Colorado	1,358	1,301	1,415
14	Illinois	1,340	1,327	1,353
15	Nevada	1,279	1,244	1,314
16	Virginia	1,278	1,257	1,299
17	Oregon	1,216	1,198	1,234
18	Minnesota	1,212	1,193	1,231
19	Delaware	1,184	1,167	1,201
20	Utah	1,173	1,153	1,193
21	Texas	1,166	1,153	1,179
22	Georgia	1,155	1,138	1,172
23	Florida	1,151	1,132	1,170
24	Arizona	1,146	1,131	1,161
25	Vermont	1,142	1,120	1,164
26	Wisconsin	1,138	1,111	1,165
27	Michigan	1,122	1,104	1,140
28	Pennsylvania	1,094	1,081	1,107
29	North Carolina	1,079	1,057	1,101
30	Ohio	1,068	1,049	1,087
31	South Carolina	1,037	1,002	1,072
32	Maine	1,025	999	1,051
33	Nebraska	1,002	977	1,027
34	Kansas	993	968	1,018
35	New Mexico	963	913	1,013
35	Tennessee	963	944	982
37	Indiana	952	934	970
38	Montana	951	921	981
39	Missouri	945	923	967
40	Wyoming	920	855	985
41	South Dakota	918	894	942
42	Idaho	917	886	948
43	Iowa	913	880	946
44	Louisiana	911	887	935
45	Kentucky	906	883	929
46	North Dakota	904	883	925
47	Alabama	871	857	885
48	Oklahoma	861	842	880
49	Mississippi	849	818	880
50	Arkansas	806	782	830
51	West Virginia	783	743	823

SOURCE: "Median Monthly Housing Costs for Specified Owner-Occupied Units (in 2003 Inflation-Adjusted Dollars)," in *2003 American Community Survey*, U.S. Census Bureau, American Community Survey Office, 2004, http://www.census.gov/acs/www/Products/Ranking/2003/R17T040.htm (accessed September 13, 2004)

TABLE 5.6

Reasons for working at home, by selected characteristics, May 2001

(In thousands)

Characteristic	Worked at home[1]	Reason for working at home						
		Finish or catch up on work	Business is conducted from home	Nature of the job	Coordinate work schedule with personal or family needs	Reduce commuting time or expense	Local transportation or pollution control program	Some other reason
Total, 16 years and over	19,759	7,375	3,770	5,937	1,076	269	4	1,224
Men	10,291	3,936	2,054	3,091	339	157	4	638
Women	9,468	3,439	1,716	2,846	737	112	—	587
Class of worker and pay status[2]								
Wage and salary workers[3]	13,856	6,431	1,115	4,508	706	226	4	795
Paid work at home	3,436	548	786	1,291	379	138	4	275
Unpaid work at home	10,278	5,855	300	3,165	317	88	—	508
Self-employed[4]	5,860	943	2,623	1,422	370	43	—	426

[1]Persons who worked at home at least once per week. This total includes persons who did not report a reason for working at home.
[2]Excludes unpaid family workers, not shown separately.
[3]Includes persons who worked at home but did not report pay status.
[4]Includes both the incorporated and unincorporated self-employed.
Note: Data refer to employed persons in nonagricultural industries who reported that they usually work at home at least once per week as part of their primary job. Dash represents zero.

SOURCE: "Table 6. Job-Related Work at Home on Primary Job by Reason for Working at Home, Sex, Class of Worker, and Pay Status, May 2001," in *Work at Home*, U.S. Department of Labor, Bureau of Labor Statistics, May 2001, http://www.bls.gov/news.release/homey.t06.htm (accessed September 14, 2004)

TABLE 5.7

Working at home by presence of children, by selected characteristics, May 2001

(Numbers in thousands)

Characteristic	Total employed[1]	Persons who usually worked at home[2]					
		Total	Percent of total employed	Percent distribution by class of worker[3]			
				Total	Wage and salary		Self-employed[4]
					Paid work at home	Unpaid work at home	
Total, 16 years and over	131,803	19,759	15.0	100.0	17.4	52.0	29.7
Married, spouse present	75,248	13,916	18.5	100.0	16.9	51.1	30.9
Not married	56,555	5,843	10.3	100.0	18.6	54.2	26.7
Never married	35,196	3,086	8.8	100.0	19.8	60.0	19.6
Other marital status	21,358	2,757	12.9	100.0	17.2	47.6	34.7
Without own children under 18	81,059	11,121	13.7	100.0	15.7	52.3	31.0
With own children under 18	50,744	8,638	17.0	100.0	19.6	51.6	27.9
With youngest child 6 to 17	29,227	5,058	17.3	100.0	18.0	52.8	28.5
With youngest child under 6	21,517	3,580	16.6	100.0	21.8	49.9	27.2
Men, 16 years and over	**69,659**	**10,291**	**14.8**	**100.0**	**16.0**	**50.5**	**32.6**
Married, spouse present	42,153	7,616	18.1	100.0	15.5	51.1	32.3
Not married	27,506	2,675	9.7	100.0	17.3	48.9	33.2
Never married	18,943	1,571	8.3	100.0	19.8	52.9	26.4
Other marital status	8,562	1,104	12.9	100.0	13.7	43.2	42.8
Without own children under 18	43,625	5,763	13.2	100.0	14.6	48.5	35.8
With own children under 18	26,034	4,527	17.4	100.0	17.7	53.1	28.4
With youngest child 6 to 17	14,216	2,652	18.7	100.0	16.8	51.0	31.6
With youngest child under 6	11,818	1,875	15.9	100.0	19.1	56.1	23.9
Women, 16 years and over	**62,144**	**9,468**	**15.2**	**100.0**	**18.9**	**53.7**	**26.5**
Married, spouse present	33,095	6,300	19.0	100.0	18.6	51.2	29.1
Not married	29,049	3,168	10.9	100.0	19.7	58.6	21.3
Never married	16,253	1,516	9.3	100.0	19.7	67.3	12.6
Other marital status	12,796	1,652	12.9	100.0	19.6	50.6	29.3
Without own children under 18	37,434	5,357	14.3	100.0	16		
With own children under 18	24,710	4,111	16.6	100.0	21		
With youngest child 6 to 17	15,011	2,406	16.0	100.0	19		
With youngest child under 6	9,699	1,705	17.6	100.0	24		

[1]Includes persons who did not provide information on work at home.
[2]Persons who usually work at home are defined as those who work at home at least once per week as part of their primary job.
[3]Unpaid family workers and wage and salary workers who did not report pay status are included in total but not shown separately.
[4]Includes both the incorporated and unincorporated self-employed.
Note: Data refer to employed persons in nonagricultural industries. Children are own children and include sons, daughters, step-children, and adopted children. Not included are nieces, nephews, grandchildren, and other related and unrelated children.

SOURCE: "Table 2. Job-Related Work at Home on Primary Job by Sex, Marital Status, Presence and Age of Children, and Pay Status, May 2001," in *Work at Home*, U.S. Department of Labor, Bureau of Labor Statistics, May 2001, http://www.bls.gov/news.release.homey.t02.htm (accessed September 14, 2004)

TABLE 5.8

Job-related work at home and use of electronic equipment, by selected characteristics, May 2001

(In thousands)

Characteristic	Worked at home[1]	Workers using electronic equipment for work				
		Computer	Internet or e-mail	Fax	Telephone	Other
Total, 16 years and over	**19,759**	**15,282**	**12,360**	**7,829**	**15,333**	**1,266**
Men	10,291	8,215	6,953	4,647	8,634	765
Women	9,468	7,067	5,407	3,182	6,699	501
Class of worker and pay status[2]						
Wage and salary workers[3]	13,856	11,059	8,872	4,668	10,246	864
Paid work at home	3,436	2,795	2,422	1,813	2,865	312
Unpaid work at home	10,278	8,180	6,382	2,802	7,270	542
Self-employed[4]	5,860	4,193	3,474	3,140	5,061	402

[1]Persons who worked at home at least once per week.
[2]Excludes unpaid family workers, not shown separately.
[3]Includes persons who worked at home but did not report pay status.
[4]Includes both the incorporated and unincorporated self-employed.
Note: Data refer to employed persons in nonagricultural industries who reported that they usually work at home at least once per week as part of their primary job. The number of workers using electronic equipment at home exceeds the total number who worked at home because many of these workers used more than one type of equipment. "Other" electronic equipment includes scanners and other types of computer-related peripheral equipment.

SOURCE: "Table 5. Job-Related Work at Home on Primary Job by Usage of Electronic Equipment at Home by Sex, Class of Worker, and Pay Status, May 2001," in *Work at Home,* U.S. Department of Labor, Bureau of Labor Statistics, May 2001, http://www.bls.gov/news.release/homey.t05.htm (accessed September 14, 2004)

CHAPTER 6
CHANGING FAMILY PATTERNS

THE MOBILE SOCIETY

In the spirit of the early settlers and pioneers, Americans claim mobility as their birthright. The original colonies were not long established before expansion began for more farming land. The frontier was the next piece of unexplored land to the west, and successive generations of Americans worked their way across the continent to the Pacific Ocean. After the Civil War, many freed slaves migrated to the North in search of jobs. In the twentieth century, southern cities attracted new industries which led to a new migration of jobseekers, as well as retirees seeking warmer climates.

Migration to Suburbs Continues

The economic prosperity following World War II enabled many American families to pursue what was perceived to be a better life in the wide-open spaces of the outlying, newly developing suburbs. The ties that bound the nuclear family, the extended family, and the ethnic neighborhood—all of which existed before the war—were loosened. With government aid, most notably Veterans' Administration (VA) mortgages, newlyweds and young couples with children bought homes in the suburbs. Leaving their parents and relatives, these young families soon became self-sufficient entities tending to their own needs. By 1960, suburban residents for the first time outnumbered those living in cities.

Additionally, in 1956 the federal government enacted the National Defense Highway Act, which provided for the construction of more than forty thousand miles of interstate highway. This expansion of the nation's highway system, coupled with low gas prices, facilitated the suburbanization of America. By 1960, the Census Bureau reported that 75% of families in the United States owned a car, compared with about 50% in the late 1940s. Many businesses also left cities to move to the suburbs. It did not take long for shopping and entertainment centers to follow.

During the 1970s and 1980s more middle-class and affluent families migrated to the suburbs, Census data

showed. With the loss of many businesses and jobs to the suburbs, city dwellers began to see their quality of life diminish. Cities struggled with fewer jobs, poverty, high crime rates, and drug-related problems.

Suburban Dwellers in the Twenty-First Century

In 2002 the Census Bureau found that more than half of all households (55.5 million) were located in the suburbs. Nearly 56% (31.7 million) of married couples lived in the suburbs and another 21% (11.7 million) lived in rural areas and small towns. Regardless of where they lived, 83% of married couple families owned their homes.

New Home Construction Boom

The dream for many families is a new home, one in which they select the floor plan to meet their needs and choose everything from bathroom towel bars to light fixtures to floor coverings. Young families often bought their first new home as a completed model and looked forward to designing a future home their own way. Couples who had raised their children and were preparing for retirement will sometimes use the proceeds from the sale of the family home to build their dream house. Data collected by the U.S. Census Bureau and the Department of Housing and Urban Development (HUD) provided a glimpse into new-home purchases. Of the 973,000 new homes sold in 2002 and 1,086,000 sold in 2003, just one-fourth were already completed when sold. Nearly 40% of new home buyers (361,000 in 2002 and 406,000 in 2003) selected the location for their home, participated in the design, and purchased it before construction began. (See Table 6.1.)

New homes came with sometimes staggering price tags. Of new homes sold in 2002 and 2003, just 6% were priced under $100,000, according to Census and HUD report, while 20% of new homes sold in 2002 and 24% sold in 2003 were priced in excess of $300,000. (See Table 6.2.) Reflecting a shift in population to the South and the West, those two areas claimed nearly three-

TABLE 6.1

New home sales by stage of construction, 2002–03

[Thousands of houses. Detail may not add to total because of rounding]

		Sold during period		
Period	Total	Not started	Under construction	Completed
2002	973	356	361	256
2003	1,086	416	406	264

SOURCE: Adapted from "Table 3. New Homes Sold and For Sale by Stage of Construction and Median Number of Months on Sales Market," in *New Residential Sales in July 2004*, U.S. Department of Commerce, U.S. Census Bureau, U.S. Department of Housing and Urban Development, August 25, 2004, http://www.census.gov/const/newressales.pdf (accessed September 24, 2004)

FIGURE 6.1

Percent distribution of movers by type of move, 2002–03

(Population 1 year and older)

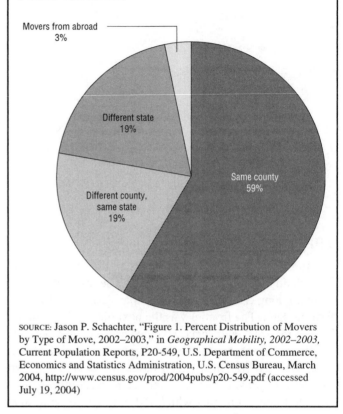

SOURCE: Jason P. Schachter, "Figure 1. Percent Distribution of Movers by Type of Move, 2002–2003," in *Geographical Mobility, 2002–2003*, Current Population Reports, P20-549, U.S. Department of Commerce, Economics and Statistics Administration, U.S. Census Bureau, March 2004, http://www.census.gov/prod/2004pubs/p20-549.pdf (accessed July 19, 2004)

quarters of all new home sales in 2002 and 2003. The South led the market with almost half of the nation's new home sales (46% in 2002 and 47% in 2003). (See Table 6.3.)

Americans on the Move

Census figures showed that between 2002 and 2003, 40.1 million Americans moved. Over half of these moves (59%) were within the same county, and 19% were to another county within in the same state. Less than one-fifth of Americans moved to a different state. (See Figure 6.1.) While overall moving rates declined from 17% in 1994 to 14% in 2003, the Census Bureau reported that long distance moves increased slightly. In 1994 just 16% of all moves crossed state boundaries compared to 19% of moves in 2003.

Moving rates varied by characteristics such as age, race, ethnicity, nativity, marital status, household type, income, ownership/rental status, and poverty. Young people in the twenty to twenty-nine age range were most mobile. Persons age sixty-five and over were least likely to move. (See Figure 6.2.) The Census Bureau reported that although they were generally less mobile than younger people, persons age fifty-five and older were more likely to move to another state. Younger people moved more frequently for jobs and to form new families; many people over fifty-five often moved to settle in a new location for retirement. Often seniors chose retirement locations near where their children had settled or opted for warmer climates and social amenities of southern retirement communities.

African-Americans and Hispanics of any race had the highest overall moving rate at 18%, while non-Hispanic whites had the lowest rate at 12%. Nearly one-third of renters moved in 2003, compared to only one in fourteen homeowners. More people in poverty (24%) moved than those with incomes above poverty level (13%). This trend may have reflected the greater likelihood that people in poverty were renters and were challenged to find adequate affordable housing. (See Table 6.4.)

More than half of all moves were done with a change of housing in mind—either to find a better home, safer neighborhood, or more affordable rental unit. These were typically moves within the same community or county. Family reasons motivated 26% of all moves—for example, a change in marital status—followed by 16% listed as job-related. People who made longer distance moves did so most often for a better job (18.6%) or family reasons (16.8%). (See Table 6.5.) People who moved to the United States from other countries did so primarily for job (38.1%) or family reasons (29.4%).

Americans continue to move out of the Northeast and the Midwest, a trend that began in the 1990s. According to the Census Bureau, between 2002 and 2003 both areas of the country experienced net population losses of about 100,000 people due to migration. Much of this loss was offset, however, by movers who came from abroad. The Northeast gained 161,000 and the Midwest gained 179,000 residents from other countries. The populations of the South and the West grew significantly from both domestic and foreign migration.

Mobile Military Families

Frequent relocations are a way of life for military families. The Department of Defense (DoD) counted

TABLE 6.2

New home sales by price, 2002–03

(Thousands of houses. Components may not add to total because of rounding.)

Period	Total	Under $100,000	$100,000 to $124,999	$125,000 to $149,999	$150,000 to $199,999	$200,000 to $249,999	$250,000 to $299,999	$300,000 and over
					Number of houses*			
2002	973	62	94	138	237	139	107	196
2003	1,086	54	96	146	264	148	112	266

*Houses for which sales price was not reported have been distributed proportionally to those for which sales price was reported.

SOURCE: Adapted from "Table 2. New Houses Sold, by Sales Price," in *New Residential Sales in July 2004,* U.S. Department of Commerce, U.S. Census Bureau, U.S. Department of Housing and Urban Development, August 25, 2004, http://www.census.gov/const/newressales.pdf (accessed September 24, 2004)

FIGURE 6.2

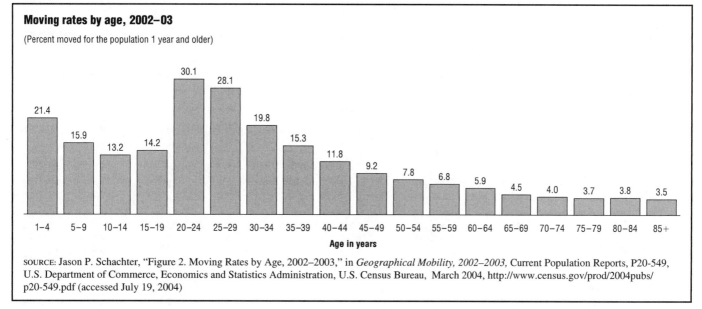

Moving rates by age, 2002–03

(Percent moved for the population 1 year and older)

SOURCE: Jason P. Schachter, "Figure 2. Moving Rates by Age, 2002–2003," in *Geographical Mobility, 2002–2003,* Current Population Reports, P20-549, U.S. Department of Commerce, Economics and Statistics Administration, U.S. Census Bureau, March 2004, http://www.census.gov/prod/2004pubs/p20-549.pdf (accessed July 19, 2004)

TABLE 6.3

New home sales by location, 2002–03

(Thousands of houses. Detail may not add to total because of rounding.)

Period	United States	North-east	Mid-west	South	West
	Sold during period[1]				
2002	973	65	185	450	273
2003	1,086	79	189	511	307

SOURCE: Adapted from "Table 1. New Houses Sold and For Sale," in *New Residential Sales in July 2004,* U.S. Department of Commerce, U.S. Census Bureau, U.S. Department of Housing and Urban Development, August 25, 2004, http://www.census.gov/const/newressales.pdf (accessed September 24, 2004)

1,434,377 active-duty military personnel with more than two million dependents on September 30, 2003.

The Department of Defense Education Activity (DoDEA) in April 2003 operated 219 public schools in seven states, Puerto Rico, Guam, and thirteen foreign countries for children of military personnel and civilian DoD employees. Enrollment in April 2003 was approximately 102,600 children in elementary and secondary levels with the majority—71,100—in overseas schools. The frequent reassignments of military personnel resulted in a 35% transient rate in DoDEA schools.

Mobility Disconnects Extended Families

One downside to increased mobility was the scattering of families that, a generation earlier, had gathered for dinner every Sunday. "These days families are all spread out and cousins don't live around the corner anymore," said Edith Wagner, founder of *Reunions* magazine, in a *New York Times* article from August 13, 2004, about family reunions. According to the article's author, Tamar Lewin, the need to revive the sense of family connection in a mobile society made reunions popular. And the gatherings "evolved into a very different affair from a simple afternoon picnic held in the grandparents' backyard," Lewin wrote. The long distances that separate far-flung relatives prompted reunions to grow into two- or three-

TABLE 6.4

Geographic mobility by selected characteristics, 2002–03

(Numbers in thousands)

| | | | | Percent moved | | | | |
| | | | | | | Different county | | |
Selected characteristics	Total, 1 year and older	Same residence (nonmovers)	Total movers	Total	Same county	Same state	Different state	From abroad
Total, 1 year and older	**282,556**	**242,463**	**40,093**	**14.2**	**8.3**	**2.7**	**2.7**	**0.5**
Age								
1 to 4 years	16,409	12,896	3,513	21.4	13.6	3.9	3.3	0.6
5 to 9 years	19,708	16,584	3,124	15.9	9.8	2.9	2.7	0.4
10 to 19 years	41,372	35,715	5,657	13.7	8.3	2.6	2.4	0.4
20 to 24 years	19,884	13,906	5,979	30.1	17.8	5.8	5.6	0.8
25 to 29 years	18,721	13,470	5,252	28.1	16.1	5.5	5.2	1.3
30 to 34 years	20,522	16,460	4,061	19.8	11.7	3.6	3.3	0.7
35 to 44 years	44,074	38,139	5,934	13.5	7.8	2.7	2.5	0.5
45 to 54 years	40,234	36,786	3,448	8.6	4.9	1.6	2.0	0.2
55 to 64 years	27,399	25,644	1,755	6.4	3.2	1.3	1.8	0.2
65 to 84 years	30,687	29,441	1,246	4.1	1.9	1.0	1.1	0.1
85 years and older	3,547	3,422	125	3.5	2.4	0.7	0.4	0.0
Sex								
Male	138,156	118,105	20,051	14.5	8.4	2.8	2.8	0.5
Female	144,400	124,358	20,042	13.9	8.2	2.7	2.6	0.4
Race and Hispanic origin								
White alone	228,198	197,953	30,244	13.3	7.6	2.7	2.6	0.3
White alone, not Hispanic	192,458	168,524	23,934	12.4	7.0	2.7	2.7	0.2
Black alone	35,333	28,981	6,352	18.0	11.7	2.8	3.1	0.4
Asian alone	11,430	9,507	1,923	16.8	8.6	2.7	2.8	2.7
Hispanic (of any race)	38,680	31,727	6,953	18.0	11.5	2.7	2.5	1.3
Nativity								
Native	249,103	214,823	34,279	13.8	8.3	2.9	2.8	0.2
Foreign born	33,453	27,639	5,814	17.4	9.9	2.6	2.9	3.5
Marital Status (15 years and older)								
Total	**225,250**	**194,594**	**30,656**	**13.6**	**7.8**	**2.7**	**2.7**	**0.5**
Married	120,349	108,051	12,298	10.2	5.5	2.0	2.3	0.4
Divorced or separated	26,396	21,694	4,703	17.8	11.2	3.5	2.8	0.3
Widowed	14,001	13,077	924	6.6	3.2	1.5	1.7	0.2
Never married	64,503	51,772	12,731	19.7	11.6	3.8	3.7	0.6
Education (25 years and older)								
Total	**185,183**	**163,362**	**21,821**	**11.8**	**6.7**	**2.3**	**2.4**	**0.4**
Not a high school graduate	28,599	25,186	3,413	11.9	7.7	1.8	1.8	0.7
High school graduate	59,292	52,953	6,339	10.7	6.2	2.1	2.1	0.2
Some college or associate degree	46,910	41,167	5,743	12.2	6.9	2.6	2.5	0.2
Bachelor's degree	33,213	28,793	4,420	13.3	6.9	2.7	3.0	0.7
Graduate degree	17,169	15,264	1,906	11.1	5.4	2.1	3.0	0.7
Household income (in 2002)								
Less than $25,000	62,143	50,336	11,807	19.0	12.0	3.3	3.2	1.0
$25,000 to $49,999	75,010	63,424	11,587	15.4	9.4	3.0	2.8	0.4
$50,000 to $99,999	95,232	83,651	11,581	12.2	7.0	2.6	2.3	0.3
$100,000 and over	50,171	45,052	5,119	10.2	5.2	2.0	2.7	0.2
Poverty status (in 2002)								
Above poverty level	248,066	216,284	31,782	12.8	7.4	2.6	2.5	0.3
Below poverty level	34,490	26,178	8,312	24.1	14.7	3.8	4.0	1.7
Household type								
In married-couple family households	180,967	162,233	18,734	10.4	5.7	2.1	2.2	0.4
In other households	101,589	80,230	21,359	21.0	13.0	3.9	3.5	0.6
Housing tenure								
Owner-occupied	200,627	185,686	14,941	7.4	4.3	1.6	1.4	0.2
Renter-occupied	81,929	56,777	25,152	30.7	18.2	5.5	5.8	1.2

SOURCE: Jason P.Schachter, "Table B. Geographic Mobility by Selected Characteristics, 2002–2003," in *Geographical Mobility, 2002–2003,* Current Population Reports, P20–549, U.S. Department of Commerce, Economics and Statistics Administration, U.S. Census Bureau, March 2004, http://www.census .gov/prod/2004pubs/p20–549.pdf (accessed July 19, 2004).

day affairs, making the distance traveled worthwhile. Some families gathered on the family farm. Ethnic roots of families with immigrant grandparents or great-

grandparents often made traditional foods, music, and religious celebrations focal points of reunions. According to Lewin, Alex Haley's *Roots* prompted a surge in family

TABLE 6.5

Reasons for moving by type of move, 2002–03

(Movers, 1 year and older)

Reason	All movers	Intracounty	Intercounty	From abroad
Total movers (thousands)	**40,093**	**23,468**	**15,356**	**1,269**
Percent	100.0	100.0	100.0	100.0
Family-related reasons	**26.3**	**24.7**	**28.5**	**29.4**
Change in marital status	6.7	6.4	7.1	5.9
To establish own household	7.0	8.8	4.5	4.6
Other family reasons	12.6	9.5	16.8	19.0
Work-related reasons	**15.6**	**6.0**	**28.3**	**38.1**
New job/job transfer	8.8	1.7	18.6	22.6
To look for work/lost job	1.9	0.7	3.0	9.0
Closer to work/easier commute	3.2	2.9	3.9	0.2
Retired	0.3	0.1	0.4	0.6
Other job related reason	1.4	0.6	2.4	5.7
Housing-related reasons	**51.3**	**65.3**	**33.5**	**8.8**
Wanted to own home/not rent	10.2	12.7	7.1	0.5
New/better house/apartment	19.8	26.2	11.3	4.5
Better neighborhood/less crime	3.8	4.7	2.7	0.5
Cheaper housing	6.5	8.2	4.5	0.6
Other housing	11.0	13.5	7.8	2.7
Other reasons	**6.8**	**3.9**	**9.9**	**23.7**
Attend/leave college	2.5	1.1	4.2	9.1
Change of climate	0.4	0.0	1.0	0.5
Health reasons	1.4	1.1	2.0	0.9
Other reason	2.5	1.8	2.7	13.2

SOURCE: Jason P. Schachter, "Table F. Reasons for Moving by Type of Move, 2002–2003," in *Geographical Mobility, 2002–2003,* Current Population Reports, P20-549, U.S. Department of Commerce, Economics and Statistics Administration, U.S. Census Bureau, March 2004, http://www.census.gov/prod/2004pubs/p20-549.pdf (accessed July 19, 2004)

reunions among African-American families as early as the 1970s and 1980s. A 2002 poll by the Travel Industry of America revealed that one in three adults had traveled to a reunion in the last three years, and nearly one-fourth had attended a reunion in the past year.

Mobility also resulted in social disconnection for some families, particularly those that moved often. In his 2000 book *Bowling Alone: The Collapse and Revival of American Community,* Harvard University professor Robert D. Putnam noted that putting down roots in a new community took time. People who expected to move again in the next five years were 20–25% less likely to attend church, join clubs, or do volunteer work. The effort to become part of the new community, only to move again and leave new friends, seemed too much for some families.

MULTIGENERATIONAL FAMILIES

Despite lower birth rates and women delaying childbirth, increased longevity has resulted in people from four or five generations being alive at the same time. A number of researchers addressed issues that resulted from multiple generations coexisting in society, the workplace, and the same family. Books such as *Generations: The History of America's Future, 1584 to 2069,* the 1991 work by

William Strauss and Neil Howe, grouped people into generations based on events and time periods in American history. The authors identified common experiences shared by members of each generation that they believed had similar influences on the life attitudes of all members of that group. They suggested a recurring sequence of generational types and recurring social indicators such as substance abuse, fertility, immigration, and economic advance and setback.

Census 2000 identified 3.9 million families, 3.7% of all households, that contained three or four generations. The most common grouping (65%) of multigenerational households included the householder and his or her children and grandchildren. Immigrant families were more likely to have more than three generations in the household. In some cases, this was cultural, while in others immigrant families could not afford separate housing accommodations.

Grandparents Raising Grandchildren

A growing trend in families is grandparents who have taken responsibility for raising grandchildren and sometimes great-grandchildren. The Census Bureau's *2003 Current Population Survey* reported that 3.8 million children (5% of all children) lived in the home of one or both grandparents. In 19% of cases where children lived with grandparents, there were three or more children in the home. Often one or both parents of the children were also present in the home. In more than one-third of cases, however, neither of the children's parents were present and the grandparent(s) were responsible for the children. In 1970, 957,000 grandchildren were being raised by their grandparents without a parent present; in 2003 that number had increased almost 50% to 1.4 million children who were the responsibility of their grandparents. (See Table 6.6.)

Denver's *Rocky Mountain News* focused on the challenges faced by grandparents raising their grandchildren in a November 9, 2002, feature, "Grandparents as Parents: The Second Time Around." In Colorado 43% of grandparents living with grandchildren were actually raising the children. In Census Tract 9.02 on the south side of Pueblo, Colorado (Census tracts are small subdivisions of a county), reporter Burt Hubbard discovered a total of 140 grandparents with grandchildren in their homes. One hundred percent of these grandparents were raising one or more grandchildren, some since birth. The reasons ranged from parents who were deceased, in prison or addicted to drugs, or those who simply could not handle the responsibility of a child. The oldest grandparent interviewed was more than ninety years old and had raised her ten-year-old grandchild since birth.

These grandparents faced financial challenges. Many were living on retirement income or Social Security stipends; some had to return to the workforce. Expecting to coddle and spoil their grandchildren, they found them-

TABLE 6.6

Grandchildren living with grandparents, 1970–2003

(Numbers in thousands)

Year	Total children under 18	Grandchildren				
			With parent(s) present			
		Total	Both parents present	Mother only present	Father only present	Without parent(s) present
2003	73,001	3,767	547	1,576	227	1,416
2002	72,321	3,681	477	1,658	275	1,274
2001	72,006	3,844	510	1,755	231	1,348
2000	72,012	3,842	531	1,732	220	1,359
1999	71,703	3,919	535	1,803	250	1,331
1998	71,377	3,989	503	1,827	241	1,417
1997	70,983	3,894	554	1,785	247	1,309
1996	70,908	4,060	467	1,943	220	1,431
1995	70,254	3,965	427	1,876	195	1,466
1994	69,508	3,735	436	1,764	175	1,359
1993	66,893	3,368	475	1,647	229	1,017
1992	65,965	3,253	502	1,740	144	867
1991	65,093	3,320	559	1,674	151	937
1990	64,137	3,155	467	1,563	191	935
1980 Census	63,369	2,306	310	922	86	988
1970 Census	69,276	2,214	363	817	78	957

SOURCE: "Table CH-7. Grandchildren Living in the Home of Their Grandparents: 1970–Present," U.S. Census Bureau, September 15, 2004, http://www.census.gov/population/socdemo/hh-fam/tabCH-7.pdf (accessed September 24, 2004)

selves instead in the role of disciplinarians. They had to navigate new cultural attitudes among the younger generation and a school system that had changed dramatically since their own children were school age.

Grandparents Assisted Financially

Many grandparents helped with child care for their grandchildren while the parents worked. Some grandparents were called upon to assist their children with financial needs of the grandchildren. A 2003 survey by Wirthlin Worldwide found that 54% of grandparents planned to contribute to their grandchildren's college education expenses. One-quarter of those surveyed expected to pay 25–50% of the costs, while 20% planned to finance as much as 75% of the expenses.

THE MULTIRACIAL SOCIETY

As America's mobile society became more racially and ethnically diverse, dating, cohabiting, and marrying a person of another race or ethnic background has become more accepted, at least among the baby boomers and succeeding generations. In 1980, 651,000 couples, 1.3% of all married couples, were identified as interracial. By 2000 interracial couples accounted for 2.6% of married couples. Between 1980 and 2002 the total number of couples increased 16.5%, but the number of interracial couples increased 137%. Of the 1.7 million interracial couples, nearly three-quarters (73%) were composed of one white person and a person of another race other than African-American. (See Table 6.7.)

The Census Bureau changed the way information on race was gathered in 2000. For the first time, individuals were allowed to identify themselves as of more than one race or of a race other than the standard choices—white, black or African-American, American Indian and Alaska Native, Asian, Native Hawaiian, and Other Pacific Islander. While 97.6% of the population identified themselves with one race, 2.4% identified themselves with two or more races. The trend in multiracial identification was most apparent among youth. Of persons reporting themselves as a mix of two or more races, 42% were under age eighteen. Figure 6.3 demonstrates visually the areas of the country in which 40–50% of youth identified themselves with two or more races in 2000.

GAY AND LESBIAN COUPLES AND FAMILIES

In the 1990s unmarried, opposite-sex couples cracked the door to gaining employer sponsored dependent benefits for live-in partners. Same-sex partners soon pursued the same benefits. In August 2000 the "Big Three" domestic automakers from Detroit—Ford, General Motors, and DaimlerChrysler—added full health-care benefits for the domestic partners of their 500,000 U.S. employees. Gannett, the largest newspaper publisher in the country (ninety-eight U.S. papers plus twenty-two television stations), introduced domestic-partner benefits beginning January 1, 2002. In September 2002 Purdue University announced that it would become the seventh Big Ten school to offer benefits to same-sex domestic partners of university employees. According to a February 2004 article in *Kiplinger Business Forecasts,* about 20% of private-sector and government employers, and more than 40% of Fortune 500 companies, offered domestic partner benefits to same-sex couples.

TABLE 6.7

Interracial couples, 1980–2002

(Numbers in thousands. Includes all interracial married couples with at least one spouse of white or black race.)

Year	Total married couples	Interracial married couples					
			Black/white				
		Total	Total	Black husband white wife	White husband black wife	White/ other race*	Black/other race*
2002	57,919	1,674	395	279	116	1,222	57
2001	57,838	1,596	360	247	113	1,173	63
2000	56,497	1,464	363	268	95	1,051	50
1999	55,849	1,481	364	240	124	1,086	31
1998	55,305	1,348	330	210	120	975	43
1997	54,666	1,264	311	201	110	896	57
1996	54,664	1,260	337	220	117	884	39
1995	54,937	1,392	328	206	122	988	76
1994	54,251	1,283	296	196	100	909	78
1993	54,199	1,195	242	182	60	920	33
1992	53,512	1,161	246	163	83	883	32
1991	53,227	994	231	156	75	720	43
1990	53,256	964	211	150	61	720	33
1989	52,924	953	219	155	64	703	31
1988	52,613	956	218	149	69	703	35
1987	52,286	799	177	121	56	581	41
1986	51,704	827	181	136	45	613	33
1985	51,114	792	164	117	47	599	29
1984	50,864	762	175	111	64	564	23
1983	50,665	719	164	118	46	522	33
1982	50,294	697	155	108	47	515	27
1981	49,896	639	132	104	28	484	23
1980	49,714	651	167	122	45	450	34

NA Not available.
* "Other race," is any race other than White or Black, such as American Indian, Japanese, Chinese, etc. This total excludes combinations of other races by other races.

SOURCE: "Table MS-3. Interracial Couples: 1980–2002," U.S. Census Bureau, September 15, 2004, http://www.census.gov/population/socdemo/hh-fam/tabMS-3 .pdf (accessed September 24, 2004)

Same-sex partners lobbied for recognition and rights—including marriage, divorce, adoption, child custody, property and inheritance, hospital visitation, and medical decision-making. In 1997, in the first state law of its kind, the Hawaii legislature gave gays and lesbians the right to participate in their partners' medical insurance and state pensions and granted them inheritance rights, joint property ownership rights, and the right to sue for wrongful death. In 1999 California recognized same-sex couples as "domestic partners." The Vermont Civil Union law, implemented in 2000, offered same-sex couples many of the legal rights available to married couples. New Jersey's legislature passed a domestic partner law in 2004 with limited rights including insurance and medical decision-making.

Domestic Partners Recognized in Survivor Rights

The plight of domestic partners made headlines after September 11, 2001, as domestic partners of individuals who died in the attacks on the World Trade Center and Pentagon found themselves ineligible for survivor benefits from Social Security, workers' compensation, and potentially from victim compensation funds. If the deceased left no will, the partner had no legal claim to the estate. Since September 11, 2001, the Red Cross, the United Way, and several other relief agencies have taken steps to assure fair treatment of gay and lesbian partners. New York Governor George Pataki issued an Executive Order on October 11, 2001, granting same-sex partners the same benefits as spouses from the New York State Crime Victims Board.

In June 2002 President George W. Bush signed a bill making domestic partners eligible for death benefits paid to survivors of firefighters and police officers who die in the line of duty. Retroactive to September 11, 2001, the new law allowed a $250,000 federal benefit paid to any beneficiary listed on the victim's life insurance policy, previously restricted to spouses, children, and parents. The new law was named for the Reverend Mychal Judge, the New York Fire Department's chaplain who died in the collapse of the World Trade Center. The law marked the first extension of federal benefits to domestic partners.

Gay and Lesbian Marriage Remains Controversial

Reflecting changing societal attitudes toward lesbian and gay partners, the *New York Times* announced in August 2002 that it would include reports of same-sex commitment ceremonies and some formal registrations of lesbian and gay partnerships in its Sunday Styles section, along with reports of opposite-sex engagements and weddings.

While insurance and survivor benefits were available to gay and lesbian partners, many couples pushed for the same marriage rights as those available to heterosexual

FIGURE 6.3

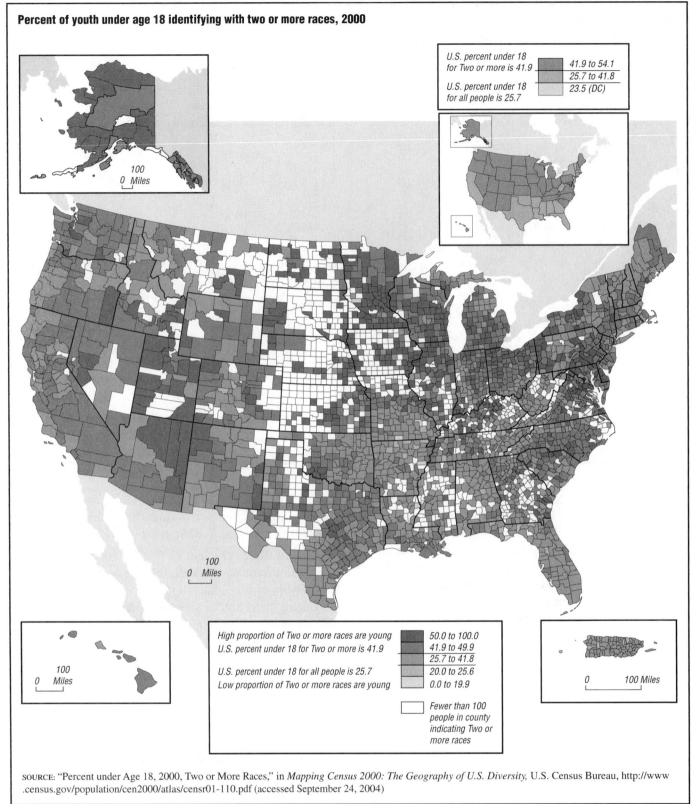

Percent of youth under age 18 identifying with two or more races, 2000

U.S. percent under 18 for Two or more is 41.9
U.S. percent under 18 for all people is 25.7

41.9 to 54.1
25.7 to 41.8
23.5 (DC)

High proportion of Two or more races are young
U.S. percent under 18 for Two or more is 41.9

U.S. percent under 18 for all people is 25.7
Low proportion of Two or more races are young

50.0 to 100.0
41.9 to 49.9
25.7 to 41.8
20.0 to 25.6
0.0 to 19.9

Fewer than 100 people in county indicating Two or more races

SOURCE: "Percent under Age 18, 2000, Two or More Races," in *Mapping Census 2000: The Geography of U.S. Diversity,* U.S. Census Bureau, http://www.census.gov/population/cen2000/atlas/censr01-110.pdf (accessed September 24, 2004)

couples. This issue became the subject of heated debate across the nation. State legislatures and courts struggled with proposals to recognize or to ban same-sex marriages and/or civil unions. In his 2004 reelection campaign, President George W. Bush proposed a constitutional amendment to ban marriage between persons of the same sex.

Gay and Lesbian Families with Children

Many gay and lesbian couples raise children—biological children of one or both members of the couple or adopted children. Of same-sex partner households in Census 2000, 22.3% of male households and 34.37% of female households included children. The National Adop-

TABLE 6.8

Type of computer activity at work, by selected characteristics, September 2001

Characteristic	Employed persons who used a computer at work (in thousands)	Percent who used a computer for:						
		Word processing or desktop publishing	Internet or e-mail	Calendar or scheduling	Spread sheets or databases	Graphics or design	Programing	Other activities
Age and sex								
Total, 16 years and over	72,277	67.0	71.8	52.9	62.3	28.8	15.2	13.1
16 to 24 years	7,087	53.6	56.1	45.6	52.2	20.8	12.2	14.3
16 to 19 years	1,532	39.8	36.9	32.1	35.7	12.8	7.4	19.6
20 to 24 years	5,555	57.4	61.3	49.3	56.7	22.9	13.6	12.8
25 years and over	65,190	68.4	73.6	53.7	63.4	29.7	15.6	12.9
25 to 34 years	17,038	68.8	74.8	56.3	66.4	30.0	17.6	12.6
35 to 44 years	20,909	68.8	73.7	55.5	65.2	31.3	16.9	12.0
45 to 54 years	18,075	69.4	74.1	53.5	62.3	29.9	13.5	13.7
55 to 64 years	7,681	66.4	71.5	47.0	57.5	25.5	12.9	13.8
65 years and over	1,488	58.0	62.2	37.2	47.2	20.6	12.1	16.6
Men	34,663	64.3	75.1	55.2	64.9	32.0	20.4	13.0
Women	37,614	69.4	68.8	50.9	59.9	25.8	10.5	13.1
Race and Hispanic origin								
White	62,063	67.4	72.1	52.7	62.7	28.9	14.7	13.2
Black	6,635	62.6	66.8	53.9	56.9	26.1	15.8	13.0
Hispanic origin	4,754	64.0	61.7	49.7	57.9	22.8	12.7	11.9
Full- or part-time status								
Usually full time on primary job	58,918	68.4	74.0	55.2	64.3	29.6	16.2	12.7
Usually part time on primary job	8,414	59.7	57.7	39.2	49.8	22.8	91	16.0
Hours vary on primary job	4,945	62.7	70.7	49.6	59.5	29.1	14.0	12.1
Educational attainment								
Total, 25 years and over	65,190	68.4	73.6	53.7	63.4	29.7	15.6	12.9
Less than a high school diploma	1,831	45.5	46.9	40.7	45.7	15.5	11.3	19.2
High school graduate, no college	14,227	55.2	59.9	46.2	53.8	19.9	11.6	14.5
Some college, no degree	12,565	64.1	69.1	51.1	60.6	26.5	14.0	13.4
Associate degree	7,013	61.6	67.4	51.2	58.2	25.9	14.9	14.9
College degree	29,553	79.6	85.2	59.9	71.5	37.4	18.6	11.1
Advanced degree	10,685	83.8	87.2	60.0	70.0	38.4	18.7	11.3

Note: Data refer to computer use on the sole or primary job. The percentage of persons who used computers for various activities may exceed 100 percent as persons may report multiple activities. Detail for the above race and Hispanic-origin groups will not sum to totals because data for the "other races" group are not presented and Hispanics are included in both the white and black population groups.

SOURCE: "Table 3. Type of Computer Activity at Work by Selected Characteristics, September 2001," in *Computer and Internet Use at Work in 2001*, U.S. Department of Labor, Bureau of Labor Statistics, October 2002, http://www.bls.gov/cps/ciuaw.pdf (accessed September 14, 2004)

tion Information Clearinghouse (NAIC) reported that gays and lesbians had always adopted children but that the number of these adoptive parents was unknown.

ADOPTION BY GAYS AND LESBIANS. Adoption rules differed in each state. Ten states (California, Massachusetts, New Jersey, New Hampshire, New Mexico, New York, Ohio, Vermont, Washington, and Wisconsin) and the District of Columbia allowed openly gay and lesbian individuals or couples to adopt. Although some joint adoption applications were successful in other states, the most common practice was for one member of the couple to apply as the legal adoptive parent of the child. In 2000 Florida and Utah were joined by Mississippi as the only states specifically banning lesbians and gays from adopting children.

TECHNOLOGY AND THE FAMILY

The Bureau of Labor Statistics reported that in 2001, 72.3 million persons used a computer at work, and two out of every five employed persons was connected to the Internet or used e-mail on the job. More women (59.6%) used a computer at work than men (47.9%), and 41.2% of women used the Internet in the workplace compared to 36% of men.

Table 6.8 illustrates typical computer functions used by people in the workplace. Internet or e-mail was the most frequent use of a computer, used by 71.8% of all workers. Other computer functions used by more than half of workers were word processing (67%), spreadsheets and databases (62.3%), and calendar or scheduling programs (52.9%). The likelihood of computer or Internet use at work was much higher among more educated workers. While less than half of workers who did not have high school diplomas used computers at work, 80% of workers with college degrees used computers for Internet and e-mail access, as well as for word processing or desktop publishing.

Computers and the Internet offered vast new resources for people seeking new jobs, and 9.2% of the population

TABLE 6.9

Job search activity using the Internet, by selected characteristics, September 2001*

(Numbers in thousands)

Characteristic	Total	Total civilian noninstitutional population		Job search activity of persons who used the Internet to search for a job (percent)					
		Total who used the Internet to search for a job	Percent of total	Read on-line ads or searched on-line job listings	Researched information on potential employers	Submitted a resume or application	Posted a resume on a job listing site or with a service	Posted on resume on own Web site	Other activities
Age and sex									
Total, 16 years and over	212,357	19,616	9.2	92.0	67.4	49.5	36.7	4.8	3.7
16 to 24 years	35,195	4,415	12.5	92.3	63.2	45.9	35.6	4.8	2.7
16 to 19 years	16,206	1,108	6.8	91.5	54.1	34.0	26.3	3.0	1.7
20 to 24 years	18,990	3,308	17.4	92.5	66.2	49.9	38.7	5.4	3.0
25 years and over	177,162	15,201	8.6	91.9	68.7	50.5	37.0	4.8	3.9
25 to 34 years	37,032	6,238	16.8	92.3	70.7	52.9	42.2	5.5	3.5
35 to 44 years	44,318	4,890	11.0	91.9	68.6	50.4	35.4	4.4	3.8
45 to 54 years	38,642	3,051	7.9	91.3	66.2	48.9	32.5	4.3	4.4
55 to 64 years	24,328	877	3.6	89.9	67.4	41.3	26.9	2.7	5.4
65 years and over	32,842	145	.4	94.1	46.5	43.2	24.6	6.6	10.0
Men	102,110	9,700	9.5	91.5	71.5	53.4	40.5	5.9	3.8
Women	110,247	9,916	9.0	92.5	63.4	45.6	33.0	3.6	3.6
Race and Hispanic origin									
White	176,220	16,018	9.1	91.9	67.1	48.2	35.1	4.5	3.8
Black	25,644	2,396	9.3	92.3	67.1	52.9	41.5	5.5	3.2
Hispanic origin	23,288	1,377	5.9	89.2	67.7	47.0	36.6	5.8	2.4
Educational attainment									
Total, 25 years and over	177,162	15,201	8.6	91.9	68.7	50.5	37.0	4.8	3.9
Less than a high school diploma	27,484	402	1.5	88.8	58.2	38.9	30.3	4.6	1.9
High school graduate, no college	57,386	2,812	4.9	90.9	59.2	42.0	31.7	3.3	3.1
Some college, no degree	30,641	3,029	9.9	92.2	63.1	48.2	34.7	3.8	3.1
Associate degree	14,779	1,667	11.3	93.7	65.4	48.3	34.7	4.7	3.7
College degree	46,872	7,291	15.6	91.9	76.0	55.9	40.8	5.7	4.8
Advanced degree	16,283	2,390	14.7	91.6	77.8	55.6	39.3	6.4	4.8

*Refers to use of the Internet to search for a job "this year," that is, from January to September 2001.
Note: The percentage of persons performing each activity may exceed 100 percent as persons may perform more than one activity. Detail for the above race and Hispanic-origin groups will not sum to totals because data for the "other races" group are not presented and Hispanics are included in both the white and black population groups.

SOURCE: "Table 5. Job Search Activity Using the Internet by Selected Characteristics, September 2001," in *Computer and Internet Use at Work in 2001*, U.S. Department of Labor, Bureau of Labor Statistics, October 2002, http://www.bls.gov/cps/ciuaw.pdf (accessed September 14, 2004)

used this resource in 2001, according to a Bureau of Labor Statistics survey. Educational level was again a significant factor in who used online job search resources. Sixteen percent of people with college degrees searched for jobs on the Internet, compared to 1.5% of persons with less than a high school diploma. Age was not a factor. Of those using the Internet to search for a job, a greater proportion of people age sixty-five and over (94.1%) searched online job listings compared to 92% of the total population. Among people who conducted Internet job searches, reading online job ads and researching employers was the most frequent activity. Half of online job seekers submitted an application or resume electronically. (See Table 6.9.)

Computers in the Home

The proportion of households with computers grew from 8.2% in 1984 to 56.5% percent in 2001, according to Census Bureau data. While only 18% of homes had Internet access in 1997, 50.5% were Internet-linked in 2000. In 2001 married-couple households with children under eighteen were most likely to have a computer (78.9%) and Internet access (71.6%). Availability of a computer and Internet connections increased with the educational level of the householder and family income. Computers were found in 72.7% of Asian-American households compared to just 37.1% of African-American households. (See Table 6.10.)

How Children Spent Their Computer Time

A majority of children from ages five to seventeen used computers at home, but their use of the Internet increased significantly with age. About 25% of five-year-olds had access to the Internet compared to more than 75% of fifteen- to seventeen-year-olds, a U.S. Department of Education study found. (See Figure 6.4.) White, non-Hispanic children had the highest rate of computer use at home (77%) and at school (84%). While just 41% of African-American and Hispanic children used computers at home, African-American children had greater access to computers at school (80%) than Hispanic children (72%). (See Figure 6.5.)

TABLE 6.10

Households with computers and Internet access, 2001

(In percent)

Characteristic	Households with computers				Households with Internet access			
	Total	Rural	Urban	Central city	Total	Rural	Urban	Central city
All households	**56.5**	**55.6**	**56.7**	**51.5**	**50.5**	**48.7**	**51.1**	**45.7**
Age of householder:								
Under 25 years old	51.1	41.3	53.0	50.9	44.7	33.5	46.7	45.3
25 to 34 years old	62.5	61.5	62.8	57.5	57.3	55.4	58.8	53.9
35 to 44 years old	69.9	71.2	69.4	62.1	62.6	62.3	63.4	54.3
45 to 54 years old	66.9	68.0	66.4	59.9	60.9	61.1	61.3	53.4
55 years old or over	39.1	38.0	39.5	35.5	33.9	32.1	35.0	29.9
Householder race/ethnicity:								
White*	61.1	58.0	62.4	60.0	55.4	51.0	56.8	54.8
Black*	37.1	31.5	37.7	33.9	30.8	24.4	30.9	27.4
American, Indian, Eskimo, Aleut*	44.7	37.6	49.5	38.7	31.4	41.5	44.1	
Asian or Pacific Islander*	72.7	69.4	72.8	67.4	68.1	68.2	64.1	63.1
Hispanic	40.0	36.6	40.3	38.1	32.0	29.9	32.6	29.8
Household type:								
Married couple with children under 18	78.9	78.6	79.0	72.4	71.6	69.7	73.6	64.6
Male householder with children under 18	55.1	53.6	55.6	51.8	44.9	39.9	47.2	44.3
Female householder with children under 18	49.2	51.0	48.9	41.6	40.0	40.9	42.3	33.5
Family households without children	58.8	55.0	60.4	55.2	53.2	48.9	55.3	49.7
Nonfamily households	39.2	31.6	40.9	41.4	35.0	26.9	36.2	37.0
Education of householder:								
Elementary	6.0	13.4	17.1	16.9	11.2	10.4	11.6	11.5
Some high school	28.2	27.6	28.4	25.5	22.7	22.4	22.6	19.8
High school graduate or GED	46.5	50.0	45.0	39.0	39.8	42.1	39.3	32.5
Some college	64.5	68.5	63.2	58.4	57.7	60.2	57.3	52.0
Bachelor's degree or more	79.8	81.1	79.5	76.7	75.2	75.1	75.0	72.0
Household income:								
Under $5,000	25.9	17.9	28.2	24.5	20.5	12.5	23.0	20.2
$5,000 to $9,999	19.2	16.4	20.1	20.6	14.4	11.0	15.5	14.5
$10,000 to $14,999	25.7	24.3	26.3	24.3	19.4	18.1	20.7	19.3
$15,000 to $19,999	31.8	29.4	32.6	33.9	23.6	21.0	25.3	24.6
$20,000 to $24,999	40.1	40.0	40.1	36.4	31.8	31.7	32.4	28.7
$25,000 to $34,999	49.7	49.4	49.9	49.9	42.2	40.5	43.7	41.3
$35,000 to $49,999	64.3	64.7	64.2	64.4	56.4	55.0	57.5	56.2
$50,000 to $74,999	77.7	78.1	77.6	75.8	71.4	70.6	71.7	70.5
$75,000 and over	89.0	89.0	88.9	86.4	85.4	84.8	85.5	83.8

*Non-Hispanic.

SOURCE: "No. 1158. Households with Computers and Internet Access by Selected Characteristics, 2001," in *Statistical Abstract of the United States, 2003,* U.S. Census Bureau, 2004, http://www.census.gov/prod/2004pubs/03statab/inforcomm.pdf (accessed September 15, 2004)

From ages five through fourteen children spent the greatest percentage of their computer time playing computer games. By ages fifteen through seventeen, the computer was used for completing school assignments (64.2%), connecting to the Internet (62.9%), and playing computer games (59.6%). Communicating with friends and family by e-mail increased with age, from 9.5% for ages five to seven to 57.7% for ages fifteen to seventeen. (See Table 6.11.)

TECHNOLOGY DISCONNECTED FAMILIES

In addition to the community disconnect brought about by mobility, Robert D. Putnam noted a disconnect among family members in his 2000 book *Bowling Alone.* Putnam attributed the problem to the availability of more individualized entertainment media. Three or four generations earlier the whole family, and sometimes the neighbors as well, gathered around the radio to hear about world events or laugh together at the antics of favorite comedians. They shared the moment and discussed it afterward. Each member of the twenty-first century family, however, could choose his/her own entertainment (TV, DVD, CD, or computer), go to separate rooms or put on headphones, and be entertained in isolation. Thus busy family members, who often grabbed something to eat on the run in their rush to get to work, school, and activities, spent less time interacting with each other during their at-home time.

A variety of organizations began to address the isolation of family members in the twenty-first-century lifestyle. Research by the National Center on Addiction and Substance Abuse at Columbia University consistently found that the more often children ate dinner with their families, the less likely they were to smoke, drink, or use illegal drugs. In 2001 the Center initiated Family Day (the

FIGURE 6.4

Percentage of 5–17-year-olds using computers or the Internet, by age, 2001

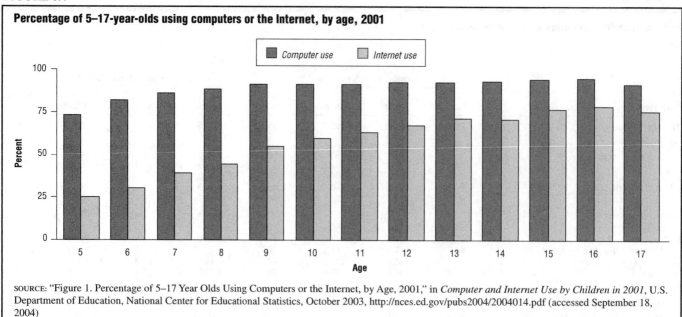

SOURCE: "Figure 1. Percentage of 5–17 Year Olds Using Computers or the Internet, by Age, 2001," in *Computer and Internet Use by Children in 2001*, U.S. Department of Education, National Center for Educational Statistics, October 2003, http://nces.ed.gov/pubs2004/2004014.pdf (accessed September 18, 2004)

FIGURE 6.5

Percentage of children and adolescents using computers at home and at school, by race/ethnicity, 2001

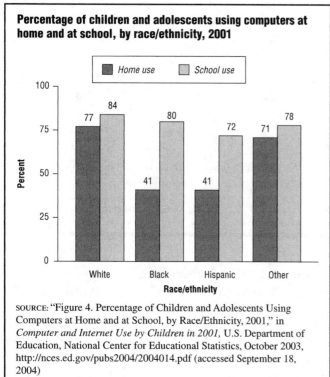

SOURCE: "Figure 4. Percentage of Children and Adolescents Using Computers at Home and at School, by Race/Ethnicity, 2001," in *Computer and Internet Use by Children in 2001*, U.S. Department of Education, National Center for Educational Statistics, October 2003, http://nces.ed.gov/pubs2004/2004014.pdf (accessed September 18, 2004)

networks featured classic TV episodes in which the show's central plot was revealed or resolved around the family dinner table.

last Monday in September) as a national effort to promote parental engagement with their children through the simple act of regular family meals. Nick at Night and TV Land cable television networks joined the promotion with a series of public service announcements (PSAs) called "The Family Table—Share More Than Meals." These PSAs were described as "a pro-social initiative designed to celebrate all of our unique families, and to encourage loved ones to reconnect." Special programming on these

TABLE 6.11

Percentage of children age 5–17 using home computers for specific activities, by child and family characteristics, 2001

User characteristics	Total number of children in thousands	Word processing Percent	Connect to the Internet Percent	E-mail Percent	Spreadsheets or databases[1] Percent	Graphics and design[1] Percent	Complete school assignments Percent	Manage household records or finances[1] Percent	Play games Percent	Other Percent
All persons age 5–17	53,013	32.4	45.6	34.4	—	—	44.2	—	59.2	2.8
Child characteristics										
Age										
5–7	11,990	9.4	22.6	9.5	—	—	13.8	—	54.0	1.2
8–10	12,455	23.8	39.5	23.9	—	—	37.7	—	58.8	1.5
11–14	16,493	42.1	54.1	43.3	—	—	56.6	—	62.9	2.6
15–17	12,075	50.9	62.9	57.7	17.1	23.6	64.2	2.9	59.6	5.7
Sex										
Female	25,835	34.7	45.7	36.1	3.9	5.6	45.4	0.7	58.3	2.7
Male	27,178	30.3	45.5	32.7	3.9	5.2	43.1	0.6	60.0	2.8
Race/ethnicity[2]										
White	33,433	39.3	55.2	42.7	4.7	6.4	52.1	0.8	70.2	3.3
Black	8,275	18.9	27.3	18.8	2.0	3.0	28.3	0.5	37.7	1.9
Hispanic	8,400	17.0	23.1	15.1	2.3	3.1	26.7	#	35.6	1.3
Asian	2,268	40.4	57.3	43.7	5.0	7.1	54.3	0.6	64.3	2.8
American Indian	637	20.7	31.7	20.8	2.1	2.3	32.0	0.5	51.7	1.9
Disability status										
Disabled	626	23.5	29.8	21.1	3.0	5.1	34.4	#	54.4	2.1
Not disabled	45,416	33.0	45.9	35.0	3.8	5.5	45.0	0.5	59.8	2.8
Family & household characteristics										
Parent educational attainment										
Less than high sch. credential	5,450	11.1	14.5	10.4	1.5	1.9	18.3	#	22.8	1.0
High school credential	13,611	22.8	35.1	27.3	2.8	3.8	35.5	#	49.3	2.0
Some college	15,665	34.3	48.7	36.0	4.0	5.8	47.5	0.7	64.6	2.9
Bachelor's degree	6,712	42.8	60.8	45.2	5.3	7.2	55.5	0.9	72.9	3.1
Graduate education	9,114	52.2	67.6	52.1	6.2	8.3	62.5	0.9	81.7	4.7
Family/household type										
Two parent household	37,230	36.6	51.6	38.8	4.4	5.8	49.6	0.7	66.6	2.9
Male householder	2,715	26.7	37.8	29.8	4.0	6.7	37.9	1.0	48.5	3.5
Female householder	12,440	21.9	29.7	22.4	2.6	3.7	30.3	#	40.1	2.1
Other arrangement	628	19.1	36.3	26.9	1.8	4.5	30.4	0.7	43.8	3.2
Household language										
Spanish-only	2,549	12.0	14.5	10.7	1.3	2.2	19.1	#	23.5	1.0
Not Spanish-only	50,464	33.5	47.1	35.6	4.0	5.5	45.5	0.7	61.0	2.8
Poverty status										
In poverty	9,277	12.5	17.2	12.1	1.6	1.9	20.1	#	28.7	1.5
Not in poverty	36,904	38.7	53.7	40.7	4.5	6.4	51.4	0.7	68.5	3.1
Family income										
Under $20,000	8,344	13.1	16.8	11.8	1.7	2.1	20.0	#	28.3	1.7
$20,000–$34,999	8,852	21.0	30.8	22.7	2.1	3.2	31.4	#	46.3	1.9
$35,000–$49,999	7,438	32.1	47.7	34.9	3.6	5.0	46.7	0.6	65.6	2.2
$50,000–$74,999	9,530	40.0	56.9	42.6	4.6	6.8	55.2	0.7	73.8	3.2
$75,000 or more	12,018	52.2	69.3	54.0	6.5	8.8	63.7	1.1	79.8	4.3

Home computer activity

TABLE 6.11

Percentage of children age 5–17 using home computers for specific activities, by child and family characteristics, 2001 [CONTINUED]

User characteristics	Total number of children in thousands	Home computer activity							
		Word processing	Connect to the Internet	E-mail	Spreadsheets or databases[1]	Graphics and design[1]	Complete school assignments	Manage household records or finances[1]	Play games	Other
		Percent	Percent	Percent	Percent	Percent	Percent	Percent	Percent	Percent
Urbanicity										
Metropolitan, city center	12,249	25.0	36.1	26.0	3.0	4.2	35.1	0.6	48.3	2.3
Metropolitan, outlying areas	23,566	36.5	50.8	38.5	4.4	5.7	49.2	0.7	64.4	2.9
Non-metropolitan	9,609	30.8	42.6	33.3	3.6	5.4	42.3	0.7	58.5	2.5

— Not available. Data were not collected.
Percentage less than 0.5.
[1]Questions about some computer activities were asked only about persons age 15 and older.
[2]White, Black, Asian, and American Indian respectively indicate White, non-Hispanic; Black, non-Hispanic; Asian or Pacific Islander, non-Hispanic; and American Indian, Aleut, or Eskimo, non-Hispanic.

SOURCE: Adapted from "Table 4. Percentage of Persons Age 5–17 Using Home Computers for Specific Activities, by Child and Family Household Characteristics, 2001," in *Computer and Internet Use by Children in 2001*, U.S. Department of Education, National Center for Educational Statistics, October 2003, http://nces.ed.gov/pubs2004/2004014.pdf (accessed September 18, 2004)

CHAPTER 7
PUBLIC OPINION ON THE FAMILY

Families provide a loving environment where children can flourish; and they help ensure that cultural traditions and timeless values are passed on to future generations. . . . Strong families play a critical role in developing the character of our Nation. They teach children important standards of conduct such as accepting responsibility, respecting others, and distinguishing the difference between right and wrong. By helping America's youth to grow into mature, thoughtful, and caring citizens, families help make our communities and our Nation safer and more civilized.

President George W. Bush, Proclamation of National Family Week 2002

STATUS OF THE FAMILY

Just before the dawn of the twenty-first century, interviewers for the Roper Institute asked Americans whether life for their family had improved since 1950. Regardless of age, gender, race, religion, or educational level, about two-thirds (63%) said that life was better at the close of the century than it had been in the past. In the public perception, women, persons with disabilities, and African-Americans had seen the greatest improvement over the previous fifty years. On the other end of the scale, 65% of respondents said farmers were in worse condition than they were in 1950, given that three out of five family farms had disappeared. The demographic group of greatest concern for the family, however, was that of children. More than half (56%) of respondents felt life had become worse for teenagers, and 44% thought it was worse for children.

"The vast majority of Americans believed that preservation of the family was critical to the future survival of the United States," according to a 2000 survey by Wirthlin Worldwide. (See Figure 7.1.) When asked to characterize the state of the American family, however, just 7% said it was "very strong and growing." Nearly one-third (32%) said the family was "weak and losing ground." While sounding pessimistic, the survey revealed an improved perception of the strength of the family compared to a 1995 survey in which 44% categorized the family as "weak." (See Figure 7.2.)

When asked to identify the causes of the decline of the family, two of the most frequent responses focused on parents' failure to teach their children discipline and respect (12%) and moral values (11%). The greater work demands on parents also ranked as one of the most serious problems for families (11%). Other factors cited included divorce (9%), economic and financial pressures (8%), decline in religious faith and church attendance (7%), mothers working outside the home (6%), and the avail-

FIGURE 7.1

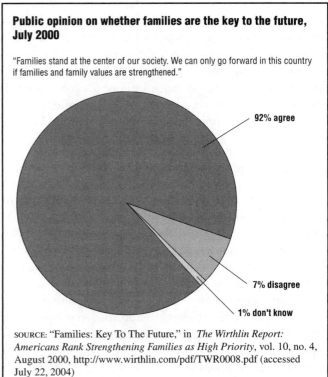

Public opinion on whether families are the key to the future, July 2000

"Families stand at the center of our society. We can only go forward in this country if families and family values are strengthened."

- 92% agree
- 7% disagree
- 1% don't know

SOURCE: "Families: Key To The Future," in *The Wirthlin Report: Americans Rank Strengthening Families as High Priority*, vol. 10, no. 4, August 2000, http://www.wirthlin.com/pdf/TWR0008.pdf (accessed July 22, 2004)

FIGURE 7.2

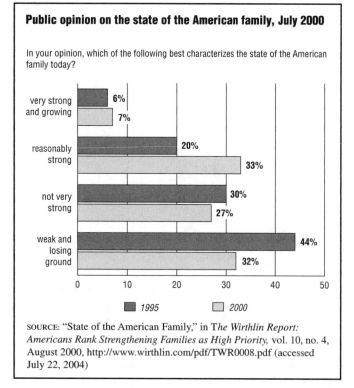

Public opinion on the state of the American family, July 2000

In your opinion, which of the following best characterizes the state of the American family today?

SOURCE: "State of the American Family," in *The Wirthlin Report: Americans Rank Strengthening Families as High Priority,* vol. 10, no. 4, August 2000, http://www.wirthlin.com/pdf/TWR0008.pdf (accessed July 22, 2004)

TABLE 7.1

Issue priorities by ethnic groups, July 2000

Which is more important...?	TOT	White	Black	Hispanic	Other
Strengthening families	64%	70%	46%	30%	68%
Increasing job opportunities	35%	29%	53%	70%	31%
Strengthening families	77%	76%	90%	64%	79%
Creating a cleaner environment	22%	23%	10%	36%	18%

SOURCE: "Issue Priority Varies among Ethnic Groups," in *The Wirthlin Report: Americans Rank Strengthening Families as High Priority,* vol. 10, no. 4, August 2000, http://www.wirthlin.com/pdf/TWR0008.pdf (accessed July 22, 2004)

FAMILY DIVERSITY

Questions about family values have generally included issues concerning the current diversity of family structures. A 1998 survey by Lou Harris and Associates asked women, "Do you think that society should value only certain types of families, like those with two parents, or should society value all types of families?" More than nine out of ten respondents (93%) thought that society should value all types of families. Only 5% indicated that society should value only certain types of families, such as those with two parents.

In the same survey 52% of women and 42% of men thought family values meant "loving, taking care of, and supporting each other." The term *family values* was described as "knowing right from wrong and having good values" by 38% of women and 35% of men. Only 2% of women and 1% of men defined family values in terms of the traditional nuclear family.

By the year 2003, families had indeed become diverse. In addition to the shrinking number of nuclear families, there were blended families that combined children from past marriages with offspring of the current marriage, cohabiting couples with children, multigenerational families, families headed by gay or lesbian couples, single-parent families, and various combinations of related and unrelated individuals who considered themselves a family.

Differing Opinions on Gay and Lesbian Marriage

In a November 2003 survey by the Pew Research Center for the People and the Press, 59% of Americans opposed allowing gay and lesbian couples to marry legally, and 51% opposed legal agreements that provided gay and lesbian couples many of the legal rights of marriage. (See Table 7.2.) People between ages twenty and thirty-five hovered just short of a 50% split in supporting or opposing gay and lesbian marriage. After age thirty-five, however, opposition to gay and lesbian marriage increased with age to a peak of nearly 90% among seventy-year-olds. (See Figure 7.6.)

ability of drugs (6%). (See Figure 7.3.) According to Wirthlin Worldwide, survey respondents in recent years named "a decline in moral values" as the most important problem facing the nation.

Strengthening the Family a Priority

Americans surveyed about priorities for political leaders named "strengthening the family" twice as important as job opportunities and three times as important as the environment. (See Figure 7.4.) Hispanic and African-American respondents, who traditionally have had strong extended families but higher unemployment and lower pay than whites, placed more importance on political leaders working to increase job opportunities than strengthening the family, according to the Wirthlin Worldwide survey. (See Table 7.1.) Concern about jobs was also a stronger focus for respondents living in the Northeast (45%) than in other areas of the country.

Among possible initiatives to strengthen the family, support for voluntary action by businesses led the way. A strong majority (87%) of persons surveyed believed business could strengthen marriages and parental attention to families by providing flexible work schedules. Recognizing the power of the media on young people's attitudes, respondents gave strong support (80%) to commending the media when efforts were made to portray positive influences of marriage. More than three-fourths (78%) of respondents supported legislation requiring counseling for couples with children before a divorce could be granted. (See Figure 7.5.)

FIGURE 7.3

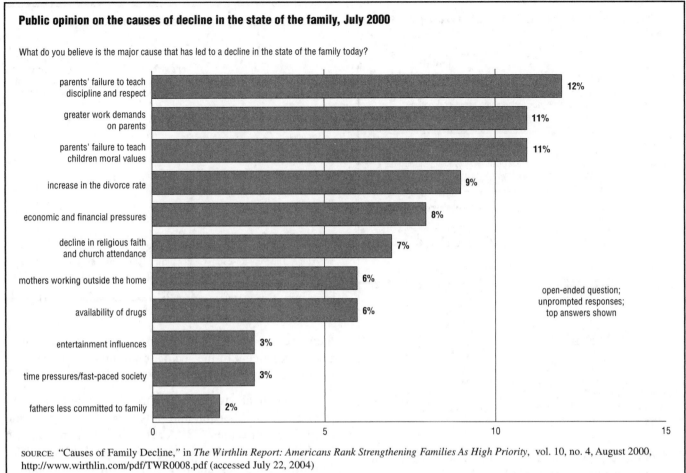

Public opinion on the causes of decline in the state of the family, July 2000

What do you believe is the major cause that has led to a decline in the state of the family today?

SOURCE: "Causes of Family Decline," in *The Wirthlin Report: Americans Rank Strengthening Families As High Priority*, vol. 10, no. 4, August 2000, http://www.wirthlin.com/pdf/TWR0008.pdf (accessed July 22, 2004)

FIGURE 7.4

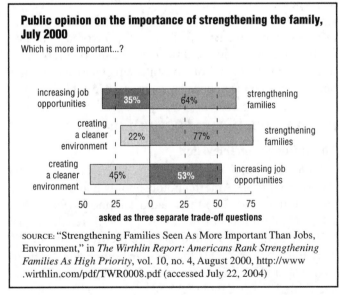

Public opinion on the importance of strengthening the family, July 2000

Which is more important...?

asked as three separate trade-off questions

SOURCE: "Strengthening Families Seen As More Important Than Jobs, Environment," in *The Wirthlin Report: Americans Rank Strengthening Families As High Priority*, vol. 10, no. 4, August 2000, http://www .wirthlin.com/pdf/TWR0008.pdf (accessed July 22, 2004)

Opposition to the gay and lesbian marriage issue was strongest in the South (67%) and in rural areas (69%). Support was strongest in the East (42%) and suburban areas (38%). (See Table 7.3.) The most cited reasons for opposition were moral and religious. Sixteen percent said

the definition of marriage involved a man and a woman. (See Table 7.4.)

While 80% of Americans surveyed said society should put no restrictions on sex between consenting adults, more than half (56%) of those surveyed believed that allowing gay and lesbian marriages would undermine the traditional American family. Fifty-four percent agreed that gay and lesbian couples could be just as good parents as heterosexuals. (See Table 7.5.) A great difference of opinion about gays and lesbians as parents occurred by age groups. By a margin of 47% to 37%, people over age sixty-five believed that gay and lesbian couples could not be as good parents as other couples. Among the under-thirty age group, 69% believed gay and lesbian couples could parent just as well as heterosexual couples. Seniors were far less likely to know someone who was gay or lesbian. Fully half of seniors could not think of the name of a single gay or lesbian person, either in their own lives or a celebrity.

Actually knowing someone who was gay or lesbian had a strong influence on individual's attitudes toward gay and lesbian marriage. Thirty-nine percent of people who favored legalizing gay marriage knew someone who was gay or lesbian compared to 21% who did not. The impact was strongest in the eighteen to twenty-nine age group where

FIGURE 7.5

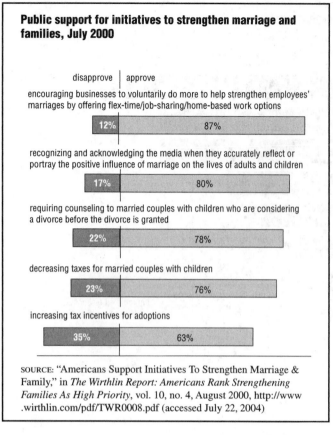

Public support for initiatives to strengthen marriage and families, July 2000

disapprove | approve

encouraging businesses to voluntarily do more to help strengthen employees' marriages by offering flex-time/job-sharing/home-based work options

12% | 87%

recognizing and acknowledging the media when they accurately reflect or portray the positive influence of marriage on the lives of adults and children

17% | 80%

requiring counseling to married couples with children who are considering a divorce before the divorce is granted

22% | 78%

decreasing taxes for married couples with children

23% | 76%

increasing tax incentives for adoptions

35% | 63%

SOURCE: "Americans Support Initiatives To Strengthen Marriage & Family," in *The Wirthlin Report: Americans Rank Strengthening Families As High Priority*, vol. 10, no. 4, August 2000, http://www .wirthlin.com/pdf/TWR0008.pdf (accessed July 22, 2004)

TABLE 7.2

Public opinion on gay marriage and civil unions, 2003

	Allowing gays and lesbians to marry legally %	Legal agreements giving many of the same rights as marriage %
Favor	**32**	**41**
Strongly	9	13
Not strongly	23	28
Oppose	**59**	**51**
Strongly	35	30
Not strongly	2	8
Don't know	**9**	**8**
	100	**100**

SOURCE: "Gay Marriages and Civil Unions," in *Opinion of Homosexuals: Religious Beliefs Underpin Opposition to Homosexuality, Part 2: Gay Marriage,* The Pew Research Center for the People and the Press, November 18, 2003, http://peoplepress.org/reports/display.php3? ReportID=197 (accessed July 26, 2004)

49% of those who favored gay and lesbian marriage knew an individual who was gay or lesbian. (See Figure 7.7.)

RELIGION AND THE AMERICAN FAMILY

Periodically, the Gallup organization interviewed Americans on the role of religion in their lives. In 2000 the poll found that 68% of Americans claimed to be members of a church or synagogue, a percentage that had changed little over the past sixty years. About one-third of Americans claimed they went to church or synagogue at least once a week, and 11% said they went almost every week. Another 11% never attended religious services. A majority of Americans believed that "religion can answer all or most of today's problems," while 17% thought it was "old-fashioned."

The debate continued over nature or nurture as the cause for homosexuality. A 2003 Pew Research Center report titled *Opinion of Homosexuals* compares 1985 and 2003 attitudes about the cause of homosexuality. In 1985 20% of people surveyed said homosexuality was something people were born with and 22% said it was a result of the way people were raised. In 2003 30% believed it was a birth factor and 14% attributed homosexuality to upbringing. A consistent 42% believed "some people just prefer to live that way." (See Table 7.6.) Seventy-three percent of Evangelical Christians, who attended religious services often and said religion was very important in

their lives, believed that homosexuality could be changed. Sixty-six percent of the secular community believed that homosexuality could not be changed. (Table 7.7.)

Evangelical churches spent the most time addressing public issues. Abortion and prayer in schools were the most frequent topics (72% each). The Roman Catholic Church focused the most attention on abortion (85%). Mainline churches spent less time discussing public issues. (See Table 7.8.)

In a series of surveys, the Pew Research Center monitored public opinion on abortion. In 1987, 41% of people surveyed favored and 51% opposed making abortions more difficult to obtain. By 2004 just 36% favored and 58% opposed making abortions difficult to obtain. (See Table 7.9.) In 2003 and 2004, 33% of women compared to 26% of men opposed greater restrictions on abortion. (See Table 7.10.)

FAMILY LIFE IN THE TECHNOLOGY AGE

The Influence of Television

The Statistical Abstract of the United States: 2003 reports that more American households had at least one television set (98.2%) than had a telephone (94.6%) in 2001. Cable television was new in 1970, reaching just 6.7% of homes, and video cassette recorders, or VCRs, were unknown. By 2003 the average home had 2.4 television sets, and 86.2% of homes had a VCR; 68% of homes had cable TV. (See Table 7.11.)

The 2003 *American Time Use Survey* conducted by the Bureau of Labor Statistics reveals that the average American spent more time watching television (2.57 hours per day) than any other activity except sleeping and working. The people with the least amount of time available for television viewing were women with bachelor's degree or

FIGURE 7.6

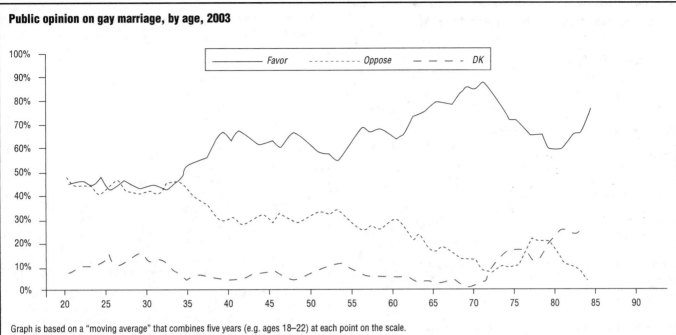

Public opinion on gay marriage, by age, 2003

Graph is based on a "moving average" that combines five years (e.g. ages 18–22) at each point on the scale.

SOURCE: "Views on Gay Marriage, by Age," in *Opinion of Homosexuals: Religious Beliefs Underpin Opposition to Homosexuality, Part 2: Gay Marriage*, The Pew Research Center for the People and the Press, November 18, 2003, http://people-press.org/reports/display.php3?ReportID=197 (accessed July 26, 2004)

TABLE 7.3

Public opinion on gay marriage by geographic characteristics, 2003

	Gay marriage		
	Favor %	Oppose %	Don't know %
East	42	50	8=100
South	23	67	10=100
Midwest	33	56	11=100
West	36	58	6=100
Urban	36	52	12=100
Suburban	38	54	8=100
Rural	22	69	9=100
White	32	60	8=100
Black	28	60	12=100
Hispanic	36	51	13=100

SOURCE: Adapted from "South, Rural Areas Opposed," in *Opinion of Homosexuals: Religious Beliefs Underpin Opposition to Homosexuality, Part 2: Gay Marriage,* The Pew Research Center for the People and the Press, November 18, 2003, http://peoplepress.org/reports/display.php3? ReportID=197 (accessed July 26, 2004)

TABLE 7.4

Main reasons for opposing gay marriage, 2003

28%	Morally wrong /a sin/ the Bible says
17	Against my religious beliefs
16	Definition of marriage is a man & a woman
12	It's just wrong/I just don't agree with it
9	Homosexuality is not natural/normal
4	Purpose of marriage is to have children
2	Bad for children
2	Opens the door to other immoral behavior
1	Undermines traditional family
1	Don't have stable, long-term relationships
1	Causes economic/legal problems
3	Other
4	Don't know/refused
100	

Based on 898 respondents who oppose gay marriage.

SOURCE: "Main Reasons for Opposing Gay Marriage," in *Opinion of Homosexuals: Religious Beliefs Underpin Opposition to Homosexuality, Part 2: Gay Marriage,* The Pew Research Center for the People and the Press, November 18, 2003, http://people-press.org/reports/display.php3? ReportID=197 (accessed July 26, 2004)

higher, women who were employed full-time, and women who had children under age six. They watched less than two hours of television per day. Men with bachelor's degrees or higher, who had children under age six, or were employed full-time watched less than two and one-quarter hours of television. Adults who spent the most time in front of the television, averaging four hours per day, were men with less than high school educations, men without jobs, and men over age sixty-five. (See Table 7.12.)

As network censorship of language and program content relaxed in the 1980s and 1990s, parents became increasingly concerned about the influence of television on children's attitudes and behavior. According to a survey by the National PTA (the National Congress of Parents and Teachers), parents of small children (age three to seven) were most worried about their children's exposure to sexual content and profanity on television. Parents of boys had almost equal fears about the effects of violence,

TABLE 7.5

Public opinion on sex, marriage and the family, 2003

Gay marriage would undermine the traditional family

Agree	56
Disagree	39
Don't know/mixed	5
	100

Gay marriage goes against my religious beliefs

Agree	62
Disagree	33
Don't know/mixed	2
	100

Gay/lesbian couples can be as good parents

Agree	54
Disagree	37
Don't know/mixed	2
	100

Society should put no restrictions on sex between consenting adults

Agree	80
Disagree	13
Don't know/mixed	6
	100

SOURCE: "Sex, Marriage and the Family," in *Opinion of Homosexuals: Religious Beliefs Underpin Opposition to Homosexuality, Part 2: Gay Marriage,* The Pew Research Center for the People and the Press, November 18, 2003, http://peoplepress.org/reports/display.php3?ReportID=197 (accessed July 26, 2004)

TABLE 7.6

Public opinion on the causes of homosexuality, 2003

	Dec 1985* %	Oct 2003 %
Why are people homosexual?		
Something born with	20	30
Way people are brought up	22	14
Way some prefer to live	42	42
Don't know	16	14
	100	**100**
Homosexual orientation...		
Can be changed		42
Cannot be changed		42
Don't know		16
		100

*Los Angeles Times

SOURCE: "Nature vs. Nurture," in *Opinion of Homosexuals: Religious Beliefs Underpin Opposition to Homosexuality, Part 1: Opinions of Homosexuals,* The Pew Research Center for the People and the Press, November 18, 2003, http://people-press.org/reports/display.php3?ReportID=197 (accessed July 26, 2004)

FIGURE 7.7

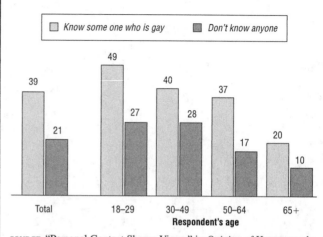

Opinions on gay marriage, by personal contact with gays and lesbians, 2003

SOURCE: "Personal Contact Shapes Views," in *Opinion of Homosexuals: Religious Beliefs Underpin Opposition to Homosexuality, Part 2: Gay Marriage,* The Pew Research Center for the People and the Press, November 18, 2003, http://people-press.org/reports/display.php3?ReportID=197 (accessed July 26, 2004)

TABLE 7.7

Public opinion on whether sexual orientation can be changed, 2003

	Can change %	Cannot change %	Don't know/ refused %
Total	**42**	**42**	**16 = 100**
White Protestant	47	36	17 = 100
Evangelical	65	23	12 = 100
High commitment*	73	17	10 = 100
Less commitment	53	33	14 = 100
Mainline	26	50	24 = 100
High commitment*	36	48	16 = 100
Less commitment	24	50	26 = 100
White Catholic	30	54	16 = 100
High commitment*	37	46	17 = 100
Less commitment	26	59	15 = 100
Black Protestant	61	26	13 = 100
Secular	21	66	13 = 100

*"High commitment" refers to respondents who attend religious services often and say religion is very important in their lives.

SOURCE: "Can Sexual Orientation Be Changed?" in *Opinion of Homosexuals: Religious Beliefs Underpin Opposition to Homosexuality, Part 1: Opinions of Homosexuals,* The Pew Research Center for the People and the Press, November 18, 2003, http://people-press.org/reports/display.php3?ReportID=197 (accessed July 26, 2004)

while parents of girls were even more concerned about programs with frightening content. For parents of children in the thirteen to eighteen range, sexual content remained the top concern with both boys and girls, and parents expressed anxiety about programs that promoted risk-taking behaviors.

Concerned parents wanted to be warned in advance about program content. And they wanted enough informa-

tion so they could decide which shows were appropriate for their children. By 1997 the television industry developed program ratings guides modeled after those used by the movie industry.

The TV Parental Guidelines included seven categories, with three specific to programs designed for children.

TABLE 7.8

What people are hearing in church about selected issues, 2003

	Total %	White Evang %	White Main %	White Cath %	Black %
Abortion*	63	72	39	85	38
Prayer in public schools*	58	72	37	49	69
Issues related to homosexuality*	55	66	36	44	42
The situation in Iraq**	53	62	38	44	63
Laws regarding homosexuals**	41	55	33	25	47
Ten Commandments in Alabama	40	54	30	25	43
The death penalty**	28	28	20	36	30
Candidates and elections	26	28	18	18	40
Number of cases, full form items	848	311	155	154	102
Min. number of cases, single form items	419	148	71	72	48

Based on people who attend religious services at least once or twice a month.
*Asked of Form 1 respondents only.
**Asked of Form 2 respondents only.

SOURCE: "What People Are Hearing about in Church," in *Opinion of Homosexuals: Religious Beliefs Underpin Opposition to Homosexuality, Part 1: Opinions of Homosexuals,* The Pew Research Center for the People and the Press, November 18, 2003, http://peoplepress.org/reports/display .php3?ReportID=197 (accessed July 26, 2004)

TABLE 7.9

Public opinion on making it more difficult to get an abortion, May 1987–February 2004

	May 1987 %	May 1993 %	Feb 2004 %
Favor	41	32	36
Strongly	18	15	17
Not strongly	23	17	19
Oppose	51	60	58
Strongly	33	35	30
Not strongly	18	25	28
Don't know	8	8	6
	100	100	100

SOURCE: "Most Oppose Making It More Difficult to Get An Abortion," in *Abortion a More Powerful Issue for Women,* The Pew Research Center for the People and the Press, April 23, 2004, http://peoplepress.org/commentary/ display.php3?AnalysisID=88 (accessed July 26, 2004)

- TV–Y All Children. Whether animated or live action, the themes and elements in this program are specifically designed for a very young audience, including children from ages two to six. This program is not expected to frighten younger children.

- TV–Y7 Directed to Older Children. This program is designed for children aged seven and above. It may be more appropriate for children who have acquired the developmental skills needed to distinguish between make-believe and reality. Themes and elements in this program may include mild fantasy or comedic violence, or may frighten children under the age of seven. Therefore, parents may wish to consider the suitability of this program for their very young children.

TABLE 7.10

Attitudes toward abortion, by sex, 2003–04

More restrictions on abortion	Woman %	Men %
Strongly favor	19	15
Favor	16	20
Oppose	26	31
Strongly oppose	33	26
Don't know	6	8
	100	100
Number of cases	2,878	2,593

Analysis based on data combined from three recent surveys conducted in August and November 2003 and February 2004.

SOURCE: "Women Feel More Strongly, on Both Sides of the Issue," *Abortion a More Powerful Issue for Women,* The Pew Research Center for the People and the Press, April 23, 2004, http://people-press.org/commentary/display .php3?AnalysisID=88 (accessed July 26, 2004)

TABLE 7.11

Home communications, 1970–2001

	1970	2001
Telephones	87.0%	94.6%
Radios	98.6%	99.0%
Televisions	95.3%	98.2%
Cable TV	6.7%	68.0%
VCRs	0.0%	86.2%

SOURCE: Adapted from "No. 1126, Utilization of Selected Media, 1970–2001," in *Statistical Abstract of the United States, 2003,* U.S. Census Bureau, 2003, http://www.census.gov/prod/2004pubs/03statab/inforcomm .pdf(accessed September 17, 2004)

- TV–Y7–FV Directed to Older Children–Fantasy Violence. This program includes fantasy violence that may be more intense or more combative than other programs in the TV–Y7 category.

- TV–G General Audiences. Although this rating does not signify a program designed specifically for children, most parents may let younger children watch this program unattended. It contains little or no violence, no strong language, and little or no sexual dialogue or situations.

- TV–PG Parental Guidance Suggested. This program contains material that parents may find unsuitable for younger children, including one or more of the following: moderate violence (V), some sexual situations (S), infrequent coarse language (L), or some suggestive dialogue (D).

- TV–14 Parents Strongly Cautioned. This program contains some material that parents would find unsuitable for children under fourteen years of age, including one or more of the following: intense violence (V), intense sexual situations (S), strong coarse language (L), or intensely suggestive dialogue (D).

TABLE 7.12

Television watching, by hours per day and selected characteristics, 2003

Average hours/day	Characteristic
1.66	Women with bachelor's degree
1.76	Women employed full-time
1.93	Women with children under 6
2.11	Men with bachelor's degree
2.14	Men with children under 6
2.21	Men employed full-time
2.29	Men age 15–24
2.39	White women
2.69	Women with no children under 18
3.07	Men with no children under 18
3.19	Women not employed
3.35	African-American men
3.47	Women without high school education
3.70	Women over age 65
3.94	Men without high school education
3.98	Men not employed
4.05	Men over age 65

SOURCE: Adapted from "Table 9. Average Hours Per Day Spent in Leisure and Sports Activities for the Total Population by Selected Characteristics, 2003 Annual Averages," in *American Time-Use Survey,* U.S. Department of Labor, Bureau of Labor Statistics, 2004, http://www.bls.gov/news.release/pdf/atus.pdf (accessed September 16, 2004)

• TV–MA Mature Audience Only. This program is specifically designed to be viewed by adults and therefore may be unsuitable for children under seventeen. It contains one or more of the following: graphic violence (V), explicit sexual activity (S), or crude indecent language (L).

A further aid to parents was the V-chip, which allowed parents to block programs they did not want their children to watch. Broadcast and cable networks encoded the ratings information into their television signals to be "read" by V-chip-equipped television sets that parents had programmed. As of January 1, 2000, all television sets manufactured with screens thirteen inches or larger in size contained V-chip technology. Television commercials, however, were not rated.

According to an April 2004 National PTA report, *Navigating the Children's Media Landscape,* parents had to make day-to-day choices among the media available to their children, including television, radio, newspapers, computers, Internet, computerized toys, video games, film, CDs, DVDs, phones, and PDAs (personal digital assistants). "With the various forms of media that children are exposed to each day, it can be difficult for parents to protect a child from inappropriate content without denying them the excellent learning opportunities that media can offer," said Linda Hodge, president of the National PTA (Parent Teacher Association). The report revealed that 36% of young children had televisions in their bedrooms and children were spending more time in front of "screens" than outside playing. The National PTA noted that more than one in four four- to six-year-olds used a computer daily. Of children with Internet access, 32% of six- to eight-year-olds

and 44% of thirteen- to seventeen-year-olds with Internet access had or planned to build their own personal Websites.

Cellular Phones Put Families in Touch

Cell phones provided go-everywhere portable access that allowed working parents and their children to keep in touch anywhere and anytime. The *New York Times* on November 18, 2002, reported that 56% of American households had wireless telephone service. Many teachers reported that "every kid seems to have a cell phone in his/her pocket or backpack." Tragedies like the 1999 Columbine High School shootings in Colorado gave evidence of the proliferation of cell phones, as frightened students called their parents from inside the school and parents called their children as soon as they heard the news reports. Media coverage of the role of cell phones in that incident perhaps spurred more parents to equip their children with cell phones. Following the September 11, 2001, terrorist attacks, news media reported victims' last calls on cell phones. A Wirthlin Worldwide survey reported that calls increased between family members and friends as Americans were touched by the need to make contact with everyone who was important to them.

Internet Access More Controversial

The Internet was perhaps a more controversial source of communication. On an average day, fifty-five million Americans logged on to the Internet. E-mail, the most common Internet activity, was used by 91% of all homes with Internet access. Research by the Pew Internet and American Life Project indicated that Internet users tended to have increased contact with family members by e-mail. Almost one-third (31%) of e-mail users reported that they had renewed contact with a family member they did not keep up with very often before Internet access.

The Internet appeared to foster extended family communication. Some 16% of Americans said they or another family member had a family Web page with pictures or information about the clan. Almost one-third (29%) said they had used the Internet to do family history research. A fourth of those who e-mailed relatives said they had learned more about their family since they began e-mailing family members.

The Internet plays a pivotal role in the lives of American teenagers, according to the Pew Internet and American Life Project. About 73% of youth ages twelve through seventeen used the Internet. Many (48%) said the Internet improved their relationships with friends, and 32% believed it helps them make new friends. However, 64% said the Internet took away time they might otherwise have spent with their families. More than half (55%) of parents of these online teens said the Internet was a good thing for their children, while 6% believed the Internet was a bad influence. A full 95% of parents of online teens believed it was important for children to learn to use the Internet in order to be successful.

EDUCATION

A 2001 Roper Center report, *To the Test,* includes a Gallup survey that asked what national issues were most important for the president and congress to address. Education topped the list, with 93% of respondents listing it as very important or extremely important. As recently as 1993, education ranked fifth on the survey list after health care, the economy, employment, and the federal budget deficit.

More than two-thirds of respondents stated that change was needed in public schools. When respondents were asked to identify the problems in schools, lack of parental involvement topped the list (78%). Undisciplined and disruptive students (73%), drugs and alcohol (69%), violence (64%), and overcrowded classrooms (61%) were identified as concerns by more than half of respondents. While 25% of respondents in another survey cited by the Roper study thought students should gain an academic background in high school, nearly half (48%) expected high school to instill discipline, morals, character, and responsibility.

YOUNG AMERICANS ON MARRIAGE AND FAMILY ISSUES

A survey of entering college freshmen conducted by the Higher Education Research Institute at the University of California—Los Angeles has long provided a glimpse of the opinions of the next generation. Support for legal abortion increased slightly from the freshmen entering in the fall 2000 to those entering in the fall of 2003 (53.9% to 54.5%). Opinions of male and female students were very similar on this issue. Support for abolishing the death penalty also grew slightly, from 2000 to 2003 (31.2% to 32.6%). In 2003 males and females were split 28.8% to 35.8% on the issue of abolishing the death penalty.

Raising a family was considered essential or very important to 75.8% of 2003 freshmen, with females rating this higher than males by just two percentage points. Being well off financially was the next most important objective for 75.4% of male freshmen and 72.5% of females.

OPINIONS ABOUT THE FUTURE

Despite predictions of natural disasters, terrorism, and environmental calamities, Americans at the turn of the twenty-first century expressed confidence that life would continue to get better. A 2000 survey by the Pew Research Center for the People and the Press reveals that more than four-fifths of Americans were optimistic about the welfare of themselves and their families. Their predictions for the next fifty years included good and bad. Eight in ten people believed there would be a cure for cancer

and for AIDS. Nine in ten expected a major earthquake in California, 64% feared terrorists would attack the United States, and 41% believed there would be a nuclear war. More than three-fourths believed the nation would elect a woman and an African-American as president.

The terrorist attacks of September 11, 2001, had a lasting impact on the nation and on American families. Certainly the families of the 2,948 individuals (official count as of October 29, 2003) who lost their lives in the four airplanes, the World Trade Center, and the Pentagon suffered permanent change. According to a September 2002 feature titled "9/11 By the Numbers" in NewYork-Metro.com (the official website of *New York* magazine and Metro TV), more than sixteen hundred people lost a spouse or partner and over three thousand children lost a parent as a result of the terrorist attacks. Researchers suggested that the events caused Americans to renew their focus on family.

In a November 2001 special edition of the *Wirthlin Report—America Responds, Part Three,* Wirthlin Worldwide noted that American's sense of security had been violated by the attacks. The report states, "The real change to American life may lie in the deeper, long-lasting effects . . . on day-to-day activities of the average citizen . . . includ[ing] family life." According to a Wirthlin survey, spending time with family and friends had taken on new significance. Planning for the holidays and for vacations was less appealing for many. (See Figure 7.8.) Wirthlin described the changed habits of Americans as "burrowing"—turning to home, family, and friends for stability and security.

Another Wirthlin report, *Seeking Stability in 2003,* found that the impact of the September 11 events was "still reverberating." Forty-eight percent of Americans felt they would have to make lifestyle changes in the next five years due to terrorist activity, compared to 61% shortly after the attacks. (See Figure 7.9.) The same report noted that Americans wanted to put their financial houses in order. In a Wirthlin survey people were asked what they would do if they won $2,000. Rather than buying some longed-for possession, 41% said they would pay off debts and 32% would save or invest the windfall. (See Figure 7.10.) Wirthlin projected that the trend of turning more attention to home, family, and friends could be expected to continue. Survey data suggested particularly that parents would increasingly measure themselves by the relationships they had with their children rather than by material possessions.

In August 2003 the Pew Research Center for the People and the Press repeated a survey conducted in early September 2001. According to the resulting report, "the threat of terrorism is now part of the fabric of American life," its pollsters found. Three-quarters of Americans

FIGURE 7.8

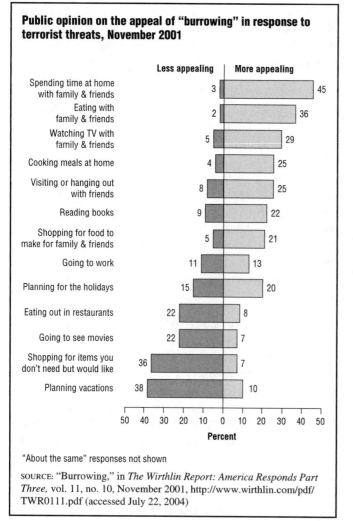

Public opinion on the appeal of "burrowing" in response to terrorist threats, November 2001

"About the same" responses not shown

SOURCE: "Burrowing," in *The Wirthlin Report: America Responds Part Three,* vol. 11, no. 10, November 2001, http://www.wirthlin.com/pdf/TWR0111.pdf (accessed July 22, 2004)

FIGURE 7.9

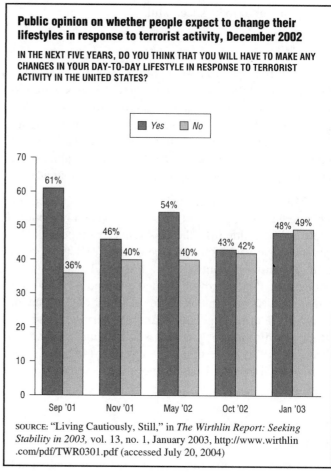

Public opinion on whether people expect to change their lifestyles in response to terrorist activity, December 2002

IN THE NEXT FIVE YEARS, DO YOU THINK THAT YOU WILL HAVE TO MAKE ANY CHANGES IN YOUR DAY-TO-DAY LIFESTYLE IN RESPONSE TO TERRORIST ACTIVITY IN THE UNITED STATES?

SOURCE: "Living Cautiously, Still," in *The Wirthlin Report: Seeking Stability in 2003,* vol. 13, no. 1, January 2003, http://www.wirthlin .com/pdf/TWR0301.pdf (accessed July 20, 2004)

found the world to be a more dangerous place than it had been ten years earlier. (See Table 7.13.) The majority of Americans continued to worry about another terrorist attack. (See Figure 7.11.) When Cold War tensions still kept the world on edge in 1987 and 1988, about six in ten Americans said they often worried about a nuclear war. In August 2003 a little more than half worried about nuclear war and just 40% worried about the chances of nuclear attack by terrorists. (See Table 7.14.)

FIGURE 7.10

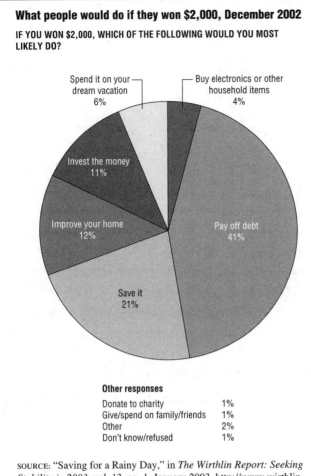

What people would do if they won $2,000, December 2002

IF YOU WON $2,000, WHICH OF THE FOLLOWING WOULD YOU MOST LIKELY DO?

- Spend it on your dream vacation 6%
- Buy electronics or other household items 4%
- Invest the money 11%
- Improve your home 12%
- Pay off debt 41%
- Save it 21%

Other responses

Donate to charity	1%
Give/spend on family/friends	1%
Other	2%
Don't know/refused	1%

SOURCE: "Saving for a Rainy Day," in *The Wirthlin Report: Seeking Stability in 2003,* vol. 13, no. 1, January 2003, http://www.wirthlin.com/pdf/TWR0301.pdf (accessed July 20, 2004)

TABLE 7.13

Public opinion on whether the world is more dangerous than ten years ago, September 2001–August 2003

HOW DANGEROUS IS THE WORLD COMPARED TO TEN YEARS AGO?

	Early Sept 2001* %	Aug 2003 %
More dangerous	53	75
Less dangerous	14	5
About the same	30	20
Don't know	3	*
	100	100

IS THE DANGER OF AN ATTACK ON THE U.S. GREATER NOW THAN TEN YEARS AGO?

Greater	51	64
Less	12	5
Same	34	29
Don't know	3	2
	100	100

*In early September 2001 the question was preceded by: "It has been ten years since the end of the Cold War".

SOURCE: "A More Dangerous World," in *Two Years Later, The Fear Lingers,* The Pew Research Center for the People and the Press, September 4, 2003, http://peoplepress.org/reports/display.php3?ReportID=192 (accessed July 26, 2004)

TABLE 7.14

Public opinion on whether there will be a nuclear war, May 1987–August 2003

OFTEN WORRY ABOUT THE CHANCES OF NUCLEAR WAR...

	Agree	Disagree	Don't know/ refused
Aug 2003	53	45	2=100
Aug 2002	56	42	2=100
Sept 1999	52	46	2=100
Nov 1997	48	50	2=100
July 1994	48	51	1=100
May 1990	52	45	3=100
May 1988	61	37	2=100
May 1987	62	27	2=100

OFTEN WORRY ABOUT THE CHANCES OF A NUCLEAR ATTACK BY TERRORISTS...

Aug 2003	40	59	1=100

SOURCE: Nuclear Nightmare," in *Two Years Later, The Fear Lingers,* The Pew Research Center for the People and the Press, September 4, 2003, http://peoplepress. org/reports/display.php3?ReportID=192 (accessed July 26, 2004)

FIGURE 7.11

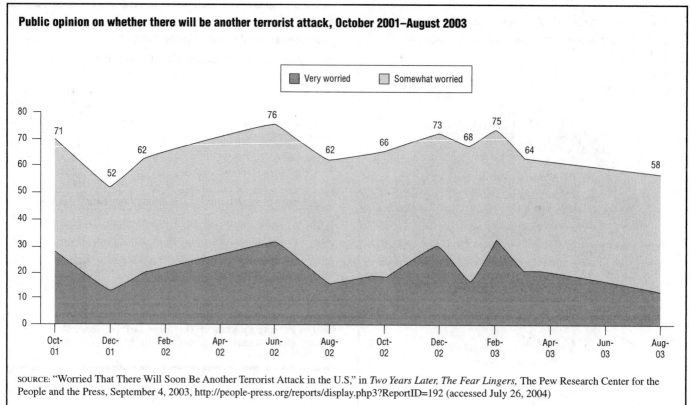

Public opinion on whether there will be another terrorist attack, October 2001–August 2003

Legend: Very worried / Somewhat worried

SOURCE: "Worried That There Will Soon Be Another Terrorist Attack in the U.S," in *Two Years Later, The Fear Lingers,* The Pew Research Center for the People and the Press, September 4, 2003, http://people-press.org/reports/display.php3?ReportID=192 (accessed July 26, 2004)

IMPORTANT NAMES AND ADDRESSES

AARP (American Association of Retired Persons)
601 E St. NW
Washington, DC 20049
(202) 434-2320
Toll-free: 1-888-687-2277
E-mail: member@aarp.org
URL: http://www.aarp.org

Administration for Children and Families
U.S. Department of Health and
Human Services
370 L'Enfant Promenade SW
Washington, DC 20201
(202) 619-0257
Toll-free: 1-877-696-6775
URL: http://www.acf.hhs.gov

Annie E. Casey Foundation
701 St. Paul St.
Baltimore, MD 21202
(410) 547-6600
FAX: (410) 547-6624
E-mail: webmail@aecf.org
URL: http://www.aecf.org

Barna Research Group, Ltd.
1957 Eastman Ave.
Suite B
Ventura, CA 93003
(805) 639-0000
FAX: (805)658-7298
E-mail: barna@barna.org
URL: http://www.barna.org

Bureau of Labor Statistics
U.S. Department of Labor
Postal Square Bldg.
2 Massachusetts Ave. NE
Washington, DC 20212-0001
(202) 691-5200
FAX: (202) 691-6325
E-mail: blsdata_staff@bls.gov
URL: http://www.bls.gov

Center for Family Policy and Practice
23 N. Pinckney St.
Suite 210
Madison, WI 53703
(608) 257-3148
FAX: (608) 257-4686
URL: http://www.cffpp.org

Center for Nutrition Policy and Promotion
U.S. Department of Agriculture
3101 Park Center Dr.
Room 1034
Alexandria, VA 22302-1594
(703) 305-7600
FAX: (703) 305-3400
E-mail: infocnpp@cnpp.usda.gov
URL: http://www.usda.gov/cnpp

Center for Research for Mothers and Children
National Institute of Child Health and
Human Development
Building 31
Room 2A32, MSC 2425
31 Center Dr.
Bethesda, MD 20892-2425
(301) 496-5097
Toll-free: 1-800-370-2943
FAX: (301) 496-7101
E-mail: NICHDInformationResourceCenter@mail.nih.gov
URL: http://www.nichd.nih.gov/

Center on Budget and Policy Priorities
820 First St. NE
#510
Washington, DC 20002
(202) 408-1080
FAX: (202) 408-1056
E-mail: center@cbpp.org
URL: http://www.centeronbudget.org

Centers for Disease Control and Prevention
1600 Clifton Rd.

Atlanta, GA 30333
(404) 639-3311
Toll-free: 1-800-311-3435
URL: http://www.cdc.gov

Child Trends, Inc.
4301 Connecticut Ave. NW
Suite 100
Washington, DC 20008
(202) 572-6000
FAX: (202) 362-8420
E-mail: webmaster@childtrends.org
URL: http://www.childtrends.org

Children's Defense Fund
25 E St. NW
Washington, DC 20001
(202) 628-8787
FAX: (202) 662-3510
E-mail: cdfinfo@childrensdefense.org
URL: http://www.childrensdefense.org

Families and Work Institute
267 Fifth Ave.
2nd Floor
New York, NY 10016
(212) 465-2044
FAX: (212) 465-8637
E-mail: mlambert@familiesandwork.org
URL: http://www.familiesandwork.org

The Federal Citizen Information Center
Pueblo, CO 81009
Toll-free: 1-800-333-4636
URL: http://www.pueblo.gsa.gov

Federal Interagency Forum on Child and Family Statistics
URL: http://www.childstats.gov

Gallup Inc.
502 Carnegie St.
Suite 300
Princeton, NJ 08540
(609) 924-9600

Toll-free: 1-800-888-5493
FAX: (609) 924-0228
URL: http://www.gallup.com

Harris Interactive
135 Corporate Woods
Rochester, NY 14623-1457
(585) 272-8400
Toll-free: 1-800-866-7655
E-mail: info@harrisinteractive.com
URL: http://www.harrisinteractive.com

Health Research & Educational Trust
c/o American Hospital Association
One North Franklin
30th Floor
Chicago, IL 60606
(312) 422-3000
FAX: (312) 422-4568
E-mail: mpittman@aha.org
URL: http://www.hret.org

Higher Education Research Institute
3005 Moore Hall
Box 951521
Los Angeles, CA 90095-1521
(310) 825-1925
FAX: (310) 206-2228
E-mail: heri@ucla.edu
URL:
http://www.gseis.ucla.edu/heri/heri.html

Joint Center for Housing Studies
Harvard University
1033 Massachusetts Ave.
5th Floor
Cambridge, MA 02138
(617) 495-7908
FAX: (617) 496-9957
URL: http://www.jchs.harvard.edu

Joint Center for Poverty Research
Northwestern University
Institute for Policy Research
2046 Sheridan Rd.
Evanston, IL 60208
(847) 491-3395
FAX: (847) 491-9916
E-mail: ipr@northwestern.edu
URL: http://www.jcpr.org

Kaiser Family Foundation
2400 Sand Hill Rd.
Menlo Park, CA 94025
(650) 854-9400
FAX: (650) 854-4800
E-mail: cpeacock@kff.org
URL: http://www.kff.org

**Lambda Legal Defense and
Education Fund**
120 Wall St.
Suite 1500
New York, NY 10005-3904
(212) 809-8585
FAX: (212) 809-0055

E-mail: members@lambdalegal.org
URL: http://www.lambdalegal.org

**National Academy of Sciences Institute
of Medicine**
505 Fifth St. NW
Washington, DC 20001
(202) 334-2352
FAX: (202) 334-1412
URL:
http://www.nationalacademies.org/nas/nash
ome/nsf

**National Adoption Information
Clearinghouse**
330 C St. SW
Washington, DC 20447
(703) 352-3488
FAX: (703) 385-3206
Toll-free: 1-888-251-0075
E-mail: naic@calib.com.
URL: http://naic.acf.hhs.gov

National Alliance for Caregiving
4720 Montgomery Ln.
5th Floor
Bethesda, MD 20814
(301) 652-7711
E-mail: info@caregiving.org
URL: http://www.caregiving.org

**National Campaign to Prevent
Teen Pregnancy**
1776 Massachusetts Ave. NW
Suite 200
Washington, DC 20036
(202) 478-8500
FAX: (202) 478-8588
E-mail: campaign@teenpregnancy.org
URL: http://www.teenpregnancy.org

National Center for Children in Poverty
215 W. 125th St.
3rd Floor
New York, NY 10027
(212) 284-9600
FAX: (212) 284-9623
E-mail: info@nccp.org
URL: http://www.nccp.org

National Center for Education Statistics
U.S. Department of Education
1990 K St. NW
Washington, DC 20006
(202) 502-7300
FAX: (202) 502-7466
E-mail: valena.plisko@ed.gov
URL: http://www.nces.ed.gov

National Center for Health Statistics
3311 Toledo Rd.
Hyattsville, MD 20782
(301) 458-4000
Toll-free: 1-866-441-6247
URL: http://www.cdc.gov/nchs

**The National Center on Addiction and
Substance Abuse at Columbia University**
633 Third Ave.
19th Floor
New York, NY 10017-6706
(212) 841-5200
URL: http://www.casacolumbia.org

**National Clearinghouse on Child Abuse
and Neglect Information**
330 C St. SW
Washington, DC 20447
(703) 385-7565
FAX: (703) 385-3206
Toll-free: 1-800-394-3366
E-mail: nccanch@caliber.com
URL: http://nccanch.acf.hhs.gov/

**National Coalition against
Domestic Violence**
P.O. Box 18749
Denver, CO 80218
(303) 839-1852
FAX: (303) 831-9251
E-mail: mainoffice@ncadv.org
URL: http://www.ncadv.org

National Coalition for the Homeless
1012 14th St. NW
#600
Washington, DC 20005-3471
(202) 737-6444
FAX: (202) 737-6445
E-mail: info@nationalhomeless.org
URL: http://www.nationalhomeless.org

National Fatherhood Initiative
101 Lake Forest Blvd.
Suite 360
Gaithersburg, MD 20877
(301) 948-0599
FAX: (301) 948-4325
E-mail: vdicaro@fatherhood.org
URL: http://www.fatherhood.org

National Housing Institute
460 Bloomfield Ave.
Suite 211
Montclair, NJ 07042-3552
(973) 509-2888
FAX: (973) 509-8005
E-mail: nhi@nhi.org
URL: http://www.nhi.org

National Low Income Housing Coalition
1012 14th St. NW
Suite 610
Washington, DC 20005
(202) 662-1530
FAX: (202) 393-1973
E-mail: info@nlihc.org
URL: http://www.nlihc.org

National Parent Teacher Association
330 N. Wabash Ave.
Suite 2100

Chicago, IL 60611
(312) 670-6782
Toll-free: 1-800-307-4782
FAX: (312) 670-6783
E-mail: nldi@pta.org
URL: http://www.pta.org

Office of Applied Studies
Substance Abuse and Mental Health
Services Administration (SAMSHA)
Parklawn Building
Room 12-105
5600 Fishers Ln.
Rockville, MD 20857
(301) 443-1038
FAX: (301) 443-9847
E-mail: info@samhas.gov
URL: http://www.oas.samhsa.gov

**The Pew Research Center for the People
and the Press**
1150 18th St. NW
Suite 975
Washington, DC 20036
(202) 293-3126
FAX: (202) 293-2569
E-mail: mailprc@people-press.org
URL: http://people-press.org

Public Agenda
6 East 39th Street
9th Floor
New York, NY 10016
(212) 686-6610
FAX: (212) 889-3461
URL: http://www.publicagenda.org

**The Roper Center for Public
Opinion Research**
341 Mansfield Rd.
Unit 1164
University of Connecticut
Storrs, CT 06269-1164
(860) 486-4440
FAX: (860) 486-6308
E-mail: rcweb@ropercenter.uconn.edu
URL: http://www.ropercenter.uconn.edu

**Stanford Institute for the Quantitative
Study of Society**
Stanford University
Encina Hall West, Room 104
Stanford, CA 94305-6048
(650) 723-7242
FAX: (650) 723-7351
E-mail: nhnie@stanford.edu
URL: http://www.stanford.edu/group/siqss

Travel Industry Association of America
1100 New York Ave. NW
Suite 450
Washington, DC 20005-3934
(202) 408-8422
FAX: (202) 408-1255
E-mail: membership@tia.org
URL: http://www.tia.org

U.S. Census Bureau
Washington, DC 20233
(301) 457-4608
FAX: (301) 457-4714
E-mail: webmaster@census.gov
URL: http://www.census.gov

U.S. Conference of Mayors
1620 I St. NW
Washington, DC 20006
(202) 293-7330
FAX: (202) 293-2352
E-mail: info@usmayors.org
URL: http://www.usmayors.org

**U.S. Department of Defense—Directorate
for Public Inquiry and Analysis**
1400 Defense Pentagon
Room 3A750
Washington, DC 20301-1400
URL: http://www.dod.gov

**U.S. Department of Housing and
Urban Development**
451 7th St. SW
Washington, DC 20410

(202) 708-1112
URL: http://www.hud.gov

U.S. Department of Justice
950 Pennsylvania Ave. NW
Washington, DC 20530-0001
(202) 514-2000
E-mail: askDOJ@usdoj.gov
URL: http://www.usdoj.gov

U.S. Department of State
2201 C St. NW
Washington, DC 20520
(202) 647-4000
URL: http://www.state.gov

Urban Institute
2100 M St. NW
Washington, DC 20037
(202) 833-7200
FAX: (202) 261-5709
E-mail: paffairs@ui.urban.org
URL: http://www.urban.org

Wirthlin Worldwide
1920 Association Dr.
Suite 500
Reston, VA 20191
(703) 480-1900
FAX: (703) 480-1905
URL: http://www.wirthlin.com

Women's Bureau
U.S. Department of Labor
Frances Perkins Bldg.
200 Constitution Ave. NW
Room S-3002
Washington, DC 20210
(202) 693-6710
FAX: (202) 693-6725
Toll-free: 1-800-827-5335
URL: http://www.dol.gov/wb

RESOURCES

The Bureau of the Census of the U.S. Department of Commerce is probably the single most important collection point for demographic information about American life. Many of its publications were essential for the preparation of this book, including: *Geographic Mobility: 2002 to 2003* (2004), *Fertility of American Women: 2002* (2003), *Children and Households They Live In: 2000* (2004), *Custodial Mothers and Fathers and Their Child Support: 2001* (2003), *Children's Living Arrangements and Characteristics: 2002* (2003), *Current Population Survey, 2003 Annual Social and Economic Supplement* (2003), *Households, by Type: 1940 to Present* (2003), *Households by Size: 1960 to Present* (2003), *Structural and Occupancy Characteristics of Housing: 2000* (2003), *Statistical Abstract of the United States 2003* (2004), *Marital Status by Sex, Unmarried-Partner Households, and Grandparents as Caregivers: 2000* (2000), *Marital Status of the Population 15 Years Old and Over, by Sex and Race: 1950 to Present* (2003), *Household Type among Foreign-Born Households by Size and by World Region of Birth of the Householder: 2003* (2003), *The Foreign-Born Population in the United States: 2003* (2003), *America's Families and Living Arrangements: 2000* (2001), *Multigenerational Households for the United States, States, and for Puerto Rico: 2000* (2000), *American Housing Survey for the United States in 2003* (2003), *Income, Poverty, and Health Insurance Coverage in the United States: 2003* (2004), *Health Insurance Coverage in the United States: 2002* (2003), *Emergency and Transitional Shelter Population: 2000* (2001), *Housing Characteristics: 2000* (2001), *2003 American Community Survey* (2003), *New Residential Sales in July 2004* (2004), *Interracial Married Couples: 1980 to 2002* (2004), *Grandchildren Living in the Home of Their Grandparents: 1970 to Present* (2004), and *Mapping Census 2000: The Geography of U.S. Diversity* (2000).

The different agencies of the U.S. Department of Health and Human Services (HHS) produce important publications on a wide variety of statistical data. The Administration for Children and Families annual study, *Child Maltreatment 2002* (2004), provided statistics about victims of child abuse and neglect. *Foster Care National Statistics* profiled children in foster care. The 2004 HHS Poverty Guidelines appeared in the *Federal Register*. The Federal Interagency Forum on Child and Family Statistics presented a variety of data on births to unmarried women and the status of children through its Childstats Web site and the report *America's Children* (2004).

Another agency of the HHS, the Centers for Disease Control and Prevention (CDC), provided sobering information about obesity trends in adults through *CDC at a Glance* (2004). Youth risk behaviors were studied in *Youth Risk Behavior Surveillance—United States, 2003* (2004). The CDC's National Center for Health Statistics (NCHS) is another valuable resource. The NCHS periodical *National Vital Statistics Report* supplied data on marriage, divorce, birth, and death trends. Additionally, some data was gleaned from *Provisional Vital Statistics for the United States; Births, Marriages, Divorces, and Deaths: Provisional Data for 2003* (2004). Life expectancy tables from 1900–2000 were found in the report *Health, United States 2003*. The Substance Abuse and Mental Health Services Administration (SAMHSA), part of HHS, provided valuable information on driving under the influence of illegal drugs in *Drugged Driving: 2002 Update* (2003).

The U.S. Department of Education's National Center for Educational Statistics compiled valuable information about the impact of poverty on student achievement in *The Nation's Report Card 2003* (2004). Other reports, including *1.1 Million Homeschooled Students in the United States in 2003* (2004), *Indicators of School Crime and Safety, 2003*, *National Postsecondary Student Aid Study* (2002), and *Computer and Internet Use by Children in 2001* (2003), shed light on diverse issues relating to education.

The U.S. Department of Labor's Bureau of Labor Statistics was also a vital source for this work. The graphics

Unemployment Map 2000 and *Unemployment Map 2003* (2004) offered a visual account of the rise in unemployment after the turn of the new century. Studies including the *National Compensation Survey 2003* (2003), *Work at Home 2001*, *Computer and Internet Use at Work in 2001*, and *Employment Characteristics of Families in 2003* (2004) provided important data about the workplace. *Women in the Labor Force: A Databook* (2004) gave an historical perspective of women's changing roles and earnings in the workplace. The *American Time Use Survey* (2004) revealed how the average American uses a twenty-four-hour day.

We are also grateful for the in-depth research of the U.S. Department of Agriculture's (USDA) Center for Nutrition Policy and Promotion, which released the report *Expenditures on Children by Families, 2003,* part of an annual series that helped quantify the cost of raising a child in today's economy. The USDA's publication *Family Economics and Nutrition Review* offered data on the cost of food in 2004 and the agency's poverty threshold schedule. The agency's 2003–04 income eligibility guidelines for public school free and reduced-price lunch programs were published in the *Federal Register.*

The U.S. Department of State maintains valuable foreign adoption information in its list *Immigrant Visas Issued to Orphans Coming to the U.S., Top Countries of Origin: 1989–2003*. The Department of Defense report *Worldwide Manpower Distribution by Geographic Area, September 30, 2003* provided perspective on locations of military families, while the *2002 Survey of Spouses of Activated National Guard and Reserve Component Mem-bers* offered a window into the challenges faced by families of reservists called to active duty.

Thomson Gale is also grateful to the National Adoption Information Clearinghouse for its in-depth information and statistics on adoption and foster care in America. The National Coalition for the Homeless gathered important but alarming data on the dangers of homelessness in *Hate, Violence and Death on Main Street USA* (2003). Thomson Gale appreciates the valuable information compiled by the United States Conference of Mayors–Sodexho report *Hunger and Homelessness Survey: A Status Report on Hunger and Homelessness in America's Cities—A 25-City Survey* (2003).

Thomson Gale thanks The Pew Research Center for the People and the Press for permission to reproduce graphics from *Opinion of Homosexuals: Religious Beliefs Underpin Opposition to Homosexuality, Part 1: Opinions on Homosexuals and Part 2: Gay Marriage* (2003), *Two Years Later, the Fear Lingers* (2003), and *Abortion a More Powerful Issue for Women* (2004).

Thomson Gale appreciates the permission of the American Association of Retired Persons (AARP) to reproduce graphics from *Money and the American Family* (2000). We also thank Wirthlin Worldwide for permission to reproduce material from *The Wirthlin Report: Who Made Me Fat? Seeking Answers to Complex Questions* (2003), *The Wirthlin Report: Seeking Stability in 2003* (2003), *The Wirthlin Report: America Responds, Part Three* (2001), *The Wirthlin Report: Workplace Issues in the 21st Century* (2001), and *The Wirthlin Report: Americans Rank Strengthening Families as High Priority* (2000).

INDEX

D

E

F

G

H

I

L

Y

Youth
 dieting, 54*t*
 fights and weapons, 56–57, 59(*t*4.9)
 leading causes of death, 56
 motor vehicles, 56

multiracial identification, 86*f*
opinions on marriage and family issues, 101
risk behavior, 55–57
sexual behaviors, 52–53, 55(*t*4.7)
suicide, 57
teen pregnancy, 7–8, 8*t*–9*t*, 15, 54–55

tobacco, alcohol and drug use, 57, 62(*t*4.10)
violence, 58–61, 60(*f*4.11), 61*t*
working, 41–42, 43*t*
Youth Gangs in Schools, 59–60
Youth Risk Behavior Surveillance (CDC), 51–53, 55–57, 58